BOMBSHELLS

To Colleen,
With Love and Best
Wishes,

Sheena xx

BOMBSHELLS

FIVE WOMEN WHO SET THE FIFTIES ON FIRE

SHAR DAWS

The
History
Press

First published 2020

The History Press
97 St George's Place, Cheltenham,
Gloucestershire, GL50 3QB
www.thehistorypress.co.uk

British Library Cataloguing in Publication Data.
A catalogue record for this book is available from the British Library.

ISBN 978 0 7509 9218 3

Typesetting and origination by The History Press
Printed and bound in Great Britain by TJ International Ltd.

MIX
Paper from
responsible sources
FSC
www.fsc.org   FSC® C013056

CONTENTS

ACKNOWLEDGEMENTS

Dreams that come true are rarely achieved without help, and this book is the perfect example of love and support that was given collectively to make a dream come true.

This book is about strong, talented, brave and adventurous women. I am privileged and honoured to have women with such attributes that I can call my closest friends.

One such woman is the incredibly gifted actress and radio broadcaster Christine Nagy. I would like to take this opportunity to thank Christine for her unwavering belief in everything I do, for giving me pep talks at any hour of the night or day, and for cheering me on and showing me nothing but love, encouragement and enthusiasm. Christine has lifted me out of some dark times, while happy times are so much brighter with her in my life. I am so grateful to you and this is a journey that I couldn't have made without you in my life. Christine, I love you!

I would also like to thank my bombshell soulmate Heather Garner. An expert on Jayne Mansfield, Heather is modest about her knowledge, but I'm not – I can say with complete confidence that there is no one I know who knows more about Jayne's life! She has been a great source of encouragement and hasn't let me wallow in self-doubt. We have spent hours together going over every detail of the bombshells and their lives; Heather has helped me to organise my thoughts and been a constant inspiration – igniting lots of different avenues to explore. Best of all, thank you for the times we get to spend together, watching old films and raising several glasses of champagne to the bombshells! I love you!

To my brother David Greenaway, for telling me for years that I should write this book! For believing in me and cheering me on, for being my writing buddy when we were both at university and for our coffees in Arundel when we would discuss writing and laugh constantly, I love you!

A special thanks to Pat and Bill Greenaway, my amazing parents. The women in this book all had issues with their fathers – my dad helps me to understand what they missed, because I have been so incredibly blessed with a strong, loving father that would do anything in the world for me. I love you, Dad!

My mum is another warrior woman in my life, yet not a bombshell fan! This makes it even more special and valuable to me that she painstakingly read every single chapter, giving me constructive well-thought-out honest criticism and feedback. Her encouragement has been incredible, and I thank her for believing in this project and asking me to hurry up with each chapter because she couldn't wait for the next instalment! I love you, Mum!

To my beautiful daughters, Sara Jeffery, Hayley Daws and Victoria Daws – I love you all more than words can say. Every single day your support and encouragement have meant everything to me. Your enthusiasm has driven me on – the excitement, the cups of tea and coffee, the bags of chocolate have all been welcomed and accepted gratefully. Thank you also for your advice and guidance when the going got tough – and for helping me in every way possible. Thank you not just in relation to the writing of this book but for accepting a daily diet of Marilyn Monroe et al. for as long as you can all probably remember! I love you all!

I would like to say an enormous thank you to my proofreader, critic, best friend and love of my life, my husband, John Daws. I honestly couldn't have written this book without you – your encouragement and belief in me is something for which I am ever grateful. You are my problem-solver and troubleshooter, keeping me going during technological disasters and keeping me fed and watered! Thank you for chauffeuring me to Ruth Ellis spots and Daws Dors tours! For accompanying me to Marilyn Monroe haunts and even for your amazing (not!) photography skills! Thank you for looking after Heathcliff – even though you said you'd never be seen walking a chihuahua! And thank you for putting up with my tears, tantrums and diva strops, and for listening to my endless whingeing! Dare I tell you now I already have the next book idea lined up? I love you with all my heart.

Finally, I would like to say special thanks and appreciation to Chrissy McMorris and The History Press for recognising the potential and helping me bring the book to life and make it a reality.

INTRODUCTION

You never forget your first encounter with a bombshell and my first time left a deep and lasting impression that is still with me now, nearly fifty years later, a faithful and enduring love affair with the alluring blondes.

I was just 6 years old in 1969 when I left London with my parents and younger brother for the sunshine and open spaces of Australia. We progressed from a Nissen hut in Sydney to a detached bungalow in Avondale Heights, Melbourne. The same day we moved in I followed my dad into the garage, where the previous occupants had left various personal bits and bobs scattered around the place.

And there she was on a calendar on the wall – a beautiful platinum-haired woman with a dazzling smile who looked like an angel to me. A barely dressed angel, I admit, but an 'otherworldly' vision all the same. I don't know what happened to the calendar but I do remember questioning my dad, and the answers he gave.

He told me her name was Jayne Mansfield and that she had recently died in a car crash; my eyes widened and my fascination grew.

Our time in Australia was brief and we returned home to England after two years. The sunshine had bleached my blonde hair practically white, and when my great aunt Ivy saw me she exclaimed, 'Well I never, she looks just like Marilyn Monroe.' I didn't know who Marilyn Monroe was but I instinctively felt this was a good thing!

Of course, my next question was, 'Who is Marilyn Monroe?' You wouldn't have to stretch your imagination too far to know how happy it made me when I found out what Marilyn looked like, but yet again I received the terrible news – Marilyn was dead, she died of an overdose, suicide and, like the news of Jayne's death, this had a profound effect on me.

As a young child I began to learn everything I could from the limited resources that were available back then, and I spent much of my time in the library.

Diana Dors had long since been on my bombshell radar as my great-uncle had known her and she was more prevalent in the media, who deemed her to be a scandalous woman, confirming what I already thought: a blonde bombshell was truly fast, dangerous and utterly fascinating!

It wasn't long before I discovered Jean Harlow and eventually Ruth Ellis, who seemed to me to be the epitome of the 'bad blonde' who had aspirations to become a famous actress but became infamous for shooting her lover instead. However, she was without a doubt a bombshell who shared the same traits as her peers.

There was, of course, no internet in the 1970s and '80s, so I relied on researching biographies, magazines and newspaper articles to gratify my insatiable appetite for information about the lives of these exciting women. I found their personalities even more captivating than their images.

With the advent of the internet the bombshell has had a revival. People across the world come together at events to celebrate the lives of these women, and social media groups are thriving with both men and women who want to learn more about these incredible females.

This book aims to explore the concept of the bombshell, tracing the origins and the influences that enabled ordinary women to become immortal goddesses. We look at their history, the gender stereotyping they utilised and satirised, and how they faced the changing times in the context of feminism. *Bombshells* tells the story of five women who contributed to shaping the history of sexuality and women's rights, within a society that both enabled them and fought against them.

The dichotomy was that their ultimate success was also their downfall; they were not as flawless as they were presented. The bombshells were living, breathing human beings who were unable to live up to their celluloid perfection. They experienced serious lapses of judgement, and some made fatal errors.

But is this perhaps the secret of their immortality? It made them relatable, to the extent that their mistakes and not just their beauty enhanced their rise to eternal fame. And whilst their personalities were vastly different, there was a multitude of similarities that have, until now, been overlooked. They transcended the constrictions of being a working woman in a 'man's world' during the 1950s, which deserves to be admired and celebrated.

Bombshells is the first in-depth introduction and exploration in one book of five unique women of strength, integrity and courage who led exceptional lives that may have ended too soon but serve as an example of what any person can achieve under impossibly difficult conditions or circumstances.

Shar Daws, June 2019

PART ONE

JEAN HARLOW

1

THE GODMOTHER OF BLONDES

The Godmother of Blondes had a short life, but one of the longest and furthest-reaching influences of any woman whose fame arose from the Hollywood Silver Screen.

Her mother, Jean Harlow, had married Mont Clair Carpenter in 1908. Three years later Harlean Harlow Carpenter was born in Kansas City, Missouri, on 3 March 1911. She was a beautiful child with cotton-white hair and green eyes, and her mother Jean rapidly lost interest in her husband as 'The Baby' (Harlean was called this throughout her life) soaked up her every moment and became her very reason for existing.

Brought up by wealthy parents and grandparents, Harlean had everything her heart could desire, and by the age of 10 she had developed a voracious appetite for reading and a passion for writing. She was particularly fond of the poetry of Lord Tennyson. In her 1920–21 school yearbook, she was thrilled to have one of her short stories published, titled 'An Elf's Adventures'.

However, Harlean was not to become a great writer; her destiny was to light the torch of the blonde bombshell as she created a unique image and persona that would be emulated and passed on for generations to come.

Preoccupied as she was with The Baby, Jean's relationship with Mont Clair was not a happy one and on 29 September 1922 she was granted a divorce that he did not contest. Jean was given sole custody of 10-year-old Harlean and in the same year she remarried a dubious character named Marino Bello, a smooth-talking Italian who had no credentials of merit and was universally disapproved of by the Harlow family.

Mother Jean (as she became known) was vivacious and attractive; she had her heart set on finding fame in Hollywood so together Marino, Jean and The Baby set out on the journey to California in 1923. When Jean arrived it soon became glaringly apparent that at the age of 30 she was too old to break into films, regardless of her drive and ambition, so the trio returned home disappointed to the Midwest in 1925.

By 1927, Harlean had developed into a stunning natural blonde with a penchant for fun and an adventurous nature, which at the age of 16 led her to elope on 20 September with 21-year-old Charles Freemont McGrew II.

Charles, who was known as Chuck, had lost both parents in a tragic boating accident when he was 16. Chuck's grandparents took over his upbringing and placed his inheritance in a trust fund for him, which matured two months after his wedding to Harlean. He received $200,000 as the first instalment.

Despite marrying without their respective families' permission, both were forgiven, and the young couple made their home in Harlean's favourite place, Hollywood, with the aid of Chuck's inheritance.

Mother Jean could not be separated from her daughter, and so she and Marino followed the young couple to Hollywood, where a chance meeting and a fun dare would change the life of both the Bellos and the McGrews forever.

In 1928, Harlean's friend Rosalie Roy, who was an aspiring actress, had an appointment at Fox Studios but no means of getting there. Harlean, who was always a kind and generous friend, offered to drive Rosalie and the offer was gratefully accepted. While waiting for her friend to conclude her interview, Harlean was spotted by Fox executives, who approached her thinking she was there looking for work.

When she explained that she was just waiting for her friend, they insisted she took a letter of introduction to the casting department. Harlean accepted the letter but had no intention of doing anything about it. Sometime later over lunch with friends, the story was retold.

Her friends chided her, saying she obviously didn't have the nerve to take the letter to casting and they wagered as much. Rising to the bet, she did indeed take the letter of introduction to casting, with one small detail changed – she applied in her mother's maiden name, Jean Harlow.

The career of Jean Harlow had begun, and the marriage of Harlean McGrew ended. On 11 June 1929, she left her husband and returned to her mother. Eventually, she and Chuck divorced.

Jean was regularly cast as an extra in high-profile films. She never took it too seriously, and she enjoyed the fun, was good-humoured and full of the joys of life. Everyone loved having her on set, and her youth and energy were positive and uplifting.

At the beginning of her career, Jean decided it would be an excellent time to reassess her appearance and she wanted to set herself apart from the competition. Her naturally blonde hair was growing darker with age and the film industry had always loved a blonde. There were many shades of natural blonde in the business and a few unnatural blondes, mainly because they were always more noticeable in crowd scenes.

So Jean went a light ash blonde and it paid off when, in 1929, Caddo, the film company owned by the millionaire Howard Hughes, was looking to cast a significant female role in his production of *Hell's Angels* and Jean fitted his visual expectations.

The publicity director was looking for a promotional angle, and Jean's hair was the obvious choice as a focus for the tag line. Although she was more ash blonde at this time, she became known as the Platinum Blonde – this was a label Jean wasn't fond of, but she understood its importance and necessity.

During a time of depression and economic decline, she contributed to sales of peroxide increasing by 35 per cent, although, it has to be said, not without several disasters that often ended with women having to shave their heads. Undeterred by such a possibility, Jean went even lighter, soon achieving the platinum look for which she was famous.

To attain platinum hair took some serious chemistry, beginning with a hydrogen peroxide and ammonia wash/bath to strip the hair of its pigment – sometimes Jean would need two such baths. The mixture would irritate her scalp, causing burning and itching. Once the colour was stripped entirely, she would then have a platinum rinse.

Her hairdresser Alfred Pagano, who mixed and applied the dangerous concoction, said in a television interview, 'We were creating the platinum blonde ... it was the first real glamour.'[1] In the same interview, Pagano revealed he also used Clorox and Lux flakes. He recalled, 'I'd say to Jean "is this hurting you?" and she'd say, "Yeah a little bit", and I'd use a blower on her sometimes to cool it off, sometimes with magazines to fan it off.'

Harlow herself maintained she never bleached her hair. She told a reporter, 'It can't be good to bleach hair with chemicals ... as for mine, it's never touched with anything but soap and water.'[2] On another occasion, she told a reporter that she just added a few drops of liquid bluing (a substance used in laundry to make clothes whiter) to her shampoo soap but not the rinse.

The consequence of such a drastic hair colour meant that every Sunday, due to the pressure of close-ups, Jean was at Jim's Beauty Studio on Sunset Boulevard, having Pearl Porterfield, who was later to help maintain Marilyn Monroe's hair, apply bleach to her roots in order to keep them white and her hair bright and camera-ready.

Jean knew her hair was a significant factor in her popularity, once stating, 'If it hadn't been for the colour of my hair, Hollywood wouldn't know I was alive.'[3]

Way ahead of her time, and long before Marilyn Monroe was declaring the benefits of being 'au naturel', Jean rarely wore underwear and often made controversial fashion choices. Hairdresser Alfred Pagano remembered, 'She never wore undergarments and I used to say to Jean, "My God, you don't have anything on underneath that jacket," and she said, 'No, I hate lines.'[4]

Arthur Jacobson, assistant director on *The Saturday Night Kid* recalled, 'She was wearing this black crocheted dress with not a stitch under it. From where I sat, you couldn't tell whether she had put it on or painted it on.'[5]

On one occasion, when asked to remove her jacket on set, she did as asked and revealed that, once again, as with Pagano, that she wore nothing underneath; everyone was left in stunned silence. After the event, Anita Loos, the writer of *Gentlemen Prefer Blondes* and who adapted the script of *Red Headed Woman* for Jean Harlow, recalled, 'Nudity was rarely seen in those days … the lighting crew almost fell out of the flies in shock.' Insisting Jean's act was not exhibitionism, Loos went on to say, 'She had no vanity whatsoever.'[6]

Jean relied heavily on her appearance, as her acting skills were at times worse than mediocre. Ridgeway Callow, the assistant director on *Hell's Angels*, described her as 'one of the world's worst actresses'.[7] It was her attractive looks and her easy-going nature that moved Jean forward from extra to leading lady.

Jean's eagerness to learn and her enthusiasm about doing whatever was necessary to improve endeared her to fellow actors and crew. Sound mixer Bill Edmondson described Jean, saying, 'Everybody loved her … so sweet and thoughtful, and always on time. She was a doll.'[8]

Although Jean could relate well to people in small groups, she struggled when making a public appearance when touring to promote films. She would tremble in fear, barely able to speak and often crying. She would say, 'I can't make up words … I have to study them, I have to have a script.'[9] Audiences were expecting the character she played, but Jean was poles apart from the onscreen vamps she portrayed. In real life she was naïve and unsophisticated, inexperienced in handling the general public.

Eventually she overcame her nerves, the public adored her for who she was and her popularity soared. However, Howard Hughes was not entirely enamoured with Jean and would readily loan her out to other studios. Unhappy with the roles she was playing, she told the press, 'I've played a series of abandoned wretches whose wickedness is never explained, never condoned … How can I expect audience sympathy when I have none for the parts I've been forced to play?'[10]

One of the loans was to Columbia Pictures to make *Gallagher*, later retitled *Platinum Blonde*. Jean played the title role, and her comedic timing was close to pure genius. The director Frank Capra was impressed with her dedication, helpfulness and professionalism.

2

'DEAREST DEAR'

Shortly before *Hell's Angels* premiered, Jean met Paul Bern, who was the assistant to Irving Thalberg, producer at MGM. Paul and Jean became firm friends and he saw her potential, bringing her to the attention of MGM, who negotiated with Caddo to borrow Harlow for a small part in the film *The Secret Six* (1931). On seeing Jean in *Platinum Blonde*, both Bern and Capra suggested that MGM consider taking her. After interviewing her, Mayer and Thalberg agreed to proceed with buying out her contract from Caddo, despite still being unsure, mostly due to the respect and trust that they had in Paul Bern's opinion.

Jean was thrilled to sign with MGM. She had felt unappreciated and used by Caddo and did not have a particularly good relationship with Howard Hughes. Her new studio began grooming her straight away and the publicity machine cranked into action. Howard Strickling, head of publicity, was well aware that Harlow had been hired as MGM's resident vamp, but he saw that she had a rare quality; she was able to throw out comedic lines while still exuding sexual appeal and innocence all at the same time.

Unfortunately for Jean, her stepfather Marino Bello was a thorn in her side. He became Jean's self-appointed 'manager', interfering and strutting around the studio. To make matters worse, Jean found herself working to support both him and Mother Jean. She began her contract on 19 March 1932 on a weekly salary of $1,250 for the first year with the promise of regular rises until she reached $4,000 a week by 1938. She handed her pay packet to Mother Jean, in return she was given just $125 a week to spend.

Jean's contract with MGM required her to stay in tip-top condition; she could be released at a moment's notice were she to suffer any physical defect to her appearance or her voice for more than two weeks. Her presentation was carefully constructed and crafted by the studio and for the studio.

During this time, her relationship with Paul Bern developed into something more serious, and six weeks after Bern had escorted her to the premiere of *Red Headed Woman* they attended a gathering at the home of David O. Selznick.

Selznick's wife, Irene, was pregnant, and she and Jean struck up a conversation, during which Jean confided in her that she too would like a baby of her own. Directly after their discussion, Jean sought out Bern at the party and told him she would like to marry him.

Her relationship with Bern surprised many people; he was significantly older than her, with a twenty-two-year age gap. He was also short, balding and considered by many as somewhat unattractive. However, he took Jean seriously and they had a deep connection. She was also impressed that Bern was interested in her as a person and was not trying to be physical with her.

Unfortunately, Paul Bern came with considerable emotional baggage. His mother had taken her own life and he had a morbid obsession with suicide. It was also rumoured that Bern had attempted to end his own life in the past. Furthermore, he had been living with an actress named Dorothy Millette in New York who had mental health issues.

Although he did not marry Dorothy, the law in New York gave couples who lived together the security of being 'common law' spouses. While Dorothy was at the Blythewood Sanatorium, which Bern paid for, he left to start a new life in Hollywood, but he continued to support her financially.

Despite all of this, on Saturday, 2 July 1932, the wedding went ahead, and Jean married Paul Bern. Many mysteries surrounded their relationship. Over the years, there have been numerous rumours regarding Bern that focused on a lack of development of his genitals and a theory that he was homosexual.

Such gossip was given fuel when he was found dead on 5 September in their Beverly Hills home with a gunshot wound to his head, just two months after his marriage to Jean. Although the coroner ruled Bern's death to be suicide, there had been sightings of a woman at the house that night. It was thought to be Dorothy Millette looking to confront her common-law husband.

A note discovered at the scene added to the mystery. On page 13 of Bern's guest book, a curious message written by Paul Bern has come to be accepted as a suicide note:

Dearest Dear,

Unfortuately [*sic*] this is the only way to make good the frightful wrong
I have done you and to wipe out my abject humiliation. I Love [*sic*] you.
Paul

You understand last night was only a comedy[1]

According to the author David Stenn in his 1993 biography *Bombshell:
The Life and Death of Jean Harlow*, the note was not a suicide note at all.
Stenn wrote:

> As Henry Hathaway suspected and Howard Strickling later admit-
> ted, the 'suicide note' in Bern's guest book was actually an apology
> to Harlow, whose chance meeting with Millette 'last night was only a
> comedy'. Had he lived, Bern's words would have been sent with a bou-
> quet ('the only way to make good the frightful wrong I have done you')
> to Harlow's studio dressing room, where Sada's Flowers of Culver City
> made daily deliveries. After his suicide, the note assumed a significance
> it was never intended to have.[2]

However, at the time gossip and rumours about events that night spread
like wildfire through the Hollywood community and the flames ignited
like petrol-soaked straw when, seven days after Bern's death, the badly
decomposed body of Dorothy Millette was pulled from reeds off the
Sacramento River by two fishermen. Dorothy had boarded the *Delta King*
riverboat the day after Bern had apparently shot himself; her hotel room
key still in her pocket enabled her to be identified. An autopsy revealed
that Millette had died by asphyxiation due to drowning, and the coroner's
report stated suicide.

While Dorothy's relatives were keen to make a claim on the estate
of Paul Bern, no one would take responsibility for her burial. When
Jean learned of the sorry situation, she took charge and arranged not
only a funeral but also a gravestone upon which she placed the name
'Dorothy Millette Bern' in recognition of Dorothy's relationship
with Bern.

Jean's husband had left more debts than assets; his estate was bankrupt,
and so she quietly worked to pay off all the debts. The financial stress and
the scandal surrounding his death could have destroyed her, but she held
her head high and her tongue still.

Returning to work on her current film *Red Dust* with Clark Gable, she threw herself back into life. This contributed to the press raising their estimation of Jean and giving her a great deal of respect that she had so obviously earned. Reviews of *Red Dust* were full of praise; she was given the accolade of admiration as she rose up from under the weight of adversity.

A year after Paul Bern's death, Jean's private life became quite complicated, to the point that the studio began to worry and became keen to have her married and settled down. Harlow chose MGM cameraman Hal Rosson, who was sixteen years older than Jean and not dissimilar in appearance to Paul Bern. It seemed Jean definitely had a type and that type had a lot in common with her father, Mont Clare, in age and appearance. While filming *Bombshell*, Rosson and Jean decided to elope, and on 18 September 1933 they were married.

Shortly after the marriage, Jean came into conflict with the studio over the roles she was being offered and her salary. Although this was the era of the Depression and Jean was on an astronomical wage compared with the average man in the street, she had expenses that went along with her status of being a movie star, including the need for clothes, hairdressing appointments, and photographs to send to fans, a secretary, etc. Jean also had the burden of having to continue to provide for the upkeep of her mother and stepfather.

At the beginning of 1934, while complaining the studio was going to put her on suspension, she decided to use holiday she had accrued to avoid being suspended while negations took place. Free from the constraints of working, she was able to indulge in her first love – writing – and proceeded to spend most of 1934 working on a novel. She had been keeping notes and dreaming up plots since Bern had suggested she write a screenplay, so she had stockpiled a considerable amount of material.

It was believed that Jean asked one of the studio's top writers, Carey Wilson, for guidance and advice. Wilson was happy to oblige in nurturing Jean's creative desires, although some people believed the resulting novel was ghostwritten by Hollywood publicist Tony Beacon and edited and polished by Carey Wilson.

By 26 January 1934 the studio was ready to compromise and increased her salary, also agreeing to renegotiate Jean's more minor artistic requests. Jean was keen to get back to work and signed a new seven-year contract. Busy with work and writing, her marriage was not getting the attention it required, and it was becoming evident that things were not as they should be between her and Rosson.

Jean sold the rights to her book *Today is Tonight* but felt disappointed with what she had produced. It fell short of her personal expectation, and she spent a great deal of time redrafting but never reached a level of satisfaction with it. The novel was not published during her lifetime; only when Mother Jean inherited it was it sold to Grove Press in 1965. It then took a brutal bashing from the critics for its implausible plot and crazy twists and turns.

Rosson's primary grudge was his in-laws, and the amount of time Jean spent with Mother Jean and Marino. Jean divorced Rosson on the grounds of mental cruelty and incompatibility; she also mentioned that Rosson read in bed, keeping her awake, which made her tired on set the following day. The press had a field day with this information and it was the focus of the divorce, which Harlow was granted; she was once again free by 12 March 1935.

3

'DADDY, I DON'T FEEL GOOD'

Jean had been friends with the actor William Powell since spring 1934, before her divorce from Rosson. There was a deep mutual attraction between them and once again it seemed that she had chosen another father figure; at 42 years old, Powell was nineteen years older than Jean.

William Powell was reluctant to propose marriage; he had tried it before, twice, and each time had been unsuccessful. Jean also had three failed marriages, but Powell would become the love of her life, and there was nothing more she wanted than to be Mrs William Powell.

Once again, Mother Jean and her husband became a problem in Jean's relationship. She loved her mother dearly and accepted Marino for her mother's sake, even though Jean had grown to dislike him. Powell, on the other hand, did not love Mother Jean and certainly wasn't prepared to tolerate Marino.

Powell was suspicious of Marino's dealings in Jean's affairs, so much so that he employed a private detective. It quickly became apparent that Marino Bello was embezzling from Jean (amongst others) and she was broke. He had been taking money from Jean's bank accounts and had almost bankrupted her. He also claimed to have a mining business and was taking investment from people for a company that never existed.

Powell endeavoured to help Jean, but the house at Club View Drive in which the Bellos had been living had to go. Jean took it well, brushing it off with, 'Mother and I weren't cosy there,' and 'We didn't feel comfortable.'[1]

Jean rented a house at 512 North Palm Drive, Beverly Hills. Several years later Marilyn Monroe was to make Palm Drive her home on two occasions – once with her agent and lover Johnny Hyde of the William Morris agency and then with her second husband Joe DiMaggio in April 1954.

At this point, Jean began to scale down her life, watching her finances. She still loved the classic movie-star white interior décor, even though it wasn't always compatible with her menagerie of beloved pets. She also found it impossible to compromise with her adored perfumes; her favourites were Guerlain's Mitsouko and L'heure Bleue, which she would order by the boxload.

On 27 May 1936, Jean legally changed her name to Jean Harlow. Within a few days of her name change, she was admitted to the Good Samaritan Hospital as 'Mrs Jean Carpenter' accompanied by a 'Mrs Webb', who was, in fact, Mother Jean. Later, in a statement, the hospital described Jean as being there for a rest when, in fact, she was there for an abortion. Pregnant with Powell's child, and knowing that he did not want to commit, Jean took it upon herself to quietly have an abortion without telling Powell or the public.

Naturally depressed after the abortion, Jean, who was previously a social drinker, began to drink more frequently. She abstained while working but would binge drink at the first opportunity, her favourite tipple being Graves Gin. During a drinking session she would become overemotional, and was heard to declare that she would have rather have been a wife and mother than a movie star.

The blonde bombshell had felt ill at ease with the colour of her hair since around 1932, when she began wearing darker wigs. By the time she had met William Powell, she had opted for a more honey blonde that was closer to her natural hair colour. Jean believed this gave her more options artistically and in *Wife vs. Secretary* in 1936, alongside Myrna Loy and Clark Gable, she appeared in the film as a brunette. This was a more serious role for Jean and a move away from the bombshell.

Mother Jean had always kept a close watch on her only child, but she was now in a relationship with a new lover, Henry 'Heinie' Brand, and her attention was distracted.

Despite the drinking binges and Jean's personal distress that she was unable to convince Powell that marriage was the best thing for them both, her career was going from strength to strength. She was able to put aside her private life and the fact that she had fought off several episodes of ill health. Her face would puff up in the mornings, giving her skin a deathly pallor, and this combined with some severe fatigue. When Jean stepped on the studio floor she gave unrivalled performances but she would still hit the bottle with gusto when not working.

During 1936 Jean made a total of four films. Her penultimate film, *Personal Property*, released on 19 March 1937, was to be the last she completed. Jean starred alongside Robert Taylor. At the end of January Jean went on the road with Taylor to publicise the film. As soon as the tour came to an end, she travelled back to Hollywood with the most horrendous bout of flu, which knocked her off of her feet and took her the whole of February to recover from.

In her last and uncompleted film, *Saratoga*, a romantic comedy set in the racing community, Jean took the starring role and was working again with her dear friend Clark Gable. The only apprehension she had was with working with the horses on the set as she had a fear of them.

Preliminaries for the film such as wardrobe tests, etc., were due to start in March 1937. Around this time, Jean was dealing with the chronic pain of impacted wisdom teeth. With a dislike of hospitals and time in short supply, she left the problematic teeth until it became a crisis situation and she had to have them dealt with.

Instead of having one or two out at a time, Mother Jean encouraged The Baby to have them all removed at once. The effect was devastating and Jean developed septicaemia. As a result, she was dosed up with pain-killers; there was little else that could be done.

By April it was becoming imperative to MGM that *Saratoga* was back up and running. Fortunately for the cast and crew, Jean was able to return to set on 22 April, although she was tired and drained. It took all the skills of the make-up artist and the cameraman's artistic ingenuity, but at the beginning of shooting Jean looked much improved. However, on closer inspection it is clear that she is simply not well.

Previously unheard of, Jean began arriving late on set and her tone became snappy at times. This was entirely out of character for the 'sugar and spice and all things nice' girl who still had her heart set on marrying William Powell, but he was still shying away from serious commitment. Almost as if teasing, he did buy her two rings during their relationship, but neither was a proclamation of forthcoming wedding bells.

On 25 May, after filming a scene with Gable, Jean returned to her dressing room for lunch with her friend Barbara Brown. She asked Barbara if it would be OK for them not to talk as she felt unwell. This took Brown by surprise, and she is quoted as saying, 'In all the years I'd known her, it was the only time I ever heard her say that.'[2]

Jean was in continuous pain from the wisdom teeth extraction, and due to the resulting infection she had to drain her mouth regularly, including while on set.

By 29 May, it was apparent to everyone involved with *Saratoga* that Jean was ill. The nurse on set saw her and told her to go home, but Jean refused, as she was worried that she would cause the production to be delayed. Professional pride and thoughtfulness towards the other actors made Jean want to keep the film on track.

Due to work on a scene with Walter Pidgeon, she insisted that they carry on, although she had to ask Pidgeon to hold her gently as she was in so much pain. Eventually, she collapsed in his arms and was sent back to her dressing room, never to return to the set again.

In her dressing room, Jean changed into her regular clothing and went to the set of *Double Wedding*, the production that William Powell was working on. The director, Richard Thorpe, recalled, 'When she came by and said, "Daddy, I don't feel good. I'm going home."

"Okay honey," Powell replied. "I'll be over as soon as I can."'[3]

Jean went directly to Powell's mansion, where she stayed over the weekend while he was working. Everyone initially thought she had flu, but there was no improvement by the end of the weekend, so on Sunday night, Powell contacted Mother Jean, who was having a break on Catalina Island with Brand. She returned on Monday, 31 May and organised Dr Ernest Fishbaugh to come and take tests and assign nurses from the Good Samaritan Hospital to take care of Jean.

On 1 June Jean managed to phone into the studio to tell them she was sick. She found this extremely hard because she knew delaying production would be a problem, even though they assured her they would film around her scenes. As the consummate professional, Jean Harlow felt she was letting everyone down.

Dr Fishbaugh diagnosed flu and cholecystitis (inflammation of the gall bladder). He told Mother Jean that there was nothing to worry about.

By 3 June, Jean appeared to take a turn for the better and was sitting up in bed, eating a light meal. Mother Jean and some of her daughter's work colleagues thought it might be alcohol that had caused this illness, which was how one of the most persistent myths surrounding Jean's death became widespread.

Mother Jean was trying to protect The Baby from the press and the outside world. Assuming that it might possibly be alcoholism, Mother Jean said it was not necessary for The Baby to go to the hospital because they were Christian Scientists but in actual fact, Jean's home had been turned into a hospital with a licensed physician and three nurses attending her regularly.

Harlow's body was swelling up, and when Clark Gable visited Jean and kissed her he could smell urine on her breath, which was a symptom of kidney failure. Mother Jean decided it was time for a second opinion and called in Dr Chapman, who noted Harlow's high blood urea and immediately diagnosed acute nephritis, failure of the kidneys.

The dextrose fluid Dr Fishbaugh had been prescribing had been making things worse for Jean. It is believed that her kidneys had been failing for years since she contracted scarlet fever at the age of 15. This was followed by glomerulonephritis, which damages the tiny filters inside the organ (the glomeruli).

By 5 June, Jean was in full kidney failure; unable to urinate, the toxic waste was leaving her body via her skin, sweat and breath.

William Powell visited Jean at her Palm Drive home on 6 June, still not unduly worried until she told him he looked fuzzy. He held up his hand and asked her how many fingers she could see. Jean responded that she could not see any and this alarmed Powell.

An ambulance was called, and Jean asked for the novel *Gone with the Wind* to be packed so that she could finish reading it in hospital. At 6.30 p.m. she was admitted to the Good Samaritan Hospital, but by the time she arrived, her body was so swollen it was a shock to the doctor who admitted her. She was immediately placed in an oxygen tent, and it was confirmed she was suffering from cerebral oedema.

Jean went into a state of semi-consciousness. Loved ones and friends were called to say their last goodbyes as it was clear that The Baby would not be making a recovery. Her Aunt Jetty held her hand, begging her to get better. Jean replied, 'I don't want to.' Overcome with emotion, Aunt Jetty left the room, and Jean Harlow's final words were, 'Where is Aunty Jetty? Hope she didn't run out on me …'[4]

William Powell and Mother Jean were distraught. As The Baby slipped into a coma, Powell fled the room in tears, but Mother Jean stayed with her Baby to the end, which came at 11.38 a.m. on the morning of 7 June 1937. Jean was just 26 years old.

The cause of death was given as respiratory infection, acute nephritis and uraemia. Harlow's skin pallor, severe sunburn and recurring illnesses had been signs that were easily missed and put down to other things when they were, in fact, symptoms of kidney disease.

When the studio learned of her sudden death, screenwriter Henry Ruskin remembered years later, 'The day the Baby died there wasn't one sound in the MGM commissary for three hours ... not one god-damn sound.'[5]

Announcing her death on CBS radio that evening, the presenter was clearly upset as he told the world:

> A few hours ago, Miss Jean Harlow was graduated by death to whatever the next stage may be. The Screen has lost one of its most brilliant personalities and we who knew her, a kind and gentle friend. Hollywood tonight holds many heavy hearts.
>
>   This is the Columbia Broadcasting System.[6]

Jean was attended through the night by the MGM grips and lighting assistants because 'Baby didn't like to be alone in the dark.'[7]

Initially, Mother Jean chose the white satin gown from *Libelled Lady* to dress Jean for her final appearance. However, on the day of her funeral, she had a last-minute change of heart. Instead of the white gown, Jean was dressed in the pink silk robe and white sandals that she wore in *Saratoga*. MGM hairdresser Peggy McDonald helped with the preparation and styled a wig for Jean. In her hand was placed a white gardenia and a note written by Powell that read 'Goodnight my dearest darling.'

Jean's casket was covered with 1,500 lilies of the valley and 500 gardenias supplied by the studio. Flowers were also sent by everyone that knew Jean from the studio heads to the extras on *Saratoga*.

Her funeral took place on 9 June at Forest Lawn Memorial Park. Hollywood studios observed a minute's silence at 9 a.m. as Jean Harlow's service began – it was the biggest funeral in the history of Hollywood up to that point. The Hollywood stars shone brightly for Jean, including Clark Gable, Carole Lombard, Myrna Loy and Spencer Tracy. There were so many people that the 150-capacity church could not hold everyone. People were standing in the entrance and outside, and there were also hordes of fans and onlookers in attendance.

On the Saturday after the funeral service, Jean Harlow was laid to rest at Mother Jean's behest – but paid for by William Powell – in Forest Lawn's Sanctuary of Benediction mausoleum in a marble-lined mortuary chamber where three crypts were reserved, one for The Baby, one for Mother Jean and one for Powell. The Baby and Mother Jean now reside together forever, but Powell never took up deathly residence in the mausoleum. He died of heart failure on 5 March 1984 aged 91 and is buried at Desert

Memorial Park, California, near his third wife, Diana Lewis, and his son, William David Powell, who committed suicide in 1968.

After Jean's death, the studio wanted to shelve *Saratoga* or possibly re-film it with another actress. The public were enraged and wanted to see Jean Harlow's final film. Her fans collectively encouraged MGM to finish the movie with stand-ins so they could have one last look at their idol on screen.

In this film, her acting is dulled down, lethargic and her features appear puffy and undefined. However, after her death MGM went ahead and cast Jean 'lookalikes' and 'soundalikes', obscuring their view with binoculars, large hats and distant camera angles. Even though Jean was clearly not at her best during this film, when the stand-ins appear the magic vanishes. Jean had that indefinable star quality; her presence on the screen, in good health or bad, was undeniably bewitching. Larger than life, she occupied the entire screen, and her luminosity and vibrancy left the observer no eyes for anyone else when she was present.

The stand-ins lacked lustre. They were pretty women with Harlow-esque figures in Jean's costume and with the same hair, make-up and glamour, but no glow. The whole package fails as the stand-ins' fellow actors struggle to bring the script to life. They are unable to interact in the same way, their performance declines and the film sadly crashes and limps to its conclusion.

Jean had done it all first – nude photos, fights with the studio and three marriages. Who knows what would have come had Jean made it beyond the age of 26. Jean Harlow's flame reignited in the 1950s with the most notorious blondes of all time and, like Jean, each has left a legacy that has ensured the fire will never be wholly extinguished.

PART TWO

RUTH ELLIS

4

ANGEL OR HARLOT

Hair colour is often the first thing we notice about someone. If you have to give a description to the police, you would certainly be asked what colour hair the suspect has. If we're describing a new love, hair colour is generally the starting point – many a first impression or a judgement made will be about hair colour, and no hair colour has been more judged over the centuries than blonde.

With blondes historically being associated with youth, health, fertility and love, these characteristics became a natural choice for prostitutes to replicate in an endeavour to entice their customers; therefore blonde hair became a prostitute's trademark, which helped to establish the 'bad girl' image of the blonde.

The 'angels or harlots' judgement was especially prevalent in the 1950s: natural blondes were angels and artificial blondes were harlots. When this distinction was applied it gave rise to the 'bad girl' blonde, and it could be argued even contributed to the death of one of history's most infamous bottle blondes, Ruth Ellis, who shot dead her lover David Blakely in 1955.

Following her short trial, Ellis was sentenced to death and became the last woman to be hanged in Britain.

While Ruth was on remand she experienced prejudice regarding her appearance. She was assigned to the prison hospital at Holloway on Easter Monday 1955. Her hospital case notes show that Ruth was examined that day and then interviewed. The person who conducted Ruth's interview described her as 'a heavily made up woman' with 'bleached platinum hair'. He or she also described her as 'composed but rather hard faced and abrupt in manner'.[1]

The wardresses who worked with Ruth had initially expected her to be deceitful and 'brassy', which was how the popular press had portrayed her. They found a very different woman to the blonde harlot they were expecting. Wardress Evelyn Galilee was surprised by this reality:

In came this fragile girl, a Dresden doll. She was my age and tiny – no more than 5ft – and so very slim. Her skin was like porcelain. They had taken away her false nails, eyelashes and glamorous clothes and put her in baggy prison issue clothes. But they could not strip her of her dignity. Not once did she break down, scream or cry. Ruth had this acceptance of what she'd done and felt the punishment fitted the crime. Her eyes ... were bewitching the most beautiful violet-blue, the colour of forget-me-nots.[2]

Being an artificial blonde on remand, it was noted that Ruth's hair was 'now changing colour patchily as a result of continued neglect' and that 'it is of considerable importance to the Accused that she should be able to look her best at the trial'.[3]

While she was awaiting trial in May, Ruth was relieved to hear that permission had been granted for her hair to be bleached, on the condition that she signed a note to say that she would hold no one responsible for bleaching her hair.

Determined to look her best during the trial, Ruth wanted to discuss what she should wear with her defence counsel. They raised concern, suggesting that freshly bleached hair would cause the press, public and jury to view her with disdain. But Ruth was adamant, and her regular hairdressers, Shack's of Shaftsbury Avenue, provided instructions and chemicals for the wardress to carry out the application.

The hospital case notes recorded: 'She used to get her hair bleached twice a week in a hairdresser's as it grew so fast ... Bleaching of her hair appears satisfactory. Prisoner says quite good, but cold rinsing has made hair a little too blue.'[4]

On arriving at the Central Criminal Court, at the Old Bailey, on Monday, 20 June 1955, Ruth wore a black suit with astrakhan fur collar and cuffs and a white silk blouse. Her perfectly set platinum hair complemented her flawless make-up. A voice boomed from the public gallery 'Blonde tart'. Ruth remained composed and did not baulk, offering an almost imperceptible smile.

This vision in the dock did not correspond to what an abused woman was expected to look like, cowering with mousey hair and taking no care over her appearance.

During the trial the complexities of Ruth's relationship with Blakely were ignored and her pregnancy/miscarriage, which occurred ten days before the murder after David had allegedly punched her in the stomach, was not taken into consideration. Ruth was a blonde scorned, a woman who was open about her sex life during a decade that valued sexual repression. She did not present as a victim but instead was cool, calm and precise, with her clipped upper-class voice that was as false as her dyed blonde hair.

Ruth had felt socially inferior; she had desperately wanted to escape her working-class roots to socialise with the upper classes, where she thought she was destined to belong. Her mother told reporter Godfrey Winn in the *Sunday Dispatch* after the murder:

> Ruth hated us to be poor. She hated boys, too at that time. That seems so strange now. But she always liked clothes, and she would borrow mine and dress up in them. She wasn't like my other children. She was so very ambitious for herself. She used to say 'Mum, I'm going to make something of my life.'[5]

Evelyn Galilee, who worked in the condemned cell, warmed to her charge, finding Ruth helpful. She was impressed with Ruth's calmness under extreme conditions and in Evelyn's eyes, Ruth Ellis was 'first class'.

Ruth had been born on 9 October 1926 in Rhyl, North Wales. Her father, Arthur Hornby (the family surname was changed to Neilson in 1925), was a travelling professional musician. Ruth's mother, Elisabertha or 'Bertha', had been a Belgian refugee, and when she met Arthur she was also a single parent. Bertha had worked in domestic service and was allegedly raped by the son of the family she worked for. In 1918, as a result of the rape, she gave birth to a boy whom she named Julian.

Arthur and Bertha married in 1920, when she was three months pregnant with Arthur's child. Arthur's family disapproved of the union; they were not happy that Bertha was already a single parent, and being pregnant at the time of her marriage confirmed to them that she had no morals.

Within six months of getting married, Bertha delivered a daughter named Muriel, who was closely followed by her younger siblings Granville, Ruth, Jacques and Betty. In total, Bertha gave birth to nine children, four of whom died during childhood of disease such as measles;

she also suffered numerous miscarriages, which was not unusual at this time.

Arthur was doing well as a cinema pianist who accompanied the silent movies. However, this was the period just before the advent of the 'Talkies' in October 1927. Once a motion picture was synchronised with sound, Arthur's job became redundant.

The struggling young family was struck by a double tragedy in 1929. Ruth's uncle, who was Arthur's twin brother, died suddenly as did Ruth's younger brother, Jacques. The lack of work and recent bereavements prompted Arthur to move his family from Wales to Bramley, a village in England between Basingstoke and Reading. Arthur secured a job as a telephonist and hall porter at the Park Prewitt Mental Hospital.

The main reason Arthur accepted the job was that it came with a house big enough to accommodate the family. Possibly as a coping strategy, Arthur began drinking heavily, which resulted in outbursts of violence. Unfortunately, this was the beginning of a socially downward spiral for the Neilson family.

Ruth's sister Muriel claimed in later years that their father Arthur sexually abused both Ruth and herself. For Muriel, the sexual abuse, which continued for many years, culminated in the birth of a son by her father, whom she named Robert. Ruth never mentioned this at any time and it cannot be verified one way or another now, though it seems unlikely that Muriel would make such horrific claims against her father were they not true. As all of the people involved are now deceased, including Muriel, there is no way of attempting to confirm what happened all those years ago.

Close to her mother, Ruth was an introverted child. She experienced an extremely unsettled home life in the late 1930s and during the start of her teens her behaviour began to change; she grew insolent and brazen, and would run off unexpectedly. Ruth lacked interest in school and left as soon as she legally could at the age of 14 without any qualifications.

While Ruth had no academic aspirations, she did have social ones. Ambitious to make something of herself, she was independent and she aspired to do the unthinkable in the 1940s: to break out of her class and move up the ladder of stratification on to the upper level where she thought the real fun was.

Her passion in life at this time was dancing and socialising, which increased when she moved to London.

Arthur had taken a new job in London with the intention of establishing himself and acquiring suitable accommodation so that Bertha and the rest of the family could join him. Ruth, however, could not wait, and arrived at her father's flat in the capital at the age of 14 with her older brother and his girlfriend.

With the Second World War having broken out, those who stayed in London had to endure the Luftwaffe's bombing raids; people were being injured and homes were being destroyed. Everyone was living on their nerves with air raids and the constant threat of gas attacks.

But for Ruth, it was an exciting move; she was blossoming into a pretty young woman with natural auburn hair, she had an enviable figure with measurements of 34-24-34 – the perfect hourglass – and London provided a social life and unlimited possibilities.

Although life was at times precarious, Ruth was a strong-willed, determined girl and, prophetically, she had adopted the motto 'a short life and a gay one', a line borrowed from a British Pathé newsreel of 1921 that had been shown in the cinemas and referred to turkeys being reared for Christmas.[6]

Work was not difficult to come by: Ruth tried a variety of jobs but found many of them severely tried her low boredom threshold. She took a waitress position in a Lyon's Corner House Restaurant, near Trafalgar Square. It suited her outgoing personality and it could be considered as her first step towards a career as a hostess.

Ruth loved the social interaction of being a waitress and she thought that this would be the life for her, with the dream of owning a chain of restaurants. She soon realised that the more she turned on the charm, the more she received in tips to supplement her wages and, well-versed in the art of flirtation, she was especially popular with the men.

Things were going well for the girl-about-town until in March 1942. Having been admitted to hospital with chronic severe pains in her fingers, knee, and ribs, Ruth was diagnosed with arthritis, which was later confirmed to be acute infective arthritis. Several weeks in hospital followed but eventually when she was well enough to be discharged, on 3 May, Ruth could not believe her luck when the rheumatology consultant advised her to use dancing as therapeutic exercise. She assured everyone that she would follow the instructions to the letter, delighted to dance on doctor's orders!

By this time Bertha and the rest of the family had moved to London, sharing a Victorian house in Brixton. With her sister Muriel, Ruth would hit the town, having a ball, charming the US and Canadian serviceman and feeling very grown up and sophisticated. However, things were soon about to change for Ruth and the now flighty 17-year-old really would have to grow up.

5

YIELD TO THE NIGHT

On one of her nights out with her sister Muriel, Ruth met a handsome young French-Canadian serviceman named Clare Andrea McCallum. There was an unmistakable attraction between them and very quickly their flirtation led to them embarking on a sexual affair. Possibly at another time it would never have happened, but the young couple were caught up in the moment.

The terror of war provided a backdrop of fear and urgency. War made people reckless and less inhibited. They were aware that 'tomorrow' wasn't a certainty and they were driven to fill their 'today' with passion and fun. But Ruth wasn't as mature and sophisticated as she pretended to be, and very quickly found herself pregnant with Clare's baby.

The Canadian promised Ruth eternal love and marriage, and maybe her life would have turned out very differently – but Clare was unable to provide the promised marriage as he was already married with three children back in Canada. Ruth was about to join the ever-increasing statistics of single mothers of illegitimate children conceived during the war years.

Blissfully unaware of Clare's marital status, Ruth refused to be ashamed, even when her parents' disapproval was made clear to her. While the love of her life was posted abroad, he continued the charade, sending her love letters with talk of their forthcoming marriage.

She continued to work throughout her pregnancy and a few weeks before her due date she was packed off to spend her confinement at the Gilsland Nursing Home in Cumbria, away from the dangers of the bombs and air raids in London. The home was in fact originally a luxury hotel and spa, but during the Second World War it was used as a maternity hospital.

Not yet 18 years old, before she was able to spread her wings and fly, Ruth was grounded by the difficult birth of her first child on

15 September 1944, a boy she named Clare Andrea Neilson (known as Andre or Andy) after his father.

Due to the baby's father avoiding setting a date for the wedding, Bertha contacted his military unit, and was duly informed that Clare was married with children. When Ruth found out about her lover's wife and family in Canada, she was devastated by the brutal initiation into how cruel love could be and it had a transforming effect on her; the experience with Clare crushed her rosy-coloured outlook and destroyed her naivety, and she began to develop a prickly hard shell.

She said of that time, 'I no longer felt any emotion about men ... Outwardly I was cheerful and gay. Inwardly I was cold and spent.'[1]

Many women were forced to give up their illegitimate babies because 'good girls' didn't have a child out of wedlock. It became the biggest social shame; men could avoid responsibility but women were left literally carrying the baby. Marriage was sacred and only children born within wedlock had status. An unmarried mother faced condemnation in the community.

Ruth was fully aware of the expectation placed on a female in the 1940s and the life that any illegitimate child might face. Adoption or the biological grandparents acting as pseudo-parents were common choices when the family wanted to keep the baby. The guilt was immeasurable but the secret could well remain uncovered; at that point in time there was, of course, no DNA testing.

Regardless of the circumstance she found herself in, and the discrimination she knew she would have to deal with, Ruth was a powerhouse of courage and she was determined to keep her son. She had fallen in love with the tiny dark-haired boy and no one was going to take him away from her.

Weaving a story about Andy's father being killed in action, Ruth returned to work with the help of her family, who all took a share in the childcare.

It wasn't long before the young mother decided she wanted more from life and the birth of her baby was not enough to prevent her from progressing. Her ambition burned and she was driven with self-motivation to pursue the glamorous life. Ruth enrolled at drama school and began taking elocution lessons. For a while she also sang in a band, but, most of all, this resourceful young woman wanted to become an actress.

The reality of her chosen career prevented her from obtaining the desired outcome. Tuition fees were high and impossible to meet. Ruth had no financial support; she had to provide the money for her son's expenses and contribute to her parents' household.

Undeterred, Ruth explored the different avenues available to her, which resulted in her responding to an advert for an evening model with the Camera Club. Knowing it would mean semi-undressed or nude photographs didn't faze the open-minded, easy-going Ruth, who was instantly accepted by the club.

She saw the Camera Club as an opportunity to gain more illustrious assignments and to meet influential people with whom she could network. Socialising with the photographers, she deftly moved into their circle of friends and associates. It was during this time that Ruth came under the influence of the notorious London club owner Morris Conley, who owned the Court Club in the West End of London.

Conley offered Ruth a glimpse of glamour, with evening gowns and sparkle and a promise of the high life. Mixing in upper-class circles, he effectively coerced Ruth into prostitution under the guise of her becoming a club hostess. The job entailed encouraging patrons of the club to attend and buy drinks, and the hostess was also expected to sleep with customers on occasion. The club amounted to little more than a brothel with Conley as a pimp and the girls as his prostitutes.

Ruth could not resist: she would be receiving a phenomenal salary of £20 per week as well as clothes suitable to her position. Ruth's previous wage had been £2 a week plus tips, so £20 a week was life changing, although she gave the majority of her pay to her parents for the care of Andy.

Taking the sexual side of the job in her stride, which included sleeping with the unattractive Conley, she kept her eye on the prize, which was a glamorous lifestyle socialising with the rich, famous and influential. Her appearance was crucial to her position, and so she did not have to justify expensive clothing and accessories, beauty treatments and pampering.

Vivacious and fun, Ruth soon had a large circle of friends, including one young woman who was to become particularly special to her. Vicki Martin (1931–55), whose real name was Valerie Mewes, was inducted into the world of being a hostess by Ruth. They were kindred spirits and together they were a beautiful and formidable force on the social scene in London.

In 1950, a 39-year-old dental surgeon called George Ellis walked into the Court Club and was immediately captivated by Ruth. George pursued her relentlessly, despite the fact he was still in love with his ex-wife. Unknown to Ruth at the time, George was also an alcoholic who suffered from dark unpredictable episodes of depression.

Seventeen years her senior, George lavished Ruth with gifts, holidays, meals out and money. After a whirlwind romance, which was sometimes volatile, he managed to convince her to marry him. The wedding took place on 8 November 1950, but one unfortunate event after another culminated in the breakdown of their relationship, and in less than a year the marriage was over.

Subsequently, in the spring of 1951, when they had already separated, Ruth discovered she was four months pregnant with George's child. The pregnancy did not hold her back; she continued to follow her dream of being an actress and she secured a small walk-on part in the film *Lady Godiva Rides Again* (1951), which stared a young and already famous Diana Dors.

Doubtless Ruth felt star-struck! There was a myth that Ruth and Diana had been good friends and that Diana had obtained the small role of a beauty contestant for her, but there is no evidence to support this. It is unlikely that Diana's interaction with Ruth on the film set was any more than polite acknowledgment.

Ruth was not in Diana's sphere, although some years later the two young women would be linked again when Diana played the part of Mary Hilton in *Yield to the Night* (1956), a film about a young blonde shop girl who is in a jealous love triangle. After her lover commits suicide, Hilton takes revenge on her love rival, shooting her in cold blood. Mary Hilton eventually hangs for her crime.

Many people have thought *Yield to the Night* was inspired by Ruth Ellis, a belief that is still perpetuated to this day, but this is inaccurate. Joan Henry wrote the novel long before Ruth shot David Blakely dead.

When filming ended, Ruth made one last attempt at saving her marriage, but it was too late. Returning to London heavily pregnant on 2 October 1951, and in a state of anxiety and distress, Ruth gave birth to a daughter whom she called Georgina Jayne. The delivery was not straightforward for either Ruth or Georgina, and Ruth required sedation for some time after the birth.

Ruth felt listless and confused, and it is highly likely that she was also suffering from postnatal depression, which was not taken seriously in the 1950s. Often described as a 'nervous condition', it was sometimes treated with electroshock therapy and Valium, a drug that is known to cause dizziness, tiredness, blurred vision, hallucinations, confusion and depression amongst its many side effects.

A woman would be considered neurotic, and the symptoms of post-partum depression were not recognised as they are today. The consequence of being labelled 'neurotic' in the 1950s meant that women kept symptoms, thoughts and feelings to themselves for fear of being seen as insane.

Following Georgina's birth, George Ellis wanted Ruth to agree to putting their daughter up for adoption. He was also eager to get a divorce as quickly as possible. Ruth engaged the services of solicitor Victor Mishcon. George was giving Ruth an allowance of £4 a week, which did not cover her living expenses. Weighing up her choices, she felt the only way forward was to go backwards, to return to the best way she knew of making money. She went to see Morris Conley, who welcomed her back with open arms.

Conley had refurbished and renamed his nightclub, and it was now known as Carroll's Club. The hours had changed, and Conley had obtained a licence allowing him to open until 3 a.m. This proved a stumbling block for Ruth, as transport to the home of her parents was not available at that early hour. Conley, however, had the perfect solution: a room in a flat near to the club.

Ruth did not have to weigh up the pros and cons for long. She accepted Conley's offer and was soon ensconced at Carroll's while her parents took care of the children when she was working. Not fully recovered from Georgina's birth, the long hours took a toll on her health but she continued on regardless.

At Carroll's Club, Ruth was the most popular hostess. She had an abundance of feminine charm and a class that set her apart from the other girls. Her elocution lessons had not gone to waste and she was not out of place in any well-to-do environment.

In March 1952, Ruth applied for her first passport. She had a bevy of admirers, with one gentleman patron of the club in particular whisking her abroad for a holiday and supplying her with everything she would need, including a large post-holiday payment for service rendered.

In the run-up to Christmas that year, Ruth was admitted to hospital with what she thought was gastric flu. Sadly she was diagnosed with an ectopic pregnancy; the baby was developing in the fallopian tube. An emergency operation was required and Ruth was left with a permanent scar as a result of the surgery. The procedure had a lengthy recovery time and she was to remain in the hospital for two weeks over the New Year period. However, her hostess friends, including her best friend Vicki, came to visit bringing flowers and fun.

As the New Year dawned it brought with it a storm of emotion that was to change the course and the length of Ruth's life.

6

'MY LOVE AND HATE'

It was 1953 when Marilyn Monroe exploded on to the big screen in the film *Niagara* (released in London on 24 April), an American film noir telling the story of Rose Loomis. Monroe plays the blonde femme fatale, who is vacationing at a cabin in Niagara Falls with her husband George (Joseph Cotton) while she is also secretly meeting a lover; together they plan her husband's murder.

Ruth, along with the vast majority of the population at the time, was a frequent cinemagoer who would have been influenced, without a doubt, by the glamorous Hollywood stars such as Monroe. It just so happened that in the summer of 1953 Ruth took the decision to transform her auburn hair to platinum blonde, replicating Rose Loomis's short blonde wavy bob.

Looking at photos of both Ruth and Marilyn at this time, you can see a definite likeness in style. Ruth told the *Woman's Sunday Mirror* on 26 June 1955 that the colour change in 1953 had been an impulsive decision. Having woken up one morning with the desire to change what she saw in the mirror, she felt her hair colour and style were drab and needed updating.

Her sister, Muriel, thought the new colour suited her; she had also lost weight and wore her hair much shorter in the Monroe-esque curled bob. The overall effect on Ruth was quite ageing. At 26 she looked much older and it also gave a slightly hard edge to her appearance.

Ruth also began posing for more risqué photographs, and she began socialising with a different crowd of glamorous, wealthy people from the motor racing set who normally frequented the Steering Wheel Club, just off Park Lane, Mayfair. Her friend Vicki Martin had already established herself within the group and their ethos was fun, heavy drinking and motor sports. Patrons of the club included such luminaries as Stirling Moss, Douglas Fairbanks Jnr and Peter Ustinov.

When the Steering Wheel Club closed in the afternoon, the drinking and merriment would continue at other nearby establishments, including

Carroll's Club. One of the racing enthusiasts who belonged to the club was 24-year-old David Blakely. David came from a privileged background. His father was a doctor in Sheffield, and his wealthy stepfather encouraged David's love of motor racing, contributing to his financial ability to pursue a racing life.

In February 1952, David's father had died unexpectedly of coronary thrombosis. He left his son an inheritance of £7,000, which David received in 1953, exactly one year after his father's death. The legacy enabled David to live his dream and build a racing car with the help of his friend Anthony Findlater, a 31-year-old mechanical engineer.

David had previously had an affair with Ant Findlater's wife Carole, a journalist and sub-editor on *Woman* magazine. Carole left Ant temporarily but soon reconciled with her husband and returned to the marriage. Several years later when questioned about the affair Ant said, 'If he'd had the opportunity, David wasn't the sort of man to pass it up.'[1] The marriage settled down, and a strong friendship flourished between the three of them, with Ant fully forgiving his errant wife and philandering best friend.

As a child, David had not been particularly popular at school. One of his peers said of him in 1955, 'The young David Blakely took a positive delight in hurting others. His mercy did not seem to me to exist …'[2]

A slim 5ft 9in, David had grown into a reasonably pleasant-looking man: clean-shaven with a mop of unruly dark hair, and with an arrogance and a charm that many women fell for. Another regular of the Steering Wheel Club and an acquaintance of David's was a man named Desmond Cussen. Desmond was on the margins of the racing set; he was interested but not active within the sport. Desmond had a smart conservative appearance, with a thin moustache and neatly slicked-back hair.

Born in Epsom, Surrey, Desmond Cussen had received a boarding-school education and trained in accountancy. He too came from a wealthy background and he had served in the RAF as a bomber pilot during the war, being demobbed in 1946.

Desmond had a two-bedroom flat at 20 Goodwood Court, a private mansion block in Marylebone. He was a serious and polite gentleman who appeared somewhat out of place within the scene he had chosen to be part of, although he did drink heavily on occasions and at those times he was rather a morose drunk.

Together, David and Desmond were destined to change the course of Ruth's life. It is not known precisely when she met them both, although it is believed to have been just before October 1953 at Carroll's Club.

Ruth remembers seeing David for the first time casually propped up against the bar making inappropriate and distasteful remarks about the venue and its hostesses. He called the club a den of vice. Ruth recalls this memory in an interview with the *Sunday Mirror*, headlined 'My Love and Hate', on 26 June 1955. She describes that initial meeting towards the end of 1953:

> Slowly and offensively he turned to the girls, looked them up and down and said, 'I suppose you are the hostesses?' I said to my friends, 'Who is that pompous little ass?' My party was composed mainly of racing drivers. Somebody said, 'Oh, that's David Blakely. He's a driver too.' Mr Blakely was really mad with me. He said, 'I suppose you're another of these hostesses?' I smiled politely and said, 'No, as a matter of fact, I'm an old has-been.'[3]

Ruth intentionally spoke loud enough for David Blakely to hear her derogatory comment. She also stated in the same interview that she hoped she would 'never have to see that little shit again'.

About this time Conley offered Ruth the position of manager of one of his other clubs in Knightsbridge, called the Little Club. Ruth accepted the position and relished the idea of being in charge of the club, which also came with accommodation above the premises.

David was Ruth's first customer to walk into the Little Club and order a drink from her. They both put the previous spats behind them and, within two weeks of meeting David, Ruth had moved him into her flat above the club. The interior of the flat revealed Ruth's movie star aspirations; her bedroom was painted white, with a flourish of Hollywood glamour. Andy and Georgina would also stay at the flat from time to time when they weren't at her parents or with her sister Muriel.

Although Ruth and David's relationship began with antagonism on both sides, they quickly fell into a passionate love affair that, at this early stage, appeared to be more of a physical attraction than a love match. David was reported to have told his racing driver friend Cliff Davis that Ruth was 'one of the best fucks in London'. Davis, who had also allegedly slept with Ruth, was able to concur that Ruth was rather talented in the bedroom and a skilled lover, calling her an 'artist' with particular reference to the deployment of her tongue.[4]

During Ruth's trial Cliff Davis spoke out in Ruth's favour, commenting that, sex aside, he held Ruth in very high esteem and that she was a woman of principles, unlike David Blakely who was severely lacking in the fundamental ethics. Davis also accurately (with hindsight) described the couple's relationship as 'unstable as a stick of dynamite'.[5]

Desmond Cussen was also beginning to take a prominent role in Ruth's life. He was captivated by her charm and personality, and his obvious desires began to cause friction with David. Desmond and Ruth got on exceedingly well and, like the other men in Ruth's life, he was ready and willing to lavish gifts on her and help her out financially.

One puzzling aspect of their relationship was that, while Desmond proclaimed his love for Ruth (it was reported he never had another woman in his life after Ruth's death), he also claimed that she was emotionally unresponsive in bed, that her lovemaking was a series of actions that she repeated in a perfunctory manner. Significantly, he is the only man that Ruth slept with to say such a thing, although it did not appear to dampen Desmond's ardour for her, which invariably accelerated his conflict with David.

However, David was also pursuing other women, despite the intensity between Ruth and himself. Within a month of knowing David, Ruth had caught sight of a notice that appeared in *The Times* in the 13 November edition announcing David's engagement to a Miss Mary Dawson of Yorkshire.[6]

He had managed to keep his 25-year-old fiancée separate from his wild London lifestyle and nights with Ruth, which was probably not too tricky as Mary lived a good distance from London, although she did attend various social events and sporting fixtures as David's significant other.

There isn't any real evidence of Ruth's reaction to finding out that David was engaged but we do know that Ruth became pregnant in December 1953, presumably with David's child. When she was questioned at her trial regarding the pregnancy and asked about David's reaction to it she stated, 'he was very concerned about my welfare. Although he was engaged to another girl, he offered to marry me, and he said it was quite unnecessary for me to get rid of the child, but I did not want to take advantage of him.'[7]

Ruth also told the court that she was not in love with David at the time, and she felt that it would be quite easy to resolve the problem, which she referred to as a 'mess'. When hearing Ruth's response to the marriage proposal it should be remembered that at this point she was still legally married to George Ellis. On 8 March 1954, Ruth terminated the pregnancy, without financial help from David.

Under Ruth's management, the Little Club rapidly became the place to go for politicians, actors, the racing set and journalists alike. It also became a favourite gathering place for gay men; they felt safe at the Little in an era when homosexuality was still a taboo and a punishable offence in law. She had taken the Little to great heights, rapidly increasing the revenue, and giving the club a smarter appearance and an atmosphere that was previously lacking.

The problem was the love triangle that Ruth had encouraged. David was reluctant to introduce Ruth into his family life, which fed into her inferiority complex; while, in stark contrast, Desmond wanted to marry her. He took her to race meetings, social events, restaurants and parties. Desmond was also financially supportive, whereas David was becoming a financial sponge, with Ruth funding his lifestyle.

She was flattered by Desmond's attentiveness and generosity. There also seems an element of Ruth being somewhat manipulative, playing Desmond and David against each other. Each man was jealous of the other, and this boosted Ruth's self-esteem. It seems likely that, while her heart lay with David, her head was fixed on Desmond.

In March 1954, Ant and Carole Findlater moved into 29 Tanza Road, Hampstead. David persuaded Ant to give up his job at Aston Martin and work on David's racing-car project, the Emperor, full time for a wage of £10 per week. David finally introduced Ruth to the Findlaters at Ant's thirty-third birthday party. Carole and Ruth took an instant dislike to each other. Carole observed that Ruth spent the evening flirting with other men while Ruth thought of Carole as a 'Mother Superior'.

Very soon, the Emperor began to drain David's inheritance. Initially he was a generous buyer of rounds at the Little Club, possibly in an attempt to improve his popularity. As his funds diminished, Ruth foolishly allowed him to drink for free at the club, and he was already practically living there full time for free.

When Morrie Conley found out about the living arrangements, he was so angry that he demanded that she pay £10 a week in rent from there on in. Previously, the flat had been a free perk of the job.

David was seriously compromising Ruth's lifestyle. She could no longer afford the beautiful clothes; weekly visits to the hairdressers; and her favourite signature scent, Miss Dior. Saving was not in Ruth's nature; if she saw something she had to have it, and she was also generous with her friends. However, now, to be able to afford her relationship with David, she had to re-establish afternoon liaisons with gentlemen to top up her income.

It was not unusual for the patrons of the Little Club to witness violent rows between the couple, which were escalating during the autumn of 1954. David would often arrive at the club already fuelled with drink, looking for a fight and ready to cause an explosive scene. Ruth would attempt to calm the situation, but David would have none of it, verbally belittling and abusing Ruth and on occasions physically striking her.

On one occasion David's sexual jealousy got the better of him and he accused Ruth of sleeping with Desmond. He threw the accusation at Ruth in front of other club members, much to Ruth's anger and embarrassment. When members attempted to step in and stop the abuse, Ruth indicated that she would prefer to manage the situation herself, protecting him from the wrath of her customers. Urging David to go with her upstairs to her flat, the row continued and noisy bumps and bashes would ensue, suggesting that the physical assault had continued.

After such events as this, Ruth would reappear sometime later, obviously upset and thoroughly depressed. However, she seemed incapable of making a stand and ending the cycle of violence in which the couple found themselves entangled.

At the beginning of December, it was becoming obvious that this situation would not be able to continue. The Little Club's takings were being adversely affected by this toxic relationship. Ruth was chasing David day and night and David was equally obsessive and jealous; he began more and more to show his resentment in front of and towards the customers of the Little Club.

Ruth had to face financial facts, and with the plummeting club takings, the inevitable parting with Conley arrived. Out of a home and almost out of a job, Desmond picked up the pieces again and took Ruth into his home at Goodwood Court. Ruth moving in with Desmond caused David to go into a spasm of anger. She had promised Conley she would stay *in situ* as club manager until he could find a suitable replacement.

Ruth had already agreed to Georgina moving to Warrington to live with a childless professional couple who George Ellis had recommended, although Ruth drew the line at the suggestion they should adopt her. With their daughter's custody agreed, George filed for divorce.

When Ruth moved into Desmond's flat she suggested that boarding school would provide Andy with a good start in life, and it would also get him out of the overcrowded flat. Desmond, who had become a father figure to Andy, agreed and it seemed a natural progression that by August 1954 he was also paying Andy's boarding-school fees.

7

1955 – A BAD YEAR

It must be acknowledged that 1955 was always going to be a bad year for Ruth. On 9 January 1955, her beautiful and vibrant best friend, Vicki Martin, died in an automobile accident, aged 23. The fun-loving beauty died of a broken neck and spinal injuries. This tragedy shook Ruth's world and had a profound effect on her mental and emotional well-being.

Vicki's funeral took place on the morning of Friday 14 January, at Golders Green Crematorium. In the afternoon her ashes were buried and the service took place in her real name of Valerie Mewes at the little parish church in Englefield Green, Surrey. Ruth's grief was overwhelming and it was also the day her divorce from George Ellis became final.

By early January 1955 Ruth and David were back together again, but their relationship had not improved, and the drunken brawling between the couple became even more of a frequent occurrence. Both accused the other of being unfaithful; both were completely accurate.

David had been invited to drive for the Bristol Works Team at Le Mans on 11 June 1955 (a date David would not live to see), and even though he knew he was in an utter mess both financially and with Ruth, in his excitement he asked Ruth to join him in France. Of course, Ruth said yes and immediately organised French lessons at Desmond's expense. She began her private tuition on 17 January; however, she was not a dedicated student and therefore made little if any progress.

Ruth's paranoia was increasing; she was regularly instructing Desmond to drive her around to look for David's car or discreetly following him from one place to another. It is only in recent years that stalking, which in effect was what Ruth and Desmond were doing, became a criminal offence.

There was a particularly nasty scene on 7 February 1955, when she located David at Penn, near his family home in Buckinghamshire. An altercation took place, resulting in Desmond having to take her to Middlesex hospital to be examined.

There were no apparent internal injuries and no broken bones, but Ruth had sustained bruising and a blackened left eye. She would tell other people she had been in an accident. A spray of red carnations arrived from David with an apologetic note.

Strangely, both men made an attempt to be civil with each other. On one occasion David even invited Desmond to be his co-driver at a rally in Brighton. It is possible that David, who had experienced being in a love triangle with the Findlaters, had hoped for a similar outcome with Ruth and Desmond.

During February, and with extraordinary powers of persuasion, Ruth, who was still working at the Little Club in Brompton Road, convinced Desmond to provide her with a furnished room in Egerton Gardens, which was just a five-minute walk from the club as opposed to the hour-and-a-half walk from Goodwood Court.

Desmond agreed and duly paid the rent, while Ruth, unbeknown to Desmond, moved David in and introduced him to her landlady as her 'husband'.

Ruth saw her relationship with Desmond from a practical point of view; he helped her out and she had sex with him. Ruth was adept at gaining the sympathy vote, knowing just what to say to make men feel protective towards her. This was a woman who was skilled at obtaining money from gentlemen friends by making them feel special, appearing to take them into her confidence and weaving a sad story to elicit sympathy for her plight. The men involved thought they were the only one to whom she had turned for help in her hour of need, and of course they were unable to resist this delicate fragile doll of a woman who just needed a strong shoulder and a little bit of help to get her out of her troubles.

On Monday 7 March, Ruth began a modelling course at the Margery Molyneux Agency, Woodstock Green, just off Oxford Street. The agency was owned and run by Cherry Marshall, who recalled:

[She] was never a model in the professional sense, although she was always described as one. She'd done a few pictures for a provincial magazine … When I interviewed her I told her she was too short and that she almost certainly wouldn't get any work … She was quite pretty and heavily made up in a theatrical way, but when we got rid of her pancake makeup she had a rather refined little face, and she looked very good in swimsuits too. Maybe, I said, if a manufacturer wants a petite size model she would be given a chance.[1]

Desmond was very encouraging of Ruth taking the modelling course; he hoped once again that it would take her mind away from David and give her a new focus and a possible career.

Cherry Marshall described Ruth's attendance on the course as being erratic, and at one point during a beachwear rehearsal she noticed that Ruth was not taking part. Cherry was surprised because she thought this would be Ruth's area to shine. When she spoke to Maggie Wood, who was in charge of the school at that time, the response was that Ruth was in a poor state and covered in bruises from head to toe, therefore she couldn't possibly parade in a swimsuit and, furthermore, she had red-rimmed, swollen eyes from crying.

After this incident, Marshall had a word with Ruth and suggested she made up for the lost classes in the next course, and that she should have her passing-out show with that intake of girls instead. Ruth seemed happy at this suggestion, but unfortunately it was the last time she attended the course and they did not see her again.

The Little Club had been a focus for Ruth, but when she came to the end of her notice David became even more central to her world than ever before, and while he was telling friends that he wanted out of the relationship, he was sending altogether different signals to Ruth. By now, friends of David were under the distinct impression that he was staying in the relationship with Ruth primarily out of fear. Ruth's violent and jealous nature frightened David and he claimed he was petrified that Ruth would seek out his family and explode.

David had been having another long term relationship with a married woman in Penn, which he realised was going nowhere and couldn't continue. At the same time he felt his affair with Ruth was doomed but he was unable to square his shoulders and straighten out his life.

Ultimately, at 25, David did not have the maturity or the life experience that enabled him to cope with the complexity of his relationship with Ruth. He was perplexed; he didn't want to stay with Ruth, but he was unable to leave her. Ant and Carole Findlater were astounded at the situation and could not understand why their friend was continuing an affair with someone they considered to be such a vulgar woman and to whom they referred to as a 'common tart'.[2]

Not long after Vicki had died, Ruth discovered she was pregnant again and she believed the baby was David's. When she shared the news with him, this time he didn't offer to marry her. Instead, according to Ruth they got into a violent argument that resulted in David attempting to strangle her.

Ruth admitted the fight was spurred on by sexual jealousy on her part. David hit her soundly around the head, causing temporary loss of hearing, and then grabbed her tightly around the throat with one hand and punched her in her stomach with the other until she blacked out.

On 28 March, possibly as a result of the beating, Ruth said she lost the baby. It is not clear whether Ruth had a natural miscarriage, as she used the term 'abortion' when talking about the circumstances surrounding this event. Later at the trial, she said that David had become very violent and she did not know whether this had caused the 'miscarriage', but in her written statement she said:

On 28th March, I had an abortion, and I was not at all well. On that occasion, David took no interest in my welfare and did not even bother to inquire if I was all right. I was very hurt indeed about this, and I began to feel a growing contempt for him. The results of my abortion continued until Tuesday 5th April.[3]

It does seem more likely that an abortion took place when examining the evidence of David's words when he attempted to reassure Ruth, telling her on 30 March that he 'wished I had had enough money to keep little David. But I haven't.'

According to Marks and Van Den Bergh, in their 1977 book *Ruth Ellis: A Case of Diminished Responsibility?*, Mr Justice Havers had since said that, had he and the jury known of her abortion and that she had been taking tranquilisers before drinking Pernod, she would never have hanged.[4]

It is clear that the balance of Ruth's mind had become disturbed. It would be an unusual person who could lose a best friend and a baby within months of each other and not find it traumatic. To take a severe beating from the man you love, to be disregarded and cast aside, treated as an inferior, would have added to Ruth's feeling of her life being worthless and living untenable.

At around this time, David began insistently telling friends he wanted to leave Ruth for good. David's friend Cliff Davis recalled that David had told him, 'I'd do anything to get away from her, but as soon as we meet it all starts again.'

Ruth also shared her concerns with Cliff, telling him she was certain David was seeing other women. One night while she and Cliff were drinking at the Esmeralda's Barn nightclub she told him that, 'she had given David some money and that he was probably out somewhere having sex with some tart.'

8

THE FINAL SCENES

It was now April and, despite earlier concerns, the Emperor was almost complete; however, Ant Findlater and their mutual friend car enthusiast and salesman Clive Gunnell expressed concerns over whether it was ready to race. Time and money were almost exhausted, David was desperate and, ignoring his friends' reservations, he entered the Emperor in the forthcoming race at Oulton Park in the north of England.

Entering the race meant less time available to spend with Ruth, who was in bad shape after the loss of her baby. She continued to pester David, phoning him obsessively. To buy himself some time and space, he once again promised to marry her when the car was completed. When it was time to take the Emperor to Oulton Park, Ant put his concerns behind him and he and Carole made an unlikely foursome with Ruth and David. Carole attended the race in her capacity as women's editor for the *Daily Mail*, writing an article about women's fashion at the track.

The event was to be a non-starter; the Emperor broke down during practice and was never to race again. David was beside himself with anger and frustration, and he accused Ruth of jinxing the car, reminding her that she had once said he would have no luck because of the way he treated her. During their altercation, she warned him she would not accept him walking over her for much longer. David's response was to tell Ruth that she'd always stand it because she loved him.

During this time, Desmond had been away in Wales and he thought Ruth was at home. On his return, he found a note from Andy's school. Ruth had forgotten to pick Andy up from boarding school for the holidays. When Desmond phoned Ruth at Egerton Gardens, her housekeeper explained that Mrs Ellis was at a race meeting with her 'husband'. Desmond was furious. It was only later that the housekeeper discovered a note from Ruth to say that if Mr Cussen rang she should tell him that she was visiting Georgina. Tempers were frayed all around.

On Wednesday 6 April, after they had returned, David's temper improved considerably when he had received his team photo previously taken on 25 March for Le Mans. He was very proud of the picture and gave a copy to his mother and a copy to Ruth. He signed Ruth's copy 'To Ruth, with all my love – David'.

Ruth, who understood the financial predicament he was in with the breakdown of the racing car, told him that he should give up his idea of becoming a professional racing driver. David, buoyed by this team photo and a new enthusiasm, suggested that she should persuade Desmond Cussen to consider loaning the £400 needed for repairs.

There are two quite distinctly different versions of what happened at the beginning of the Easter Holidays. On Good Friday, 8 April 1955, Ruth claimed that David Blakely left Egerton Gardens around 10 a.m. He was in a very positive mood and told Ruth he was going to talk to Ant Findlater about saving the Emperor. He said to her that he would return the same evening so that they could take Andy out. Ruth said that they had parted on the very best of terms.

The Findlaters, on the other hand, described that evening in much more detail and their version of events did not correlate with Ruth's.

The couple recalled that they had visited the Magdala pub on 8 April with David. When, around 8 p.m., he had looked at his watch to return to Egerton Gardens, he had told them Ruth had been bothering him, that she had wanted him to take her out that evening but he could not cope with her any longer. Ant Findlater advised David he should break off the relationship and that he was stupid to continue seeing her.

David explained that her tantrums were becoming too difficult to handle, and he said he was desperately unhappy and frightened at her increasing violence. Feeling that he needed a clean break, he would usually have headed to his family home at Penn, but after the last showdown there he was afraid that Ruth would follow him and there would be another violent scene.

He stated that he did not want to cause his mother and stepfather any further embarrassment. On hearing David say this, Carole Findlater snapped at him, 'For God's sake! Don't be so bloody spineless and silly. Any man can leave any woman. What can she do about it?'

David resented being rebuked and replied to the effect, 'It's easy for you to talk like that, but you don't know her. You don't know what she can get up to!'[1]

Carole's patience was wearing thin and by this point she shrugged off David's excuses, feeling somewhat defeated by the whole situation. They had been telling David that Ruth was a bad lot for some time now and he wasn't paying attention to the answers they were giving him.

Ant felt sorry for David and suggested that David should come and stay at Tanza Road with them for the Easter holiday. Ant also told David that, should Ruth harass him, he would personally make sure that he and Carole would deal with her. David felt relieved at this suggestion, gratefully accepting his friend Ant's solution to this sticky relationship problem.

Ruth later maintained that the Findlaters were responsible for what eventually happened. They had taken it upon themselves to unite and form a human shield between Ruth and their friend. Humiliated and angry, this fuelled her jealousy and made her frustrated and volatile.

Desmond Cussen collected Ruth and Andy from Egerton Gardens and took them to his flat at Goodwood Court for lunch. In the afternoon they all went to the cinema and in the evening Desmond returned them to Ruth's flat and left. Ruth put Andy to bed and made herself up to go out that evening with David. She poured a drink and waited for him to pick her up around 7.30.

By 9.30, Ruth was angry as David was two hours late and she thought that maybe he had drunk too much at the Findlaters, so she rang Tanza Road. The Findlaters' au pair answered the phone and explained that the couple were out and that she was alone there with the baby. Ruth demanded to know if David had gone out with them. The au pair replied that she did not know.

Ruth gave it an hour and then called back. This time Ant Findlater answered the phone. He told her Blakely was not there. Ruth told Ant that she had been waiting for David since 7.30, the time he told her he would pick her up to go out. Ant was non-committal as Ruth began pushing him for answers regarding David's whereabouts.

Ant eventually told her he had seen David but that his friend had driven on, without telling him where he was going. Ruth believed Ant Findlater was lying and at her trial she recalled his attitude towards her as being 'cocky' and that she felt both Carole and Ant had taken control of David.

Ruth continued to phone Tanza Road regularly that evening, although Ant's reaction to this was to hang up without talking to her. The Findlaters said the obsessive calls had begun to scare David and caused him to tremble with fear.

Ruth had tried to phone Desmond in between calls to Hampstead, but he wasn't answering either. Sometime after midnight she finally got an answer from Desmond. She asked him to come and pick her up and to drive her to Tanza Road. Desmond duly drove her over to the Findlaters' flat. On arriving, Ruth jumped out of the car, ran up the steps and rang the bell. Receiving no reply, she kept her finger on the button.

Frustrated by being ignored, Ruth walked to the nearest phone box and rang the Findlaters. Ant lifted the receiver and then let it drop back on the cradle. She went straight back to Tanza Road and repeatedly rang the bell.

At her trial, Ruth said she was confused, stating she heard giggling and that it was the au pair.

Having no satisfaction of an answer from either the phone or by ringing on the doorbell, Ruth ran to Desmond's car and grabbed a rubber torch from the glove box. She then ran over to David's Vanguard car and battered out three of the windows. During the whole episode, Desmond remained in his car, watching the drama unfold. At her trial Ruth was asked how she felt at this time. She responded by saying she was in 'rather a nasty mood'.[2]

Ant called the police. He then went out on to the street to try to occupy Ruth until the police arrived. When they did Ruth bombarded the police officer with information and complaints about David and the Findlaters. Feeling this was a run-of-the-mill domestic dispute, the officer tried to calm Ruth down and persuade her to go home to get some sleep.

The police left, and Ant went in and shut the door on Ruth, adding to her agitation. She began screaming and shouting hysterically. It was by now 2.30 a.m., and Ant called the police again. This time, the officer used stronger language with Ruth, making it clear that she would be arrested for a breach of the peace if she continued. Ruth walked away, got into Desmond's car and they both drove off.

Desmond dropped Ruth home at Egerton Gardens and returned to Goodwood Court. Ruth spent the rest of the night sitting up chain smoking, her mind going over the events of Friday and the early hours of Saturday. She felt sure that David was having several affairs, including sleeping with the Findlaters' au pair. She thought she had been unjustly treated, and felt humiliated and angry.

On the morning of Saturday 9 April, Ruth left Andy in bed, dressed and took a taxi to Hampstead. The weather was on the chilly side, miserable, windy and cloudy. Arriving early at Tanza Road, Ruth quickly found a place to conceal herself in a doorway and by now she was utterly exhausted and shivering in the cold temperature of the morning.

At around 10 a.m. her vigil paid off when she saw Ant Findlater leave the house. Looking left and right, and satisfied there was no one around, he carefully beckoned someone out of the house. It was David Blakely. Together they inspected the damage to the Vanguard, then promptly got in the car and drove away.

She felt justified; she was not paranoid and knew now for sure they were lying to her. Suspecting they were going to Clive Gunnell's garage in Mayfair, she left just enough time for them to arrive before going to a phone box and calling the garage. When the phone was answered, she gave a false name and asked for Ant Findlater. Ant came to the phone but the second he heard Ruth's voice he put the phone down.

Ruth immediately hailed a taxi to Goodwood Court. On arriving, she asked Desmond to phone the garage; he did so but was equally unsuccessful. At this point, he reminded Ruth that Andy was alone at the bedsit in Egerton Gardens. By now it was lunchtime, so together they drove to Egerton Gardens and gave Andy lunch. They then took him to the zoo in Regent's Park. When they got there, Desmond gave Andy enough money to entertain himself, with instructions for him to make his own way home.

From Regent's Park, Desmond drove Ruth directly to Hampstead and eventually they found David's car parked outside the Magdala public house. Ruth decided it would be best to head to Tanza Road as, due to the licensing laws at the time, David would have to leave the Magdala by 3 p.m. when it closed. When she left Desmond, he lost track of where she went so he began to drive around to look for her. Unbeknown to him, Ruth had struck up a conversation with some plasterers who were working on a house across the road from No. 29.

Enquiring as to why the men were working on an Easter holiday weekend, they told Ruth that it was a rush job as the vendor wanted to get the house on the market and make a quick sale.

The vendor overheard Ruth expressing an interest in buying the house and invited her in for a cup of tea and a look around. Sitting sipping her tea, in the front room of the house, Ruth had the perfect view of No. 29 and saw David and Ant return. Making her excuses to the owner, she left and slipped back into the doorway where she had hidden the previous evening.

Eventually, David and Ant re-emerged from the property with Carole and the au pair, who was carrying the Findlaters' daughter, Francesca. The small party got into David's car and headed in the direction of the Magdala. Ruth wasn't able to follow them quickly enough on foot but shortly after they had all left Desmond located her. Ruth instructed him to take her to the Magdala, but when they arrived David's car was not there.

It was getting late, so they returned to Egerton Gardens. Andy arrived back from his lonesome day out, was given dinner and put to bed. Later they again left Andy alone and Desmond drove Ruth back over to Hampstead. The Magdala was busy, but there was no sign of the Vanguard or Blakely. Ruth instructed Desmond to drive her back to Tanza Road, where they located David's vehicle outside No. 29.

There appeared to be a party going on and, as Ruth stood looking up at the flat, someone opened a window to let cigarette smoke out. She could hear David's voice, and he seemed to be talking to a woman who was doing a great deal of giggling. Ruth automatically associated the giggles with the au pair. From subsequent interviews, it was more likely to have been a friend of the Findlaters whose name was Charlotte.

According to the Findlaters, this small Easter weekend gathering of friends was to drown their sorrows regarding the state of the Emperor and to reassure David that he was among friends and did not have to fear Ruth.

Desmond sat in the car while Ruth was intently trying to listen to what was going on. Desmond found this to be embarrassing and did not want to eavesdrop.

At 10 p.m., Ant and David came out of the house with an unidentifiable woman and Ruth assumed it was the au pair. She heard David say, 'Let me put my arm around you for support.' This confirmed in Ruth's mind that the Findlaters were using their employee as a honeytrap to conspire to lure David away from her.

Ruth did not see the three return to the house; she had taken a break from her vigil, possibly for a call of nature. When she returned to her hide-out she saw the blinds at the front room window, under the Findlaters' flat, had been pulled down. At this she once again assumed that it was the au pair's bedroom and that the au pair and David had gone to bed together.

Feeling exhausted and defeated, she asked Desmond to drive her back to Egerton Gardens. With chronic sleep deprivation, her mind was not functioning logically. The Findlaters were making it impossible for her to talk to David, and her frustration and anger was building.

Returning to Egerton Gardens, she continued to smoke and drink – staying awake another night. At 9 a.m. on Easter Sunday, Ruth phoned the Findlaters again. Ant picked up the phone, and she told him, 'I hope you are having an enjoyable holiday because you have ruined mine.'[3] Ant put down the phone without speaking before she could get her full sentence finished, adding to her overwhelming feelings of frustration and humiliation.

Ruth spent the rest of the morning at her flat until just before lunch, when Desmond arrived. He took her and Andy back to Goodwood Court for lunch. At her trial, Ruth said she completely forgot what they did that day, but she recalled that her son was with them and that they amused him in some way.

Her memory kicked back in around 7.30 p.m. when she returned to Egerton Gardens and put Andy to bed. Ruth identified this as the time she first felt she wanted to kill David. At some point Ruth had obtained a revolver and slipped it into her bag. After the murder she wasn't willing to divulge where she had obtained the gun from.

Desmond had sworn on oath that he dropped Ruth off at 7.30 p.m. and did not see her again. After the trial, Ruth contradicted her initial statement. She said that Desmond drove her to the Magdala on Sunday night to find David and that he also oiled the gun, gave it to her and showed her how to fire it.

At midday on Sunday, Blakely went to the Magdala with Ant Findlater to meet their friend Clive Gunnell. David was a regular at the Magdala and was well liked by staff and customers. After meeting at the pub, the Findlaters took their daughter to Hampstead Heath fair and David went along, too. Arranging a soiree for the evening, Clive Gunnell promised to bring along his gramophone and records, so after the fair David and Carole drove to Clive's house to pick him up.

Returning to Tanza Road, they listened to music, chatted, smoked and drank. At around 9 p.m., Carole ran out of cigarettes, and the beer had also been drunk, so she asked David to go and buy some more, to which he and Clive agreed. They headed out to the Magdala in the car, which was quite surprising as both Clive and David had been drinking and the Magdala was within easy walking distance.

When Ruth arrived at Tanza Road, the car had gone, so she headed straight to the Magdala and, as she expected, the Vanguard was parked outside.

Ruth's feeling that she wanted to kill David became overwhelming. She peered through the stained glass windows of the pub, watching them order their drinks with David making his purchases at the off licence section. She watched them drain their glasses and then walk casually to the door of the pub. Ruth was now standing on the pavement with her back to the Magdala. As they emerged on to the pavement, Clive headed to the passenger side of the car and waited for David to get in and release the catch on the door so Clive could also get in.

David had noticed Ruth as he walked towards the car but turned his back on her. As he fumbled in his pocket for the keys, Ruth called out 'David'. He continued to ignore her and began to remove his keys from his pocket. Ruth called out again, but this time she took the gun out of her bag. David turned and upon seeing the gun he ran straight towards his friend. Ruth fired two shots, and David screamed Clive's name. Ruth followed him as he ran, and Ruth told Clive to get out of the way.

David did not know which way to turn. He naturally panicked and ran, but not quickly enough. As he ran past the car down the hill, there was a third shot, and he fell. Ruth ran towards him as he was sprawled face down on the ground, with blood and beer frothing around him (he had been carrying beer bottles to take back to the party) and, with less than 3 inches between David and the gun, she pulled the trigger, firing two bullets into his back.

With five shots fired, Ruth attempted to discharge the last round into her own head, but for whatever reason she did not pull the trigger. As she lowered her arm the final shot rang out, ricocheting off the pavement into the hand of a woman who was walking towards the pub with her husband. At this point Ruth turned to Clive and said, 'Go and call the police.'

9

'A LIFE FOR A LIFE'

David lay dying on the ground, moaning and bleeding from his mouth, while off-duty PC Alan Thompson cautioned Ruth.

PC Thompson had been drinking in the Magdala and was the first officer at the scene. He took the gun from Ruth, placing it into his own pocket with complete disregard for preserving evidence such as finger-prints. It is also worth considering that Thompson had been drinking, which would make one question the detrimental effect of this on his thinking and actions that night, particularly in relation to his treatment of the gun and his evidence as a witness.

Thompson accompanied Ruth Ellis to Hampstead Police Station at approximately 10 p.m., where she admitted her guilt, adding that she was 'rather confused'.

The first the police knew about her son was when she mentioned him in her statement. The police panicked and immediately dispatched officers to Egerton Gardens. Fearful she may have killed Andy, they were relieved to find him sleeping when they arrived.

There were significant gaps in Ruth's statement that were not explored to the extent that they should have been. Ruth did not mention what had occurred on the Saturday before the shooting and she left Sunday's events completely blank.

When she was asked what she had intended to do with the gun, Ruth replied, 'I intended to find David and shoot him.'[1] And thus she sealed her fate.

After the Findlaters were interviewed, their statements drew Desmond Cussen into the picture and he was interviewed by the police as well.

At 12.30 p.m. on Monday 11 April, Ruth Ellis was charged with the murder of David Blakely. Later that afternoon, when brought before Hampstead Magistrates' Court, Ruth was granted legal aid and appointed a solicitor. She was then remanded in custody until 20 April and taken to

Holloway Prison, where she requested a Bible and a photograph of David. The hospital reports state she was heavily sedated and slept through the night.

A journalist from the *Daily Mirror*, Dougie Howell, went to No. 44 Egerton Gardens and spoke with Ruth's housekeeper, Mrs Winstanley, suggesting that Ruth would need a first-class solicitor and that a legal aid solicitor would not be helpful to her.

Howell persuaded Mrs Winstanley to encourage Ruth to accept the solicitor recommended by the *Daily Mirror* and that they would pay for his services in return for Ruth's life story. Ruth agreed and John Bickford of Cardew-Smith & Ross was engaged to act for her. Ruth's own solicitor, Victor Mishcon, did not handle criminal cases.

One of the first things Ruth did from her cell was to write a letter to David Blakely's mother apologising for what had happened.

Ruth had prepared herself for death. However, with a few exceptions, most murderers at that time were not hanged; they were usually given lengthy prison sentences in accordance with their crime. So, when Bickford accepted the case he was not unduly concerned about the outcome; he did not expect Ruth to get the death penalty.

Ruth's 'intention' on the night of the murder was fundamental to the outcome. For Bickford, this meant a plea of 'insanity' was the only possible way forward. However, he knew it would be difficult, as the legal definition of insanity meant that it was rare for anyone to fit the criteria that had been set down in 1843 without any medical advice.

While Bickford knew this would be a challenge to convince a jury he had not bargained for Ruth's attitude towards this approach; she completely dismissed any possibility of pleading insanity. Even Ruth's mother desperately tried to persuade her to enter the plea, but Ruth stood firm, telling her mother, 'It's no good. I was sane when I did it, and I meant to do it.'[2]

All that was realistically left open to Bickford to advise was the option for Ruth to plead not guilty with a defence of manslaughter. At this time, English law did not recognise diminished responsibility, but this was to change as a direct result of Ruth's case.

Bickford found himself in an unpleasant situation fighting an unfair system, while at the same time being instructed by a client who was intent on receiving the death penalty and ultimately committing assisted suicide.

In 1977, during a television interview, Bickford disclosed that he had seen Desmond Cussen on 13 April 1955, and that he confessed that he had taken Ruth to Tanza Road with the gun in her bag on the night of the murder, but neither Desmond nor Ruth wanted this to be made public. Ruth instructed Bickford that this was a matter of client confidentiality, and she did not want to involve anyone else.

Ruth had also unnerved Bickford when she showed him her wicked sense of humour, telling him, 'I gave David a lot of rope – come to think of it, he's giving me quite a bit now.'[3]

The trial judge was Mr Justice Havers, who was said to be kind and fair and not known to be a hanging judge. On behalf of the Crown, the prosecution was led by Mr Christmas Humphreys, Mr Mervyn Griffith-Jones and Miss Jean Southworth.

Ruth's defence team consisted of Mr Melford Stevenson, QC; Mr Sebag Shaw; and Mr Peter Rawlinson.

Rawlinson made a visit to Ruth in Holloway on 11 May 1955 to tell her the trial had initially been set for 14 June, although this date was to change. During an interview for a television documentary in 1999, he said that she called her life 'a bad life' and she asked him to 'make certain won't you, that I will be hanged, that is the only way I can join him [David]'.[4] Rawlinson said he was shocked by Ruth's matter-of-fact attitude about facing death.

Mr Justice Havers was also to recall the case in 1977 during an interview for the Thames Television documentary *The Last Woman to Hang*:

From the time she came into the dock until the end of the trial I must admit it rather surprised me and I came to the conclusion that she was so certain that she was going to be convicted that she had made up her mind that she'd got to face it.

The interviewer then asked: 'How strongly did you get that impression, how quickly after you had seen her?'

Havers almost shamefully replied:

Well, of course, I saw her, she came into the dock, then I saw her. I didn't look at her, I must say, hardly at all during the case for the Prosecution. Then she came into the witness box you know, one of the things we have to do is try and make out when she's telling the truth, and you have to observe their demeanour and that sort of thing. Of course, I'm bound to look at her then.

Matter of fact, she was telling the truth in most respects I'm sure. Unfortunately, the truth for her was fatal.

The viewer of the documentary cannot help but be shocked that a woman on trial for her life was subjected to a hearing that lasted less than two days, during most of which the judge was unable to bring himself to look at the defendant. Whether guilty or not, this seems incredibly callous.

Pleading not guilty suited Ruth for one reason alone: she was able to have her say in court. Had she pleaded guilty, she felt the truth would not come out. She was particularly keen that the Findlaters should be put on the witness stand and that her own defence should cross-examine them.

A jury of two women and ten men was sworn in at the Central Criminal Court at the Old Bailey, London, on Monday 20 June 1955. It is quite possible that never in the history of murder trials was the defendant given the worst defence team and the defence team given the worst defendant – it was an impossible job to defend Ruth, who appeared to have her mind entirely set on being hanged. She would say repeatedly 'a life for a life.'

Conversely, for Christmas Humphreys, prosecuting, it was possibly the easiest murder prosecution of his career. When he asked Ruth what her intention was when she fired at David her response was: 'It is obvious, when I shot him I intended to kill him.'[5]

The defence made a pathetic and poorly planned effort to show provocation. It called psychiatrist Dr Duncan Whittaker, who not only irritated the judge but severely compromised Ruth's situation when he admitted under cross-examination by the prosecution that Ruth was not, in his professional opinion, excessively disturbed but was emotionally immature.

In a murder case of this nature the psychiatrist should have conducted extended interviews with Ruth, but Dr Whittaker saw her for a total of two hours from 3.30 p.m. on 4 June 1955.

In 1999, during the making of the documentary *Ruth Ellis: A Life for a Life*, consultant forensic psychologist Dr Gillian Mezey was asked if two hours was an adequate amount of time for a psychiatrist to assess Ruth:

> Two hours is the sort of period you would expect to spend with someone who is charged with burglary, not with somebody who, where the stakes are so high and who stands to lose their life if the case goes against them.

Ruth's own doctor, Dr T.P. Rees, who had experience of her mental health issues and who had been prescribing her tranquilisers for some time, was not called as a witness. Dr Rees, in his professional opinion, believed that on the drugs she was taking, combined with the Pernod she had been drinking, she would not have been responsible for her actions.

There were several significant flaws in the defence throughout the trial, missed opportunities that became catastrophic. Witnesses for both the prosecution and the defence were not adequately cross-examined.

At one point while Cussen was in the dock, on behalf of the prosecution, Ruth's defence barrister, Melford Stevenson, QC, questioned Desmond briefly about the bruises that had been inflicted on Ruth by Blakely.

Desmond explained it was a common occurrence for Ruth to be beaten by Blakely but, instead of pursuing this line of questioning, Stevenson told Desmond that he didn't want to press him for details when he asked how often Desmond had seen marks on Ruth.

Ruth's life was in the balance, and her defence lawyer was saying he did not want to press a prosecution witness for details. This would be unbelievable if the official transcripts were not available to verify the facts. Ruth's solicitor, Bickford, felt that Stevenson missed the chance to capitalise on Ruth's emotional and physical abuse.

Several witnesses could have been called to boost Ruth's case, including the French teacher Mrs Marie Therese Harris, who had been giving Ruth lessons, and who had noted at the time that Ruth was bruised and unable to concentrate due to her being distressed.

Mrs Harris also had a discussion with Ruth's son, Andy, about the gun in Desmond's flat. Furthermore, according to Andy, Desmond took him and his mother on a trip to Epping Forest, where Desmond gave Ruth a demonstration of how to handle the gun, but Andy never had a chance to talk to the police or the jury. No credible witnesses were called on Ruth's behalf.

Ant Findlater was questioned by the defence with a similar lack of pressure. The defence failed to ask relevant questions, or delve deeper into the circumstances of that weekend. In the dock, Ruth was frustrated and upset, and by the time she took the witness box, it was as though she'd not only given up but was intent on undermining her own defence.

During the course of the trial Ruth was portrayed as cold-blooded. Had the court and the jury been aware of other circumstances in her life it is likely she would still have been found guilty but the judge might have been more lenient and used the option of mercy, jailing her instead of imposing the death sentence.

Disregarding the fact that Ruth paid her family to provide childcare, she was painted as an unfit parent for leaving her children at home while she worked and socialised. It was not unusual, however, for parents to allow their children much greater freedom in the 1950s than most parents would feel comfortable with today. Children roamed the streets at their leisure, and it was considered normal for them to be left at home alone. Also, it was not entirely uncommon for parents to go out in the evening leaving their children at home in bed without a babysitter, but convicting Ruth for murder was made easier for the prosecution due to the heavy slant on her poor parenting and moral conduct. The behaviour of fathers was seemingly never in question.

Towards the end of his summing up, Mr Justice Havers instructed the jury not to take a view on Ruth's moral conduct:

> There is one other observation which I should like to make, and that is that this Court is not a court of morals. You will not, therefore, allow your judgement to be swayed or your minds prejudiced in the least degree because, on her own admission, when Mrs Ellis was a married woman she committed adultery, or because she had two people at different times as lovers. Dismiss those questions from your minds.

By making this comment, it had the effect of highlighting Ruth's perceived lack of morals in an age where sex before marriage was a taboo, and adultery shameful and socially unacceptable. Ruth broke every moral code of the day: being a single parent to Andy; working as a hostess of a nightclub; and being separated from her husband, while simultaneously taking two lovers.

Mr Justice Havers directed the jury to Ruth's perceived moral flaws, while at the same time asking the jury not to take them into consideration directly after he had emphasised them. Together with Ruth admitting to shooting Blakely and offering little to no insight into her background of abuse and mental health issues, her stiff upper lip of calmness in court contributed to her being seen as having no feelings. Ruth's immaculate appearance went against her, as she made a stunning entrance into court 'like a film star'.[6]

Yes, she admitted to the murder, but it was well within the jurisdiction of the court to offer mercy; whether she wanted it or not is another matter.

Ruth showed little interest in saving her own life. With a couple of rare exceptions, she stayed calm throughout the whole process. The only time she cried was when she was shown the photograph David had given her and signed. When the judge indicated that she could sit down to calm herself, Ruth declined the offer.

On 21 June, the jury took just twelve minutes to find Ruth guilty of murder. Mr Justice Havers, placing the black cloth on his head (a tradition of English law when sentencing someone to death), asked Ruth if she wished to say anything, but she remained silent as he sentenced her:

> Ruth Ellis, the jury have convicted you of murder. In my view, it was the only verdict possible. The sentence of the Court upon you is that you be taken hence to a lawful prison, and thence to a place of execution, and that you there be hanged by the neck until you be dead, and that your body be buried within the precincts of the prison within which you shall last have been confined before your execution, and may the Lord have mercy upon your soul.

The chaplain finished with 'Amen', and Ruth quietly whispered 'Thanks'.[7]

Ruth remained calm; she smiled at family and friends in the public gallery, turned from the dock and walked out of the court accompanied by the wardress and the clicking of her own heels.

Before she left the Old Bailey, she had a brief reunion with her family. She cried, but insisted it was not because she had been given the death penalty – she was ready to embrace that – but because she was angry that the Findlaters were getting away with what she perceived to be their part in this crime. She was also adamant that she did not want to appeal.

During her incarceration, when she received a visit from her brother Granville, Ruth passed a note to him asking for a lethal drug that would quickly end her life. Granville shared the note with his father, who immediately agreed this would be the best course of action for Ruth and that he should comply with her request. However, Granville knew that after sentencing, Bickford might go to appeal, and didn't want her to end her life when there was a chance that she might not hang after all. He therefore made the decision to tear up the note.

LAST GASP OF A DYING GODDESS

Ruth's execution was set for 13 July 1955 but, while she was reconciled to her fate, her solicitor John Bickford was not. After the trial, Bickford tried to get Ruth to appeal the death sentence, but she was adamant she no longer wanted to live.

Family and friends visited daily, imploring Ruth to appeal for mercy. Her answer to them was, 'I have committed this crime. I must die for it.'[1] Ruth would not waver; she had made her decision and firmly stuck by it.

Jacqueline Dyer, Ruth's friend, begged her to come clean on how she had obtained the gun. Jackie took her concerns to her MP, George Rogers. After describing to him how Ruth was given the weapon by Desmond Cussen and other mitigating circumstances, Rogers applied for permission to visit Ruth.

Permission was granted, and Wardress Griffin was present during the meeting on 28 June, at 5.40 p.m. In a statement, Griffin wrote that Rogers introduced himself and then launched into all the reasons why Ruth should be appealing her sentence. The visit upset Ruth and she said she was too tired to argue with him.

Ruth was the perfect prisoner; she was always cooperative and polite. In her notes, she was often described as cheerful, composed, pleasant and non-complaining.

However, there was a frequent reference to Ruth showing no emotion and her detachment to the situation. Ruth slept well most nights, but she did have a restless sleep on occasions and at the time had to resort to sleeping tablets.

Ruth enjoyed discussing the books she was reading with the wardresses, and she had a small bowl containing two goldfish that she was allowed to keep on the table in her cell.

Talkative and delighted with visits from family and friends, Ruth animatedly discussed the court case with them, almost as if she was playing a part, the leading role in a movie she had always wanted to be in.

As June progressed, at times Ruth occasionally became upset, worrying about the children and that she would not live to see them grow up. But on the whole she took the situation in her stride and would happily converse with her prison guards on all manner of subjects. After a visit with her solicitor on 13 June, she returned to her cell upset and had been crying. She had insisted on seeing the photographs of David taken after the shooting. They were worse than she had imagined.

Had Ruth built up a romantic vision of David's death? Clean shotgun wounds, a movie star stagger then a handsome corpse, who would be waiting in spirit for her to join him? Was this her perception, her own reality of the only possible happy ending, which she knew that she could not have in this life?

The following day she appeared to have recovered her composure and was cheerful and talkative. By the evening, though, she expressed that she wished she did not have so much time to think and appeared sad.

The prison officers' handwritten reports make strange and uncomfortable reading. It is clear from the notes that they were only looking at the surface of the person in their care. No one was prepared to look at the inner world of the prisoner; as long as she was conforming and behaving, everything was OK.

The subtext shows you a terrified woman. Ruth was essentially not a bad person; she had made a series of disastrous decisions and increasingly destructive choices leading up to the murder of Blakely.

On 11 July, the governor of Holloway received the message that the Home Secretary would not be offering a reprieve. When this news was conveyed to Ruth, for the first time since her incarceration, and despite weeks of insisting she was ready to die, she went to pieces. Bickford was her first visitor after she had been given the news. Ruth told him she felt he had not acted in her best interests and that it was his fault she was going to be hanged. After a torrent of abuse, Ruth fired him on the spot.

Bickford was devastated by Ruth's reaction. For weeks he had been urging her to fight for her life and at each point she had reminded him it was an 'eye for an eye, a life for a life' and that she was ready to join David.

After leaving Holloway, Bickford telephoned Leon Simmons, who was the solicitor who handled her divorce along with Victor Mishcon, and explained what had taken place with Ruth and that he had been sacked by her. As a result of the call, Simmons and Mishcon arranged an urgent visit to Ruth.

Bickford later said, 'This was the thing that absolutely had a tremendously deep effect on me and, in fact, I can't say it ruined my life, but it had such a profound effect as to change my life.' He went on, 'When I went to tell Mrs Ellis that her reprieve had been refused, something which she already knew, she turned to me and said, "I know what you've been doing. You have been taking a bribe in order that I should be hanged and Cussen should go free."'[2]

Ruth had her second and final visit from George Rogers, who proposed that Andy should stay with him and his wife for the duration of what was about to take place and for Andy to have a holiday with them. Ruth accepted his proposal.

Later that day, Ruth had another visit from her friend Jacqueline Dyer. When the visitors left, Ruth was weighed in preparation for the necessary calculations to be done for the hanging and found to be 7st 5lb.

Before their appointment with Ruth, Simmons and Mishcon had visited Bickford who, although feeling he was still under client confidentiality, directed his colleagues to press Ruth about who gave her the gun.

Arriving at Holloway at 11.15 a.m. on 12 July, the solicitors spoke to Ruth in the presence of Officer Griffin. They gently persuaded Ruth to give them more details about where the gun came from. Eventually, she agreed to provide a statement telling the truth, but she asked them not to use it to try and save her life. She said, 'I don't want to get anyone else into trouble – one life for a life is enough. I didn't say anything about it up to now because it seemed traitorous – absolutely traitorous.'[3]

Ruth made a final statement at 12.30 p.m.:

I, Ruth Ellis, have been advised by Mr Victor Mishcon to tell the whole truth in regard to the circumstances leading up to the killing of David Blakely and it is only with the greatest reluctance that I have decided to tell how it was that I got the gun with which I shot Blakely. I did not do so before because I felt that I was needlessly getting someone into possible trouble.

I had been drinking Pernod (I think that is how it is spelt) in Cussen's flat and Cussen had been drinking too. This was about 8.30pm. We had been drinking for some time. I had been telling Cussen about Blakely's treatment of me. I was in a terribly depressed state. All I remember is that Cussen gave me a loaded gun. Desmond was jealous of Blakely as in fact

Blakely was of Desmond. I would say that they hated each other. I was in such a dazed state that I cannot remember what was said. I rushed out as soon as he gave me the gun. He stayed in the flat.

I had never seen the gun before. The only gun I had ever seen there was a small air pistol used as a game with target.

Signed Ruth Ellis[4]

Before putting her signature to it, she added:

There's one more thing. You had better know the whole truth. I rushed back after a second or so and said 'Will you drive me to Hampstead?' He did so and left me at the top of Tanza Road.[5]

Simmons and Mishcon asked her permission to put her new statement forward to the Home Secretary. She seemed to lose all previous determination and consented for the first time, giving them her permission if they 'wanted to' put it forward.

Time was running out; the solicitors rushed the statement directly to the Home Office.

Jacqueline Dyer arrived with her husband to see Ruth. Jacqueline described Ruth's face as looking white, with her hair silver rather than its usual ash blonde. Jacqueline found it challenging to talk, choked up with emotion. Ruth, as if to put her at ease, told her, 'All your efforts to help me have not been in vain. You will know this later.'[6]

At 2 p.m., her brother Granville, his wife, and her parents visited.

After discussions with Simmons and Mishcon, Phillip Allen at the Home Office told his secretary to phone Sir Frank Newsam, who was the Under Secretary of State, and it became imperative to find Desmond Cussen and interview him. The search began at 4.30 p.m., just sixteen and a half hours before Ruth was due to be executed.

According to Granville, Ruth was still stating that she had no hope or desire for a reprieve. In the *Daily Mail* on 13 July 1955, Granville recalled:

We could not think of what to say after her statement about being drunk at the time of the killing and the business of the gun. None of us could understand why she did not release this information earlier. Obviously, she was trying to shield someone.

Before her parents left, Ruth requested that they take good care of her son and that as he grew up, they ensured that he knew that, whatever she did, she loved him all the time.

At 9 p.m. Ruth penned a final letter to her solicitor, Leon Simmons, thanking him for attending that morning, and asking him to ask her mother to place pink and white carnations on David's grave.

Meanwhile, the search for Desmond Cussen had been abandoned just before midnight as he could not be located.

The Home Secretary, Major Gwilym Lloyd George, was standing firm on his decision that the law must take its course. One wonders if he slept on the hot and humid night of 12 July 1955.

The new day broke with warm sunshine. Ruth was up early; she may not have slept at all. There are several slightly differing accounts of Ruth's last morning on earth, but we do know for sure that one of the first things she did was to add a postscript to the letter she had written the night before to Leon Simmons:

Dear Mr Simmons, Just to let you know I am still feeling alright.

The time is 7 o'clock am – everyone (staff) is simply wonderful in Holloway.

This is just for you to console my family with the thought that I did not change my way of thinking at the last moment.

Or break my promise to David's mother.

Well, Mr Simmons, I have told you the truth and that's all I can do.

Thanks once again.

Goodbye.

Ruth Ellis.[7]

On the day a prisoner was to be executed, they were given the privilege of wearing their own clothes. Ruth chose a skirt and blouse, her blue diamante glasses and black court shoes. She applied minimal make-up, including a slick of her favourite red lipstick.

Ruth picked through a breakfast of scrambled eggs while her goldfish swam in the bowl next to her, blissfully ignorant of the fact this was the last breakfast of their golden-haired companion.

When the Rev. John Williams arrived, Ruth spent some time with him praying and asking for forgiveness. She had requested a crucifix to be fastened to the wall.

At 8 a.m. there was a scuffle of activity. Four male prison officers had arrived in the condemned cell. They were there to escort Ruth to the death chamber, but they would not stay to see the hanging; only a female governor or deputy governor could witness a woman hang.

Wardress Galilee had the task of caring for Ruth until she went into the execution chamber. Galilee had the unpleasant job of taking Ruth to the lavatory to have her take off her regular underwear and step into padded calico underwear that would need to be strapped on to her tiny frame.

This practice for condemned females about to hang was introduced after the 1923 execution of Edith Thompson, who was hanged after her lover stabbed her husband to death. There was no proof that Edith was party to his murder but when questioned she did not tell the police that she knew who did it; she said it was a stranger. Edith was arrested and charged with murder or being an accessory to murder.

When she was found guilty and about to hang, she was hysterical and collapsed; she had expected to be reprieved. The governor of Holloway, who was also the medical officer, gave Edith medication to calm her down forty-five minutes before her death. Upon execution, Thompson had either a severe haemorrhage or a miscarriage on the scaffold and from then onwards the compulsory use of calico underwear was introduced.

Returning to her cell, Ruth sat quietly at the table. A nursing sister arrived with a phial of sedative, which she tried to pass to Ruth, but she would not take it. Instead, she accepted a large tot of brandy, for which it has been claimed she was grateful.

Shortly before 9 a.m. the death party entered the cell. On sight of her executioner, Albert Pierrepoint, Ruth jumped to her feet, knocking over her chair in the process. One can only imagine the terror that was being processed internally while she worked so hard to maintain the calm exterior that she had shown since her arrest.

The infamous Pierrepoint approached Ruth's chair and picked it up. He instructed her to sit down again and to place her arms behind the chair; she did as she was told and he bound her wrists with a calf-leather strap.

Before being led from the condemned cell, Ruth removed her blue diamante spectacles and handed them to the deputy governor, stating that she would no longer need them. The prison officers slid the screen from the wall and revealed the door to the execution chamber. Ruth stood, aided by two prison officers either side of her. She searched out the eyes of Wardress Galilee, who remembers, 'It was a look of pity –

she felt sorry for me. She looked at me and mouthed "Thank you", and she went out.'[8]

Pierrepoint walked in front and led her into the chamber. He guided her on to the spot above the trapdoor, where her tiny neat ankles, still wearing her black court shoes, were bound and the strap was fastened around them.

When Ruth was positioned correctly, Pierrepoint produced a white hood from his jacket pocket. The smile she attempted to give Pierrepoint startled him for a moment. He then placed the hood over Ruth's head, followed by the noose. He adjusted the rope to make sure it was in the correct position; this was a science for Pierrepoint that he delighted in and took great pride over. Securing the noose to one side with a rubber washer, Pierrepoint swiftly and expertly pulled out the cotter pin and drew sharply on the lever.

Ruth plummeted to her death and Pierrepoint, who many consider a serial killer, committed another legalised murder.

Outside in the open air, in front of the prison gates just seconds before Ruth was executed, the crowd fell silent. A lone violinist played Bach's 'Be Thou With Me When I Die'. Inside the chamber of horror, the medical officer went down the stairs that gave entry to the room below the trap door. He pronounced Ruth dead, and her small wrecked body was left to hang by her broken neck for a full hour.

After the hour had passed, Pierrepoint went down to where Ruth was hanging. In his role as executioner, he took it upon himself to release Ruth's lifeless body from the noose. He then undressed the woman he had killed in preparation for her post-mortem, which was to take place in the next room. Burial would follow within the grounds of the prison. While he prided himself on his professionalism, his motivation should not be left unquestioned – was it essential for Pierrepoint to undress his victim? Or could this be regarded as a tendency to something more sinister? In his autobiography, Albert Pierrepoint talks of death as being an 'adventure' and execution a 'romance'.[9]

In her books, *Diana Dors' A–Z of Men* and *For Adults Only*, Diana has under 'H' 'Hangman'. She tells the story of how she came to meet Albert Pierrepoint in 1953 while filming in Manchester with Frank Randal. She was obviously intrigued by such a 'sinister figure' and was somewhat taken aback by a 'tubby little man wearing an ordinary suit, pork pie hat, loud hand-painted tie, and sporting a large cigar stump in his mouth'.[10] Dors thought he looked more like a bookmaker than a hangman. She described his behaviour on being introduced to him as 'loud' with a 'rather brash manner'.

Pierrepoint invited Diana; Dennis Hamilton, her husband at the time; and Frank Randal to his pub. Once there Diana reported being shocked by the name of the pub, Help the Poor Struggler, and a sign in the bar that said 'no hanging around the bar' and other such inappropriate notices. According to Diana, the customers treated Pierrepoint as though they were his 'loyal subjects'.[11]

Apparently, he was an exuberant host, pouring beers, cracking jokes and bursting into impromptu song as if, in Diana's words, 'the curtain had lifted on stage … with an ego bigger than any film star'.[12]

He reportedly showed his guests a book containing the names of all the people he had hanged, the crime they had been sentenced for and their statistics such as weight, height, etc.

Diana recalled in *A–Z of Men*:

Drawn like a snake to the charmer, I pursued my questions, horrified by his revelations.

When I asked him if people panicked as the moment came for them to die he grew rather irritated at my naivety, stating quite seriously, 'I go to the prison the day before, shake them by the hand and say, 'now you know who I am, do as I say, and you'll be quite all right.'

He paused as if waiting for me to digest this scene and then added, 'Yes, I've had some lovely letters from mothers, thanking me for taking care of their sons.'[13]

In *Adults Only* she added to this story: 'I could see the man loved his work … although within me there lurked a nasty feeling about Albert's real reasons for his profession.'[14]

If Ruth had chosen a different path, she and Diana might well have become friends, but Ruth was the blonde gone bad. Her desires were no different from Marilyn's, Diana's or Jayne's. She had the ingredients: personality, drive, ambition and figure – the cards were stacked in her favour. She wanted to move away from her working-class background, to make something of herself.

Ruth had struggled to fund acting lessons, and hostessing was easy and lucrative. She was a modern woman earning her own money and making her own decisions.

With a job that gave her the outward façade of a life of glamour, without having to audition for parts competing with other actresses or learn the lines of someone else's script, Ruth had already got the role. She was acting on her own stage, and she was the leading lady.

The club had provided her with a home and income that she could increase at her own discretion; all the accoutrements of a star, with the authority and power she wouldn't have had at any film studio.

Looking closely at Ruth's past and the way she conducted her relationships, it could be suggested she may have suffered from Borderline Personality Disorder (BPD). Although it is difficult to diagnose as it shares symptoms with other mental illnesses, Ruth did appear to exhibit the signs of a high-functioning BPD sufferer. The symptoms include low self-esteem and a sense of inferiority, which David highlighted and intensified by not introducing her to his family and being reluctant to include her in certain friendship circles.

There is a struggle with empathy, and there appears to be a lack of understanding about how a person's behaviour impacts on others – which was a feature in Ruth's life. BPD sufferers also frequently find themselves in chaotic relationships that become physically or emotionally abusive and they can be excessively needy, intense and mistrusting in relationships.

There is a constant fear of abandonment, and this was a feature of Ruth and David's relationship and during her marriage to George Ellis. While he was in rehab Ruth believed he was having an affair with a female doctor or nurse. She stormed into the hospital shouting that her husband was a 'fucking adulterer',[15] asking complete strangers if they had seen her husband making love to the doctor or whether he had made a pass at them.

Frequent mood swings were also evident in Ruth's life, resulting in overreactions to external events, such as David ignoring her telephone calls during the Easter holiday, which caused her to become extremely agitated. Ruth also experienced uncontrollable anger, with reactions disproportionate to the event.

There is also a tendency with BPD for people to project their problems and emotions on to others, blaming them because it is just not possible for the person with BPD to take responsibility for the rage within them.

A perfect example of this would be Ruth's obsession with the Findlaters and blaming them for David's death.

The disorder is also responsible for an inability to control one's actions, feeling dissociation, detachment and numbness. Ruth was consistently referred to by professionals after the murder as being calm, detached and cold-hearted.

Instead of dealing with depression, some people will see the logical solution to be suicide, as it will immediately stop the pain. The events had been overwhelming, Ruth had committed a crime of horrendous magnitude, and it seems plausible that she just wanted the pain to stop. She saw no other way out than by the hangman's noose.

PART THREE

MARILYN MONROE

THE BEGINNING OF THE END

The childhood and ancestry of the woman who grew from Norma Jeane (string bean) into Marilyn Monroe (movie star) is the perfect example of an urban myth. Translated from a narrative established by the adult Marilyn, it has since become deeply entrenched within her story. Almost sixty years after her death, she continues to wear the label of 'victim'. Yet, this woman was strong and determined, a mistress of manipulation and self-preservation, during a time when a woman's essential role was that of wife and mother, whose identity would be acquired through her husband.

Sifting through Marilyn's life can be likened to counting grains of sand on a beach, an infinite task given the volume and complexity, the contradictions and fabrications. Extracting grains of truth from the opinions, assumptions and widely distributed untruths is a mammoth task and enough to terrify the most seasoned researcher.

Childhood recollections were peppered with inconsistencies, and it was claimed by her foster sibling Eleanor 'Bebe' Goddard that many of Marilyn's woeful tales of neglect and abuse were a direct spin on Bebe's traumatic childhood, borrowed and reused to elicit sympathy.

What we do know of Marilyn's childhood is that her mother, Gladys, married her first husband, Jasper Baker, in 1917 aged 15, the paperwork illegally signed by Gladys's mother, Della, who declared that her daughter was 18. Gladys's father, Otis Elmer Monroe, had died eight years earlier.

Within seven months of the marriage, Gladys gave birth to a son, Robert 'Kermit', swiftly followed by a daughter, Berniece, in July 1919. When the inevitable happened and the marriage broke down, Gladys filed for divorce, which she was granted, along with custody of the children. However, Jasper claimed Gladys was an unfit mother and abducted them, taking them back to his hometown of Kentucky. With no means of fighting Jasper, Gladys accepted that she would have to give up her children.

By 1924 she had remarried. Her second husband was 27-year-old Martin Edward Mortensen. On 1 June 1926, Gladys gave birth to her third child, a daughter, in the charity ward of the Los Angeles General Hospital; she named her Norma Jeane Mortenson. While Mortensen's name was on the birth certificate, he has been discredited as the child's father due to the belief that he had disappeared from Gladys's life before her baby was conceived. Charles Stanley Gifford, a foreman at Consolidated Film where Gladys worked, is the biographers' favourite in the search for Norma Jeane's actual father. There is, however, no credible evidence that Gifford was the father; Gladys had other love interests and she did not apply for any form of support from him.

Norma Jeane was born into a robust matriarchal background of divorced working women, astute and revolutionary females who were sexually permissive. Although still dependent on men for outward respectability and hoped-for financial security, they learned how to manage the system to achieve their desires and survive, going against the tide and making their own decisions.

Gladys needed an income and returning to her job as a film cutter was the only sensible option; her close friend Grace McKee, who eventually took a leading role in Norma Jeane's life, supported her friend's decision. Gladys secured a place for her newborn daughter with foster parents Ida and Albert 'Wayne' Bolender, who lived on a small farm across the road from Della.

A well-chosen couple with a good reputation and solid religious background, Ida and Albert lived in a small but well-looked-after home. Albert worked for the post office and they supplemented their income by taking in a limited number of foster children for the sum of $25 a week.

Over the years Ida has been portrayed as a dark, evil character; an austere religious zealot who gave no affection to Norma Jeane, biting at the child when she called her Mama with, 'I'm not your Mother. Don't call me mother any more, call me aunt.' A slightly different version of this story is told by Norma Jeane's sister, Berniece, who recalls Norma Jeane telling her, 'Aunt Ida told me she had to teach me not to call her Mama because Mother had gotten upset hearing me do that. And I got totally confused after that and thought "mama" just meant "woman". I missed Aunt Ida when I went to live with Mother ...'

Berniece asked, 'You liked her? She was a good person?'

The 18-year-old Norma Jeane replied, 'Oh, yes. I was very lucky to have her. She and Uncle Wayne came to my wedding.'[1]

Gladys's mother, Della, died on 23 August 1927, aged 51. Gladys believed that both of her parents had died insane; however, Otis contracted viral syphilis and Della had acute myocarditis. Both illnesses affected brain function. Whether brought on by fear or coincidence, Gladys was to spend much of her adult life in and out of mental institutions. Described as a paranoid schizophrenic, she lived the majority of her life withdrawn from society in sanatoriums and rest homes until she died on 11 March 1984 aged 82.

Marilyn's mental health would become the focus of Hollywood hype and press attention throughout her career, and indeed reaching beyond her death and into the present day. What Marilyn thought was her family history of insanity would haunt her short life, aided and abetted by the media, which refused to let go of the belief that she was mentally unstable.

In the summer of 1933, Gladys removed 7-year-old Norma Jeane from the Bolenders. Having spent seven years with the couple, her sudden removal from the only home she had known would have been unsettling. Gladys had purchased a house and to meet mortgage payments she leased it to an English family, renting back two rooms within the house, where she lived with Norma Jeane.

Disastrously, in early 1934, Norma Jeane's mother had her first serious breakdown. Gladys had experienced several significant triggers in a short time, including the death of her only son, Robert, who had recently died of kidney failure aged 15. Whatever the underlying causes of her breakdown may have been, Gladys was admitted into a psychiatric institution aged 32.

By removing Norma Jeane from her settled environment with the Bolenders, Gladys unwittingly plunged her 7-year-old daughter into an uncertain future. Instead of the child returning to the couple, Grace took control of both Gladys's and Norma Jeane's life. Around this time Grace also met Ervin Silliman Goddard, better known as Doc, and in a rush of passion the couple married in Las Vegas that August.

For Norma Jeane it meant her life became more unstable, as she was shuttled between family members and friends, eventually entering the Los Angeles Orphans Home on 13 September 1935, signed in by Grace.

It seemed a callous move; however, for Grace to obtain legal guardianship of Norma Jeane, it was a requirement that the child would need to be in state care for a minimum of six months before the request for guardianship could be filed.

After this episode Norma Jeane was to experience at least a further five foster homes, including returning to the care of Grace and living with Grace's aunt Ana Lower on two separate occasions. Aunt Ana, a 58-year-old divorcee who owned a small property portfolio, would become a significant influence on Norma Jeane. They developed a close and loving bond. Many years later, Marilyn was to say of Aunt Ana:

> She changed my whole life. She was the first person in the world I ever really loved, and she loved me. She was a wonderful human being. I once wrote a poem about her [long since lost], and I showed it to somebody, and they cried … It was called 'I Love Her'. She was the only one who loved and understood me … She never hurt me, not once. She couldn't. She was all kindness and love.[2]

In 1940, Ana's health was failing and Norma Jeane returned to Grace and Doc Goddard, who also had custody of Bebe, Doc's daughter from his first marriage. It was around this time that Norma Jeane came to the attention of a neighbour's son, James 'Jim' Dougherty, an athletic and handsome 19-year-old who was to become her first husband.

There was a flirtatious rapport between Norma Jeane and Jim, and eventually they started seeing each other as girlfriend and boyfriend, although Jim was concerned about the age difference (Norma Jeane was only 14) and it looked as if it was going to come between them until an incident occurred. According to Norma Jeane, Doc, in a drunken state, staggered into her bedroom, sat on her bed and promptly attempted to kiss her. A frightened Norma Jeane cried out, at which point Doc hastily left the room and was remorseful and embarrassed about the episode. Norma Jeane confided in Jim and Ana and, sensing a dangerous situation unfolding, Ana took Norma Jeane back under her wing.

Doc was offered a timely job promotion that would involve relocating to West Virginia. Unable to take Norma Jeane with them, the Goddards encouraged a quick marriage between the young couple as a way of avoiding Norma Jeane returning to the orphanage.

Allegations of sexual abuse during Marilyn's childhood have sometimes appeared unclear as to who the abuser was and when the molestation took place, but throughout her lifetime Marilyn frequently spoke about the sexual abuse she had suffered as a child. In 1947, when the journalist Lloyd Shearer interviewed her, he recalled:

> She confided to us over lunch that she had been assaulted by one of her guardians, raped by a policeman, and attacked by a sailor. She seemed to me then to live in a fantasy world, to be entangled in the process of invention, and to be completely absorbed in her own sexuality.[3]

Shearer did not feel comfortable with this information at the time and decided not to write about Marilyn at all.

The first public uncovering of her abuse took place during conversations with the journalist Ben Hecht in 1953 and 1954. While working on her autobiography *My Story*, she told him about being inappropriately touched in one of her foster homes by a boarder called 'Mr Kimmel', a name she said she had changed to cover the identity of the abuser. Marilyn said this had taken place after she had left the orphanage so, while she was frightened, she didn't scream for fear of being sent back to the home. After the traumatic abuse, she ran to tell her 'aunt', who glared at her and said 'Don't you dare say anything against Mr Kimmel … Mr Kimmel's a fine man. He's my star boarder.'[4]

In 1960 she told a variation of the story to the writer and journalist Maurice Zolotow. The timing and content was slightly changed and in 1962 she told her photographer George Barris yet another alternative version on the same theme.

The changes in her story contributed to the controversy and debate, with some of her earlier male biographers being sceptical. Fred Lawrence Guiles, in his biography *Norma Jean, The Life and Death of Marilyn Monroe*, flatly dismissed her account of the 'Kimmel' incident, saying 'there are a number of reasons why it simply will not wash.'[5]

One of the reasons Guiles gives is that, according to his reckoning, Norma Jeane did not live in a house that took in boarders. He does, however, believe the incident with Doc Goddard happened; Guiles had interviewed Doc during the research for his book and he admitted an incident did take place.

What causes uncertainty is that Marilyn did embellish her life. Grace Goddard told Marilyn's half-sister Berniece about a story she and Marilyn invented:

We had to have a biographical story, and we had to have one fast! We hadn't dreamed that we would need one, and suddenly things were happening too fast. We made up a story about Marilyn having no parents and being in a lot of foster homes and spending time in an orphanage and Marilyn signed it as being the truth.[6]

Influenced by Grace, Marilyn was taught the art of subterfuge, which has over the years given us so many different variations of the woman, enabling us to choose the one that suits us best.

Marilyn repeatedly told friends and colleagues of her abuse. She confided in Hollywood director Jean Negulesco that an elderly actor had raped her at 8 years old. Again, during a party in New York, she told the husband of Peggy Fleury, who was a student with her at the Actors Studio, about being sexually abused, saying she felt lucky that the experience had not made her psychotic, as it did many victims of such attacks.[7]

It is not uncommon for someone who has been abused to vary their account of what happened over a period of time. In June 2018 it was reported that the World Health Organisation had formally recognised a complex form of post-traumatic stress disorder unique to survivors of childhood abuse. According to the inquiry's chief psychologist, Bryony Farrant, survivors of abuse have 'a complex, pervasive and rigid negative belief in themselves'.[8] They struggle with relationships, especially with trust. During a survey for this inquiry called the Truth Project it was found that 85 per cent of people subjected to abuse who had taken part in the study had mental health problems in later life, including depression, anxiety and insomnia. Many experienced either a total avoidance of sex or multiple partners. Some also experienced dependency on alcohol, with a disturbing one in five having attempted suicide.

The abuse Norma Jeane experienced took place more than eighty years ago and we are only now understanding the extent of the problem and still grappling to come to terms with how to lessen the pain and trauma for the child who has undergone such a terrible experience.

Marilyn the adult was renowned for her inability to sleep and her dependence on drugs and alcohol. She struggled with relationships and sex. Her interest in psychiatrists and her suicidal tendency became legendary, contributing to her being labeled as a 'victim', although today's modern media would have called her a 'survivor'.

During Marilyn's lifetime, the biographer Maurice Zolotow poign-
antly said:

Out of her experience of pain, Marilyn came to equate love with pity.
She believes that a man who doesn't feel sympathy for her pain cannot
love her, and her own love for people is strongly linked with pity – more
so than with lust or romantic idealization.[9]

The depth of compassion measures love. With the abuse came the erasure
of her sexuality. Was this reason for Marilyn later claiming that 'the truth
was that with all my lipstick and mascara and precocious curves, I was as
unresponsive as a fossil.'[10]

MARRIAGES OF INCONVENIENCE

Jim Dougherty

In the spring of 1942, Norma Jeane's classmates noticed a difference in her personality; she was louder and more confident. Dating Jim likely gave her a sense of grown-up kudos. Achieving good-to-average grades at school, with the wisdom of only the young, she decided to ditch education and devote her life to being a housewife. This action gave her a sense of superiority amongst her peers for the first time. Unfortunately, the consequence of such a rash teenage decision was to instil within her a strong feeling of inferiority for the rest of her life.

Sixteen-year-old Norma Jeane became Mrs Jim Dougherty on 19 June 1942. Aunt Ana sent out the invitations and the service took place at a family friend's home. Ana gave the bride away, Gladys did not attend, and neither did Grace, who was in Virginia by this time. There has been much contention as to whether this was an arranged marriage, or if it was more of an encouraged marriage of two young people who thought they were in love. Marilyn stated sometime later, 'I never had a choice. There's not much to say about it. They couldn't support me, and they had to work out something, and so I got married.'[1] Although Marilyn always claimed it was a marriage of convenience, Jim told of being 'very much in love'[2] with his new bride.

For Norma Jeane, sex was a frightening prospect that she didn't fully understand. Her previous experience had been harmful and damaging, and while Jim spoke enthusiastically about their love life, presenting Norma Jeane as an eager participant, Marilyn's recollections were less than flattering. When talking about her first marriage, she said:

> The first effect marriage had on me was to increase my lack of interest in sex. My husband either didn't mind this or wasn't aware of it. We were both too young to discuss such an embarrassing topic openly.

It was not just age that made discussions about sex difficult. During the first part of the twentieth century, women were actively discouraged from knowing too much about sexual activity. Naïvety and childlike innocence, even after marriage, was highly valued. Innocence meant respectability and superiority in a female. Too much knowledge of sex for a woman said she must be of low morals and tainted; possibly second-hand goods in a society that valued virginity in a new wife.

In marrying Jim, Norma Jeane exchanged her youth and potential for a future of domestic drudgery and childbearing. The institution of marriage in society was changing but not fast enough, and when recalling this time Marilyn perceptively stated:

> My marriage brought me neither happiness nor pain. My husband and I hardly spoke to each other ... I've seen many married couples since that were just like Jim and me. They were usually more enduring kind of marriages, the ones that were pickled in silence.[3]

In 1944, while Marilyn working at Radioplane for the war effort, a photographer named David Conover arrived with a small army film crew, tasked with taking photographs and film of women on the assembly lines. Conover saw the potential in Norma Jeane, arranging for her to model outside of work. There was no stopping her, and there was no place for Jim. When Norma Jeane joined a model agency, it advised that single girls were desired by both the agency and the studios. After four years of marriage, Norma Jeane took the agency's advice and divorced Jim.

To the end, Jim always maintained the marriage was a happy one and that they loved each other. Marilyn, however, insisted that she had always regarded Jim as a brother.

Joe DiMaggio

The marriage certificate was dated 14 January 1954, the bride was named as Norma Jeane Dougherty, but the groom married Marilyn Monroe.

In March 1951, Marilyn had a publicity photoshoot with some members of a baseball team in training, and one of the photos caught the eye of Joe DiMaggio, the most famous baseball player in America.

Thirty-seven-year-old DiMaggio had previously been married to the actress Dorothy Arnold, in 1939. Dorothy reluctantly quit acting at Joe's insistence and in 1941 she gave birth to their son, Joe Jnr. The marriage was not successful, and Dorothy filed for divorce. It was uncontested and became final in May 1944.

Joe was eager to meet Marilyn and in December 1951, after retiring due to injuries, he contacted his friend David March, who was the press agent who had organised Marilyn's publicity shoot, asking him to arrange it. It took some persuasion, but in early 1952 March succeeded and Marilyn agreed to a date.

The sexual chemistry between the couple was sizzling, but their differences were immense. Marilyn was creatively casual, Joe was obsessively organised. Joe was old school, the strong, silent type; Marilyn was progressive and emotional. To Joe, money was important. He came from a poor immigrant background, and money showed how much you were worth; it was respect and honour. For Marilyn, financial gain was not her priority.

Around the time of their first date, the news that Marilyn had posed nude for a calendar hit the headlines. Marilyn was at risk of being publicly humiliated and ruined; others before her had posed for nude photographs, but no one had admitted to it. Rather than attempt to deny the situation, Marilyn, with ingenuity and humour, faced it head on – she turned the problem into an asset, confirming to Fox executives it was indeed her 'although I really thought that Tom [Kelley] didn't capture my best angle.'[4]

Speaking to United Press correspondent Aline Mosby, she once again relied on making people feel sorry for her, as she shed a pretty tear and explained that a few years back she'd been in a dire financial situation with no money for food or rent. The public could not resist this beautiful and vulnerable young woman, pouring her heart out to them.

Marilyn's career not only survived but went from strength to strength. In a time of sexual repression, Marilyn was telling the public that sex wasn't dirty. She made fun and light of the situation, and they loved her all the more for it.

Joe had a different opinion and for a while cooled off and called less, until, in the wake of the calendar revelation, the news broke that Marilyn was not an orphan. Joe rushed to her side as again she worked her magic on the executives and the press, forestalling disaster and coming out of the experience with love and sympathy from her adoring public after she explained how she had been brought up in an orphanage and foster homes due to her mother being an invalid. Marilyn told the press that she was helping her mother and protecting her as best she could. Marilyn explained that her father had died in an automobile accident.

As 1953 dawned, Marilyn was a little more conservative in her dress as she and Joe were becoming closer. She began telling him and the press that all she really wanted was to be a housewife and to have a family. Joe expected Marilyn would give up the actor's life to raise their children and attend to his every need, but he didn't know Marilyn. She may have raised the neckline of her blouse, she may have made him promises, but when it came to the home run, Marilyn wasn't playing ball!

By 1954, with the encouragement of Joe, Marilyn refused the script for a musical comedy called *The Girl in Pink Tights*. She hated it and, fuelled by Joe, she was angry that Frank Sinatra had been signed at a rate of $5,000 per week while she was to be paid $1,500, even though she was the main draw and would receive top billing.

Marilyn said that the character she was to play was a 'dreary cliché spouting bore, who was the cheapest character I had ever read in a script'.[5]

Marilyn was suspended by the studio. She began to panic and almost gave in, but Joe decided it would be an excellent time to get married. Hasty arrangements were made for a quiet ceremony on 14 January 1954, followed by a February honeymoon in Japan that coincided nicely with a contract that stated Joe had to play exhibition baseball and coach two Tokyo baseball teams.

Before the bride left for the wedding at City Hall, she quickly phoned the press to let them know her secret.

The new Mrs DiMaggio agreed to entertain the troops in Korea. It was the first time she would be before a live audience and Joe wasn't happy, but Marilyn would describe it as the highlight of her career. However, by the time they returned from their honeymoon, the marriage was already in trouble.

The studio had lifted her suspension, and Marilyn was cut a deal: if she would play a supporting role in the musical *There's No Business Like Show Business*, she could have the lead role in the movie *The Seven Year Itch*, directed by Billy Wilder. Marilyn was elated at the prospect of playing 'The Girl' in *The Seven Year Itch*, so she accepted *Show Business*. She disliked the script, and Joe hated it even more, but Marilyn was determined to get through it for the role in *Seven Year Itch*.

On 27 August, while Marilyn was filming a Carmen Miranda-inspired dance routine for the song *Heatwave*, Joe arrived with a friend. Watching her shimmy and thrust in a way Joe considered obscene, he made his feelings clear to everyone in the vicinity as he abruptly left the set.

Show Business was a grim job set against the background of her marriage disintegrating. Marilyn compared herself to her idol, Jean Harlow, wondering if she was subconsciously steering her life towards emulating Harlow's when she said later, 'It was kind of spooky, and sometimes I thought, "am I making this happen?" But I don't think so. We just seemed to have the same spirit or something, I don't know. I kept wondering if I would die young like her, too.'[6]

As filming for *The Seven Year Itch* began, no one could know that the film was about to make history, and Marilyn's marriage was about to die.

The photographer Sam Shaw suggested the perfect publicity stunt; the press and public were alerted to the fact that Marilyn would be filming what has since become the famous scene in which her skirt was blown high by the wind from the subway below – outside the Trans-Lux Theatre, on Lexington Avenue at 52nd Street, New York. Press and public gathered and cheered take after take.

Joe had attended reluctantly, and as he watched his wife's skirt surge upwards from the blast of the wind machine, it revealed her panties. The crowds roared for more, but he could not contain his anger. Once again, he abruptly left the scene, making sure everyone knew of his rage and the reason why.

After the event, back at the hotel screams and shouts could be heard coming from the couple's room. A hairdresser on the movie, Gladys Whitten, later recalled that the next morning she was with Natasha Lytess, Marilyn's acting coach, and that it was clear Joe was angry with Marilyn and 'he had beat her up a little bit. There were bruises on her shoulders, but we covered them with make-up.'[7]

Domestic violence in the 1950s was often seen as an acceptable punishment for an errant wife. Joe's sexual jealousy would have been sufficient grounds for many a man to slap him on the back and tell him 'well done, she deserved it'. The law in both Britain and the United States had always fought to uphold the 'sanctity of the home', and terms such as the man being the 'master of his own home' and 'a man's home is his castle' were commonly used.

While some may dispute that Joe was a misogynist, he certainly ticked all the boxes regarding the profile of a domestic abuser with controlling behaviour issues. He isolated Marilyn from her friends and had a particular problem with Natasha Lytess. Natasha and other colleagues of Marilyn's were interviewed before Marilyn and Joe's marriage. While everyone else predicted it would be a great success, Natasha, who as Marilyn's acting coach shared a close relationship with her student, said in an interview for *Picturegoer* magazine:

> This marriage can't possibly succeed. Marilyn is intensely ambitious. She hungers for intellectualism, for the world of arts and letters. She wants to be stimulated mentally. She is not for DiMaggio – and DiMaggio is not for her.[8]

Joe played on her vulnerability and dependence, which in itself is a type of psychological abuse that will often precede violence in a relationship as it did when they returned to their hotel room after the location publicity shots of the subway scene. Joe appeared to be intent on damaging Marilyn's self-esteem irrevocably.

In many people this can have the effect of causing them to internalise the abuse, believing that they are the names they have been called, and they begin to visualise themselves as they think their partner sees them.

It frequently baffles people who have not experienced domestic violence why someone would stay in such a toxic and harmful relationship. Many people in violent relationships truly love their abuser, a love that may have been deeply rooted at the beginning of the relationship, and in between periods of abuse they may be offered glimpses of that perfect side of their partner that they initially fell in love with.

Fortunately for Marilyn, Joe had not eroded her self-esteem to the point of no return. After filming in New York was completed, they returned to Los Angeles. She was not prepared to be anyone's punch bag; she would not be a victim to Joe's demands or his anger, so two weeks after the altercation in the hotel room in New York took place she filed for divorce.

Years later, Susan Strasberg told Marilyn's biographer Donald Spoto that she was 'bored' with DiMaggio, elaborating that Marilyn had said, 'To tell the truth, our marriage was a sort of crazy, difficult friendship with sexual privileges. Later I learned that's what marriages often are.'[9]

The relationship that began in a blaze of publicity ended the same way on 27 October 1954. Wearing a tailored black suit with a neat black Juliet cap, looking every inch a widow at the death of her marriage, Marilyn told the Santa Monica court about the cold indifference of her husband. She petitioned on the grounds of mental cruelty and did not mention the physical abuse; this could have been to protect Joe, whom she continued to love, or maybe she felt she was a failure that somehow deserved to be mistreated, that she was the guilty party, or possibly it was a mixture of both.

'I GUESS I'VE ALWAYS HAD TOO MUCH FANTASY TO BE ONLY A HOUSEWIFE'[1]

After Marilyn married Joe, she expressed a surprising intention. Just home from the honeymoon, the new Mrs DiMaggio told her friend Sidney Skolsky, 'Sidney, do you know who I'm going to marry?'

'Marry? What are you talking about?'

'I'm going to marry Arthur Miller.'

'Arthur Miller! You just got home from a honeymoon. You told me how wonderful Joe was, how happy he made you, and what a great time you had! Now you tell me you're going to marry Arthur Miller. I don't understand.'

'You wait, you'll see.'[2]

When Marilyn set her mind on something, there was little doubt she would achieve her goal. In January 1951 Marilyn had met the playwright Arthur Miller while she was working on a small part in the film *As Young As You Feel*. Miller was eleven years older than she was and already famous for his work, which included the stage plays *All My Sons* (1947) and *Death of a Salesman* (1949). *Salesman* won the Pulitzer Prize that year.

Marilyn was mourning the recent death of her agent and lover Johnny Hyde and struggling emotionally between takes. Miller and his friend Elia Kazan were in Hollywood to discuss a future project and were on the set that day. Miller recalled that, when he was introduced to Marilyn, as they shook hands, 'The shock of her body's motion sped through me, a sensation at odds with her sadness amid all this glamour and technology and the busy confusion of a new shot being set up.'[3]

Attending a party given by Charlie Feldman, founder of Famous Artists talent agency, Arthur was Marilyn's escort for the evening. Marilyn later told Natasha Lytess:

I met a man Natasha, it was Bam! You see my toe? This toe? He sat and held my toe. I mean, I sat on the Davenport, and he sat on it too, and he held my toe. It was like running into a tree! You know, like a cool drink when you've got a fever.

Later she told the queen of columnists, Louella Parsons, 'He attracted me because he is brilliant … His mind is better than that of any other man I've ever known. And he understands and approves of my wanting to improve myself.'[4]

Miller felt he was running away from his feelings for Marilyn and as they parted at the airport he experienced pain and a sense of doom. Despite being married to Mary Slattery at this time, he had fallen in love and the distance didn't ease the troubled conscience of a married man.

Marilyn had also fallen in love with Arthur, but this wasn't their time. Instead, she embarked on an affair with Elia Kazan, also a married man but less moralistic than Arthur and more available in terms of distance.

By 1955 Marilyn had reached a point of tough self-evaluation, as the year brought romance (including a brief affair with the actor Marlon Brando) adventure and new career challenges. The photographer Milton Greene had suggested Marilyn start her own production company, and so they began Marilyn Monroe Productions together. She was also taking acting lessons with Lee Strasberg, founder of the Actors Studio. But, most important of all, 1955 was the year she reconnected with Arthur. Their relationship, no longer held back by distance (only Arthur's marriage) they became lovers.

Marilyn had been experiencing a growing need to have a child of her own, with someone she loved, and Arthur, who she had taken to calling Papa, fulfilled her requirements; she knew she wanted children with him. And as she told DiMaggio before him, she told Arthur that she wanted nothing more than to escape Hollywood and live a simple domestic life.

As she approached 30, Marilyn realised she could not maintain indefinitely the innocent yet sexy blonde bombshell image she had so painstakingly constructed. Ageing in Hollywood was unthinkable for a female who traded on her looks and figure. She knew that at some point soon she would need to shed the sex symbol tag line to work on serious dramatic parts and yet, even as her words told people she had aspirations as a serious actress, her actions showed she was clinging precariously to an impossible and soon-to-be-an outdated concept.

As 1956 dawned, Norma Jeane Mortenson legally changed her name to Marilyn Monroe and began filming *Bus Stop*, which saw a collaboration between Twentieth Century Fox and her new company, Marilyn Monroe Productions.

Arthur would soon be heading out to become a resident of Reno, Nevada, for the statutory two months to gain a quick divorce from his first wife, Mary Slattery. In the meantime, the couple were struggling to contain their passion for one another and Arthur was desperately missing Marilyn, which is evident in a letter he wrote from New York on Wednesday, 4 April, at 1.12 p.m., telling her:

> My Darling,
> The kids are here. I am working on my speech. I love you, I want you this moment. I am deeply happy and agonised that you're not in reach. The joy of the future has suddenly come on me. I kiss you. A.[5]

By 11 June 1956, Arthur's divorce was granted and he returned to New York, but on the 21st he was required to go to Washington to appear before the House Un-American Activities Committee (HUAC). Arthur's politics were left wing and America was in the grips of anti-communist hysteria. Asked to name anyone he knew that had leftist views or interests, he refused.

While he was being interviewed he was asked why he had applied for a passport to go to England. He replied that he would be going with the woman who would then be his wife. A reporter asked him, 'Marilyn Monroe?' and Arthur replied, 'That's correct.'[6] Marilyn would be making *The Prince and the Showgirl* with Sir Laurence Olivier, in England.

The press went crazy at the news, with phrases such as 'Egghead and the Hourglass' and 'Beauty and the Brain'. The words may have been slightly different, but the theme was the same: Arthur was intelligent and valued, Marilyn was beautiful but vacuous, something to look at but of little practical worth.

Telling friends that Arthur's announcement had come as a shock to her, Marilyn implied that although he had talked about marriage, he had not formally asked her. However, it seems unlikely that they had not already agreed to get married, especially as Marilyn had telephoned her lawyer shortly before Miller's revelation saying that she wanted to redraft her will, leaving everything she owned to Arthur. Furthermore, Marilyn had also been studying to convert to Arthur's religion, Judaism, even though Arthur was not a practising Jew.

On Friday 29 June, a press conference was called for 4 p.m. at Arthur's home in Roxbury, Connecticut. Before the meeting, at around 1 p.m., a female reporter was involved in a crash, while in pursuit of the car the couple was in. The reporter sustained severe injuries and died in hospital three hours later. The conference went ahead at the scheduled time with a clearly shocked Marilyn, who had witnessed the aftermath of the accident. As well as being questioned about their impending nuptials, Marilyn was also interviewed about the British actress and blonde bombshell Diana Dors by a very persistent reporter, 'Miss Monroe, a rival of yours, Miss Diana Dors, is arriving in the United States as you're going to England, just a coincidence or is it any kind of exchange arrangement? So we won't be lonesome while you're gone?'

Marilyn responded very seriously, stuttering on occasion, 'Well, I'm afraid not. We made arrangements about the *Sleeping Prince*, well … nearly a year ago it's been going on.'

Reporter: 'Have you ever seen her in films? Have you seen her act?'

Monroe: 'No, I haven't.'

Reporter: (slightly exasperated) 'Then you're not in a position to comment.'

Monroe: (nodding) 'Sorry.'[7]

Marilyn may have felt the heat as Diana Dors was a blonde bombshell five years younger than her and the studio was continually threatening her with the competition such as Jayne Mansfield and Sheree North. During the making of *Bus Stop* Marilyn had asked for one of the other actresses, 23-year-old Hope Lange, who was playing the part of a waitress, to darken her hair.

Directly after the press had left, Marilyn and Arthur headed for Westchester County Court House in White Plains, New York, where, just before 7.30 p.m., Judge Seymour Rabinowitz pronounced them husband and wife in the company of only two witnesses. This was followed on 1 July by a second religious wedding ceremony, this time with family and friends.

Passports were granted on 13 July 1956, and the Millers headed for London. If things had been difficult before their marriage, they were about to get considerably worse. Where DiMaggio did not want Marilyn to have a career, Arthur was closely involved in all her contractual activities and this began to create a certain amount of friction in Marilyn's life. Tension grew between Arthur and Marilyn's business partner, Milton Greene, and his wife, Amy; and with Marilyn's acting mentor, Lee Strasberg, and his wife, Paula, who was her acting coach. Arthur found her dependency on both of these couples insufferable and it became a reciprocal loathing. With Marilyn being pulled in all directions, her psyche could not handle this strife.

It was not a happy time, and filming was an almost debilitating trial for Marilyn; she struggled with her fellow actors and timekeeping. This put pressure on Arthur, who was unhappy with both the Greenes and the Strasbergs as he felt they were taking advantage of his wife. Miller was also trying unsuccessfully to mediate between Marilyn and Olivier, who were now embroiled in a disagreement that would endure for the rest of their lives.

Arthur, horrified by his wife's behaviour, kept a journal, a prerequisite of most writers. The pages were filled with his regret, frustration and bitter disillusion. Unfortunately, Marilyn read it and instead of accepting it was a way of dealing with difficult circumstances for Miller, she felt utterly betrayed.

Feelings of devastation overwhelmed Marilyn, and of course, it did not improve her temperament at work. It also put a further burden on those around her to bolster her ego, and Marilyn increasingly sought solace in prescribed drugs. Regardless of the chaos and catastrophes surrounding her on set and behind the scenes, the picture came in on schedule and within budget and Marilyn's performance was charming and delightful.

After returning to America, her relationship with Arthur had been shaken, but for the moment it was still necessary to her. The Strasbergs' hold on Marilyn was more potent than ever, but Amy and Milton Greene did not make the cut. Once back in New York, Marilyn was ready to dispense of their services and severed her business dealings and her friendship.

A role reversal had subtly taken place after the marriage had begun an equal partnership. Marilyn may have been swamped by references to her beauty and Arthur's brains, but she was America's dream girl. She owned her own production company, and her earning power significantly outstripped most men. Arthur was a prize-winning professional playwright, a master in his field, with *Death of a Salesman* bringing him international acclaim and considerable financial rewards. A social dramatist who did not shirk from the responsibility of exposing real-life dilemmas, Miller had already earned his place in history.

Now, however, the great playwright wasn't writing or earning. Arthur's only job was to get his wife through each day. Marilyn was the iron fist in the velvet glove; her demands were wrapped in her femininity, the image of a little girl lost, the vulnerable and helpless persona that had become her trademark.

Defying social expectations of the gender roles in 1950s America, Marilyn took the dominant role more usually reserved for the male in a partnership. Once married, women were generally expected to function primarily as wives and stay-at-home mothers. Magazines, cinema and television promoted the patriarchal system and the female domestic sphere. Marilyn was challenging society's view of a woman's place being in the home and attending to the every need of her husband and family. While the characters she played in her films were women whose sole purpose was to find a man to take care of them financially and raise a family, here was a woman who had come from challenging circumstances and was now a hugely successful, popular actress and business owner who was the financial provider in her marriage.

Where did this leave the great American dramatist? Arthur had become Marilyn's personal assistant, managing her business affairs. He was reduced to cutting out newspaper and magazine articles about his wife and pasting them in scrapbooks, taking on the role of carer. Arthur was looking after Marilyn during recurrent depressive episodes and suicidal inclinations. Keeping her alive became Arthur's priority, soothing her through pregnancies that ended in miscarriages and on one occasion an ectopic pregnancy.

Arthur found himself in the classic female trap of being economically dependent on a spouse; Marilyn was working to not only pay their own bills but also to pay for Arthur's legal expenses during the HUAC investigations and alimony for his ex-wife and children.

Marilyn completed only three more films before she died, and all of those were during her marriage with Miller. In 1959 she made what many would consider her best film, *Some Like it Hot*. During filming, Marilyn was pregnant again. She was plagued with problems and had issues remembering her lines. The director, Billy Wilder, remembered one four-word line that took almost eighty takes before Marilyn got it right. Jack Lemmon, one of her co-stars alongside Tony Curtis, recalled, 'Billy told Tony and me that we'd better get it right *every* time because the first time Marilyn got it right, that would be the one he'd print, no matter how *we* were.'[8] Rising above her anxieties and her suffering, Marilyn gave the performance of a lifetime, but the price she paid was losing the baby.

In 1960, Marilyn made the film *Let's Make Love*. Taking the title quite literally, she began a short, doomed affair with her co-star, Yves Montand.

Finally, Arthur wrote a screenplay of *The Misfits* for his wife. It was a story he'd started in Reno while waiting for his divorce, about three cowboys, misfits in the desert. Miller adapted it, writing in the character of Roslyn for Marilyn. This should have been the dramatic piece that Marilyn had been longing for.

The highly distinguished cast included Clark Gable, Montgomery Clift and Eli Wallach, and the only other woman of note in the film was Thelma Ritter, twenty-four years Marilyn's senior. Sadly, the Miller marriage had reached the point of no return, and Marilyn's drinking and ever-increasing dependence on prescription drugs all played their part in her eventual nervous collapse. Marilyn simply hated the film, and she hated Arthur. As filming ended, so did the Miller marriage. The divorce became final on 20 January 1961.

In her last interview with Richard Meryman in 1962, Marilyn declared, 'I guess I've always had too much fantasy to be only a housewife.'[9]

14

THE RELUCTANT BLONDE

A bombshell's essence may begin with her personality, but there's a list of essential ingredients, that, when brought together, signify that the woman in front of you is projecting sex to the best of her ability. You can't look at anyone and determine their political persuasion, their feminist beliefs, level of education or in some case religious leanings with just a glance but a mere glance will let you know when you are in the presence of a bombshell.

The bombshell arrives before all else, it's the vision that her immortality is built on. Everyone knows her image but few know the story behind it about the person, her feelings and her depth of character.

On Marilyn's journey, the idea that her looks would be the key to a happy life began with her guardian, Grace McKee Goddard. For Grace, Norma Jeane became a living doll, and she bought clothes for the child (with Gladys's money) and took her to the hair parlour for ribbons and curls. With Grace deftly applying make-up to the 7-year-old's fresh face, Norma Jeane quickly learned how important it was to be pretty, to dress up and please others.

After one of these pampering sessions, Grace would take Norma Jeane to visit the studio where she worked as a film cutter in the lab. She would insist on Norma Jeane twirling in front of her co-workers, and as the little girl shyly did as she was told, Grace would exclaim with pure delight, 'Tell Ella what you're going to be when you grow up. Say: "a movie star", baby! Tell her you're going to be a movie star!'[1]

Grace was obsessed with Jean Harlow, dyeing her own hair blonde, inspired by her idol. Here began Norma Jeane's own infatuation with Harlow, as Grace declared, 'There is no reason you can't grow up to be just like her Norma Jeane.'[2]

Grace would tell the little girl, 'Don't worry, Norma Jeane. You're going to be a beautiful girl when you grow up. I can feel it in my bones.'[3]

Contrary to popular belief, while Norma Jeane loved visiting the movies, she never exhibited any acting ability during her school years. If anything, her interest lay in writing. She was an average student, but in 1938, aged 12, she gained B grades in both journalism and English, and by the age of 14 she was already a regular contributor to the 'Features' column of the school newspaper.

Marrying Jim Dougherty at 16 released Norma Jeane from worry about a career, until he enrolled with the Merchant Marines in 1943. The war in Europe was under way, and Norma Jeane joined other women in working for the war effort on the assembly line in a parachute factory. It was here at the age of 19 that an unexpected photo session with the army photographer David Conover became the turning point in her ambitions. However, even after he encouraged her to make an appointment with a model agency, a cautious Norma Jeane called in sick long before she took the decision to chance her future on modelling.

Early photographs of Norma Jeane show a straight-haired, blonde, winsome child, smiling and well dressed, at odds with the image of the neglected waif Marilyn projected over the years. The Blue Book Model Agency's owner, Emmeline Snively, was introduced to the teenage Norma Jeane, who presented as a still smiling, fashion-conscious, attractive young woman, now with vibrant chestnut hair and a frizz of thick curls that sprung from the smooth widow's peak at the front of her forehead.

Membership of Team Marilyn began to assemble. Emmeline took an immediate liking to her. She was an experienced agent, representing an abundance of successful models, many of whom gained contracts with Hollywood studios. Snively advised Norma Jeane that to progress she needed to be single; studios did not like to chance investing in a married woman who could get pregnant. This, of course, assumed that sexual activity outside marriage did not exist! It is also highly probable that it would be beneficial to a starlet in the making to give the impression she was sexually available.

During a thorough appraisal, Snively pointed out a number of flaws in Norma Jeane's appearance that would need correcting, including how to improve her walk, how to better employ make-up to accentuate her best features and how to lower her smile as she showed too much gum, which gave the illusion that her nose was over long. Most importantly of all, Emmeline wanted her young protégée to lighten her hair and control the unruly curls with a permanent straightening procedure.

Excited at the prospected of self-improvement, she absorbed Snively's suggestions with enthusiasm, except for one; Norma Jeane was adamant she wouldn't lighten her hair. However, Snively persisted, telling her that blondes photographed better in a range of colours. She suggested blondes responded better to variable light conditions, which helped the photographer during shoots. But even using Jean Harlow as an example wasn't enough to persuade Norma Jeane to bleach her hair. 'I wouldn't ever want to be a bleached blonde,'[4] she asserted.

Despite her protestations, she was eventually convinced by Snively and the photographer Raphael Wolff. A shampoo assignment was available for a blonde, and the fee was much more than her regular income. Reluctantly agreeing, it turned out that Norma Jeane's hair was as resistant as she was, and it took several applications over some time to bring her to the desired golden blonde. However, with the change, as anticipated demand for Norma Jeane increased, as did her income.

As Norma Jeane's fame grew, her hair became lighter. By 1960, she was employing Pearl Porterfield, who had been Jean Harlow's hairdresser, and she would delight Marilyn with her anecdotes about her time working with the star. When she began her last film, *Something's Got to Give*, Marilyn's hair was the lightest it had ever been; she would refer to it as pillow slip white.

The journalist Pete Martin could not get over seeing Marilyn for the first time, as she bore no resemblance to the woman on the screen or in magazines. He wondered how such a radical transformation occurred. The Hollywood publicist Flack Jones told him:

> This is true of all platinum blondes or whatever you call the highly dyed jobs we have out here. If their hair isn't touched up and coiffured exactly right; if they're not gowned perfectly and their make-up is not one hundred per cent, they look gruesome. ... They are strictly a product of the twentieth century. They're created blondes, and when you create a blonde you have to complete your creation with make-up and dramatic clothes, otherwise you've got only part of an assembly job.[5]

Hair colour was not the only change for Norma Jeane; she began to have serious aspirations about becoming an actress. Emmeline contacted her friend, Helen Ainsworth, who managed a talent agency; Ainsworth arranged for Norma Jeane to meet Ben Lyons, a talent recruit at Fox, and a silent screen test was hastily organised. The outcome of the screen test was a twelve-month contract with Fox and a name change. Lyons told her she reminded him of Jean Harlow and Marilyn Miller. Norma Jeane requested that she keep her mother's maiden name Monroe, and became Marilyn Monroe, but Norma Jeane was never entirely at ease with the name, and she wished she had held out for Jeane Monroe.

Alan 'Whitey' Snyder applied Marilyn's make-up for the test, and the pair had an instant rapport. From that day forward they became close friends, working together until Marilyn's death in 1962.

It took around three hours to achieve the face that Marilyn's fans expected. Her perfectionism and insecurities would often lead to her washing the make-up off and Whitey having to restart from scratch just before key moments in filming. It has been claimed that it was because she was narcissistic; however, it's much more likely a mixture of her perfectionist nature and an avoidance technique, delaying the thing of which she was most scared – acting.

It is highly probable that Marilyn had a form of body dysmorphic disorder, also known as BDD, a condition that causes a person to focus on their real or imagined flaws; the obsession leaves the BDD sufferer distressed, with feelings of worthlessness, believing they're ugly and not good enough.

People with BDD are often self-conscious and exhibit traits such as mirror-checking up to 100 times a day, or lengthy checks while applying and reapplying make-up, etc. It has been well documented that Marilyn spent an excessive amount of time looking in the mirror. Her friend, the writer Truman Capote, told of finding Marilyn in front of a mirror. She had been sitting there for some time and when he asked her what she was doing she replied, 'Looking at her.'[6]

The Scottish singer Shirley Manson, from the 1990s pop group Garbage, revealed in an American magazine her own history of BDD:

I always turned up five hours late because I'd be fussing about my hair and make-up. I would change into a million different outfits and make them change the lighting a million times, I would spend two hours crying in the toilet – and whatever the result, I always thought I looked disgusting.

Echoing Marilyn's own symptoms, Manson was also subjected to bullying and sexual assault as a child.[7]

Several factors are thought to contribute to BDD, including being genetic predisposition, and while Marilyn's grandparents, Della and Otis Monroe, were wrongly attributed as having mental health issues, her mother, Gladys, was institutionalised with a mental health condition for the majority of her life.

Psychological personality traits are also identified as being implicated in the cause of BDD, such as perfectionism and working in an environment where there is a pressure to look a certain way, which of course describes Marilyn's life. Also increasing the risk of BDD are specific life experiences such as neglect during childhood, sexual abuse and bullying, and having certain features pointed out as different or not right.

We know that Marilyn did indeed experience a difficult childhood – even the nice parts were problematic. While Grace showed Norma Jeane affection, she was obsessed with the child's looks and dressing her up. Marilyn recalled Grace touching her nose and saying, 'You're perfect except for this little bump, sweetheart ... But one day you'll be perfect – like Jean Harlow.' Grace also told her she had a slightly receding chin, also like Harlow, 'that could also stand fixing'.[8]

Her insecurities and anxiety were only added to later, with the model agency searching for flaws to correct and the studio suggesting minor surgery to her nose, teeth and chin. Marilyn worked at keeping her body in shape with exercises such as jogging and using weights from as early as 1943. Although she always indicated she was lazy by nature, Marilyn was also very aware that, as she had professed to not wearing underclothes (although she almost always wore a bra), she acknowledged it was more relevant to keep as toned as possible. Marilyn ate a simple diet, and in 1952 she told *Pageant* magazine that she ate mostly protein, consisting of milk and raw eggs for breakfast with a multivitamin pill. For dinner, she would have steak, lamb chops or liver with raw carrots.[9]

Clothes were an integral part of Marilyn's bombshell image; she said, 'I dress for men. A woman looks at your clothes critically. A man appreciates them.'[10]

She enlarged on this in an article in the July 1952 issue of *Movieland* magazine, 'I wonder why most women dress for women? I think that's a mistake; for myself, it would be, anyway. I happen to like men, so I usually like the same things they like. Therefore it's a matter of simple logic that, of course, I dress for men!'

She went on to complain, 'The only people who have criticized my clothes so far are women.'[11]

While she refined her look and simplified her style, Marilyn certainly pushed the boundaries of what was acceptable for a woman to wear at that time. For the 1953 Photoplay awards, where she was to collect an award for 'Hollywood's Fastest Rising Star', the dress she wore caused uproar, leading to a spat with the movie star Joan Crawford. The dress, designed by Travilla, was tight fitting, full length in gold lamé with a plunging neckline. Marilyn had worn it in *Gentlemen Prefer Blondes*, although it was only shown briefly in the picture as it was far too daring to be passed by the censors of the day.

Travilla begged Marilyn not to wear it for the awards; she had gained some weight and it was extremely tight on her. Marilyn underwent two sessions of colonic irrigation to minimise her inches, but she still filled the dress to capacity. Nothing was going to stop her wearing it and as she entered the room, all eyes were on her. It was reported the next day by the columnist Florabel Muir:

> With one little twist of her derriere, Marilyn Monroe stole the show …
> The assembled guests broke into wild applause [while] two other screen
> stars, Joan Crawford and Lana Turner, got only casual attention. After
> Marilyn, every other girl appeared dull by contrast.[12]

Joan Crawford was not about to take this lightly. She called a press meeting and verbally struck out at Marilyn, saying she exploited sex, and that women 'won't pick [a movie] for the family that won't be suitable for their husbands and children'.

Marilyn subtly hit the knockout blow in reply by responding, 'I've always admired her for being such a wonderful mother – for taking four children and giving them a fine home. Who better than I knows what it means to homeless little ones?'

There has always been a belief that Marilyn was made for men by men. It could be argued that biographers, the media and the feminist movement have done a great disservice to her. Seeking father figures throughout her life, Marilyn enjoyed the company of men, but she was formed by strong, intelligent women such as Grace McKee Goddard, Emmeline Snively, Helen Ainsworth, Natasha Lytess, Paula Strasberg, Amy Greene and many others.

When asked by the journalist Pete Martin, 'Do you mind living in a man's world?' Monroe responded 'Not as long as I can be a woman in it.'[13]

15

UNDER THE INFLUENCE

'No man is an island entire of itself; every man is a piece of the continent, a part of the main.'

John Donne, 1624

Acting mentors Lee and Paula Strasberg arguably had the greatest life-changing influence on Marilyn.

In a rare 1960s interview, Marilyn talked about having secret feelings that she was a 'fake or something phoney'. She recalled her 'teacher', Lee Strasberg, asking her, 'Why do you feel that about yourself?' He told her, 'You're a human being,' to which she responded, 'Yes, I am, but I feel I have to be more.'

Strasberg told Marilyn she needed to start with herself. He gave her permission to be herself and she valued this above all else. During the interview she admitted, 'Lee Strasberg, I see, probably he changed my life more than any other human being I've met including – um, everyone.'[1]

Lee Strasberg had wanted to be an actor and a director; unfortunately he never made the grade so he sidestepped into teaching. Born in 1901 in Poland, Strasberg's family emigrated to America when he was 7 years old. Living in New York, he began acting in plays at the age of 15 and later took lessons at the Actors' Laboratory Theatre, beginning his career as an actor and stage manager. He formed the Group Theatre in 1931, along with Harold Clurman and Cheryl Crawford.

In 1935, Lee married his second wife, the actress Paula Miller, who became an acting coach. Over the years their marriage was quite volatile; when frustrated or angry, Paula would get hysterical and sometimes threaten suicide. Lee's rages were so intense that they would often end in a nosebleed. His daughter, Susan, felt that everything revolved around Lee's 'moods, his expectations and his neuroses'.[2]

Eventually, Strasberg headed to Hollywood in 1941 but returned to New York in 1948 having not achieved his goals. That year he joined the Actors Studio, which had been founded in 1947 by Cheryl Crawford, Elia Kazan and Robert Lewis, all colleagues from the Group Theatre. From 1948 until he died in 1982, Lee became artistic director of the Actors Studio, where he taught what he called the 'Method'. He modified the teachings of the Russian actor and director Constantin Stanislavski, who taught that an actor should find motivation for his character as a whole person by truly getting under the skin of the character the actor is playing.

'The Method' consisted of actors using their own life experiences when attempting to convey emotions, actions and motivations of characters. The foundation of the Method was psychological realism. One of the proponents of Strasberg's Method was Marlon Brando. Becoming members of the Actors Studio gave the students an opportunity to flex their acting ability twice a week, among their peers, during ten-minute scenes that would be critically discussed within the group, led by Strasberg.

Membership was free but the applying actor had to pass stringent interviews and auditions before being accepted into the group of around 250 members. Strasberg made his living from giving private lessons, consisting of classes of thirty students; he did not believe in giving one-to-one lessons. According to Strasberg, it was because 'actors have to work with other actors, not alone',[3] but for the same two hours of a private fee he could earn so much more from thirty members of the studio in one go.

Lee's daughter, Susan, first met Marilyn in 1953 on the set of *There's No Business Like Show Business*. Susan was 16 years old and visiting the set to watch Marilyn film a song and dance routine. She was in awe of both Marilyn's struggle to get it right and the luminous quality she radiated in front of the cameras. When she was invited to Monroe's dressing room, after a brief chat Marilyn leaned into Susan and whispered, 'I really admire your father … I'm going to come to New York and study acting with him. It's what I want to do more than anything.'[4]

Sometime later, at a dinner party attended by Marilyn and Arthur Miller in March 1955, Monroe met the Broadway producer and co-founder of the Actors Studio, Cheryl Crawford. When asked about her future plans, Marilyn confided in Crawford that she was looking to develop her acting skills and that she was interested in stepping away from the comedy roles and taking on more serious parts.

They discussed the possibility of Marilyn working with Strasberg at the Actors Studio. As this was on Marilyn's agenda, she jumped at the chance of an introduction to Strasberg.

Wasting no time, the next afternoon Cheryl took Marilyn to the home of Lee Strasberg. Marilyn was nervous and overwhelmed at the prospect of meeting him, fearful that he would not be interested in her. She needn't have worried; Strasberg was never going to turn down the current darling of the box office.

Strasberg later said of this meeting, 'I saw that what she looked was not what she really was, and what was going on inside was not what was going on outside, and that always means there may be something there to work with.'[5]

Marilyn was impressed and fascinated with Strasberg's wall-to-ceiling bookshelves and found herself in awe at her surroundings. By meeting Marilyn at his home, Strasberg put himself firmly in control; he was able to exert his dominance and, by way of his library, demonstrate his expert knowledge and intellectual superiority.

Within twenty minutes of meeting, Strasberg had agreed to give Marilyn one-to-one private lessons and he instructed her to begin therapy before he was able to work with her. Milton Greene introduced Marilyn to his own therapist, Dr Margaret Hohenberg. (Marilyn later switched to psychiatrist Marianne Kris in 1957, which was to prove a mistake.)

For Marilyn, the Method would ultimately mean reliving her worst experiences and nightmare over and over, on a daily basis.

Not everyone was enamoured with the pretentious air Strasberg displayed. Arthur Miller found the whole situation oppressive and in 1967 he told the author Fred Lawrence Guiles, 'Don't talk to me about Lee Strasberg because I can't stand the man ... I think there is something false about him ... Lee becomes a guru to these people and unless he is there they can't move.'[6]

A good teacher should encourage autonomy, to enable a student to use the skills they have learned and to develop them to suit their needs in any given situation. For Marilyn to be a true success it was essential that she was able to be independent and think for herself on a stage set. Unfortunately the reverse happened under her tutelage with the Strasbergs.

Billy Wilder told the writer Maurice Zolotow that he thought Marilyn was being misled by people in New York who were exploiting her for prestige or money. 'They are trying to elevate Marilyn to a level where she can't exist,' he went on. 'They tell her she's a deep emotional actress. I don't know who's to blame. Kazan? Strasberg? Milton Greene? Who is Greene anyway?'[7]

Wilder also said, 'The Strasbergs didn't do Miss Monroe any good, but she worshipped them like a religion.'[8]

Marilyn had two-hour lessons with Lee Strasberg, two or three times a week. These would include singing whilst staying motionless or singing whilst jumping up and down. They also spent a great deal of time discussing Marilyn's innermost fears and her feelings of not being good enough. Marilyn was vulnerable; Strasberg gave her free lessons, which would have made her feel indebted to him. He became a great man in her eyes, who could lift her to another level, and didn't want anything from her (or so she thought); a new father figure who gave so generously of himself. How enticing this must have been for someone who was experiencing such inner turmoil and wanted more than anything to be taken seriously as an actress.

Strasberg's daughter, Susan, talked of listening to the sessions from outside of the room:

Soon I'd hear laughing or weeping, sometimes an outburst of anger, a diatribe against her studio or someone who had betrayed her trust. She was very unforgiving during these bouts, it was all black and white for her – people were either for her or against her, there was no middle ground.[9]

By asking Marilyn probing questions, Strasberg was able to establish an understanding of the mechanism by which Marilyn thought. It also gave him a way of evaluating the strengths and weaknesses in her character. By showing her empathy, which is key in gaining someone's trust and support, Strasberg gained her trust, which led Marilyn to reveal more, through which he was able to understand the inner workings of her thoughts, ideas and desires.

In studio classes, Strasberg would dominate and monopolise conversation. After an actor finished a scene he would launch into an often lengthy discourse, of sometimes up to an hour. There is a psychological advantage in talking quickly under such circumstances. It overwhelms the listener, which gives the speaker greater influence and at the same time they are seen as knowledgeable and confident. People will often switch off and accept the speaker's point of view as being correct, whether it is or not.

By December 1955, Marilyn started to attend the classes at the Actors Studio as an observer. The actress Miriam Colon recalled, 'We knew she had brought a certain fame to the studio just by being there.'[10]

Strasberg gave Marilyn validation and respect as an actress. He made her believe she could rise above the giggly blonde comedienne, that she could take on dramatic roles. For Strasberg, Marilyn brought fame, celebrity and above all respect, something he had been searching for all his life. While the private one-to-one lessons were free, the financial rewards he obtained from Marilyn were phenomenal.

When Marilyn got the part of Cherie in *Bus Stop*, Strasberg was already committed to Studio classes, so he insisted his wife, Paula, be her acting coach on set. However, Natasha Lytess was still officially Marilyn's coach. Unable to deal with any confrontation, Marilyn's lawyers at Marilyn Monroe Productions sent Natasha a telegram terminating her services; Marilyn would not answer Natasha's calls or letters. Natasha Lytess had been discarded and this was a pattern Marilyn repeated to the end of her life.

Marilyn was to become as dependent on Paula as she was on Lee, to the point that she was unable to work without her being close by. Marilyn lived in constant terror as Paula made her dig deep within herself to find emotions that would correspond with the emotional needs of the character she was playing.

Arthur Miller said about Paula:

Her [Marilyn's] feelings were very ambivalent about Paula. Paula represented to her in a very real sense her own mother who wasn't there. Paula was a real kook. She was as nutty as a fruit cake, and in every sense she was very much like Marilyn's own mother, but she [Paula] was out in the world functioning. Both Lee and Paula by this time had moved in on Marilyn. They had taken her over, at least her career, and that's the way it was for some time.[11]

When Marilyn flew to England to work on *The Prince and the Showgirl* with Olivier, Lee insisted Paula be paid $25,000 for coaching her. This was as much as some of the principal actors were earning. Generally hated on set and feeling that Marilyn heaped misery on her, Paula believed she deserved the money Lee had demanded for her services.

Laurence Olivier was fascinated with the control and influence Paula held over Marilyn on set. During an interview several years later, he described how Marilyn was reshooting a scene and recalled:

> To my absolute horror she [Marilyn] took the whole of one morning remaking the first scene and she couldn't remember it and I remember she had a mentor with her, or guide, a spiritual compass, guide that came from the department kind of sanctified theatre that existed in New York, I heard her say, 'Now Marilyn all you've got to think of is coca cola and Frankie Sinatra.'[12]

Marilyn was generous. If a friend mentioned they liked something she had, Monroe would rarely think twice in giving it to them. Lee was impressed with a string of pearls Marilyn had been given by the Emperor of Japan while she was on honeymoon with Joe. Paula began complimenting the pearls, fixing her attention on them. At Christmas 1957, Marilyn sent them to Paula in a brown paper bag.

As Marilyn's marriage to Miller was breaking down, she turned to the Strasbergs for solace and advice. She was also increasing her intake of pills such as Seconal, Nembutal, Valium and Lithium, all of which she would wash down with champagne.

After finishing *The Misfits* and needing a fresh start, she and Lee put forward the idea for a television dramatisation of Somerset Maugham's classic *Rain* with Strasberg directing and Marilyn playing the lead role of Sadie Thompson. The network executives were not interested in Strasberg but were eager to sign Marilyn and give her a choice of producers. Lee was furious. Instead of encouraging her to do something that would ultimately have benefited her beyond measure, Strasberg watched her walk away from the part out of loyalty to him.

After divorcing Arthur in January 1961, Marilyn changed her will in favour of Lee Strasberg, giving him 75 per cent of her estate with the request that:

> (d) I give and bequeath all of my personal effects and clothing to LEE STRASBERG, or if he should predecease me, then to my Executor hereinafter named, it being my desire that he distribute these, in his sole discretion, among my friends, colleagues and those to whom I am devoted.[13]

Marilyn wanted her personal effects to be shared out to the people she was fond of – her request was never actioned and the Strasbergs kept a firm hold on Marilyn's personal possessions.

On 5 February 1961, a deeply depressed Marilyn was driven by her analyst, Dr Kris, to the Payne Whitney Psychiatric Hospital for what she thought was rest under medical supervision. To her horror she was locked in a padded room and prevented from leaving. She went into a blind panic and after two days she managed to smuggle out a letter to Lee begging for him to get her out of the hospital.

When his influence truly mattered to Marilyn, Lee Strasberg did not respond to her letter.

16

THE MONSTER INSIDE

'She started out with less than any girl I ever knew, but she worked the hardest.'[1]

Emmeline Snively

On realising that there were possibilities for her beyond being a wife and mother, Norma Jeane found ambition and determination. She had a serious work ethic; she knew the odds that she was up against and acknowledged, 'There must have been thousands of girls sitting alone like me dreaming of being a movie star. But I'm not going to worry about them. I'm dreaming the hardest.'[2]

As Norma Jeane transitioned into Marilyn Monroe, she went from the wholesome girl next door to a blonde bombshell in the image of her idol, Jean Harlow. Monroe's beauty and angelic blonde hair contributed to her taking on the image of a sexual and yet innocent angel of sweetness and simplicity, and people were not prepared for this ethereal child–woman to have the devil inside of her. At least, that's how she felt when, after the making of *The Misfits* and the end of her marriage to Miller, she told Jack Cardiff:

Arthur and I are finished … Arthur saw the demon in me … a lot of people like to think of me as innocent, so that's the way I behave to them … if they saw the demon in me, they would hate me … I'm not the person I'd like to be.[3]

The demon would tell Marilyn she wasn't good enough, wasn't pretty enough, wasn't smart enough or wasn't talented enough.

Most women today can identify with Marilyn's monsters. The demon of self-doubt can be a regular visitor for some, and for others, the devil of not good enough is with them all the time.

This is part of what makes this bombshell so unique and so very current. In the social media age we live in today, with the advent of platforms such as Facebook and Instagram, young women are misleading each other and themselves by posting photographs that they couldn't possibly live up to in the real world. We have the technology at our fingertips to make our photos perfect, as with applications such as Photoshop we can manipulate our image into anything we want it to be. We can be skinnier, taller, flawless versions of ourselves and we're able to delete pictures that we consider don't flatter us or that don't present the vision we have of what we want to be or what we want others to think we are.

We give strangers a window into our lives, as Marilyn did. We show them the good parts, it provides us with a feeling of control, but each time we do this, there is ever-increasing pressure to keep up our carefully crafted image. As the image spins of out of control for those that have built up vast numbers of 'followers', there is then the strain of going out in real life and having to represent your online image.

The social platforms give us a glimpse of what Marilyn's world must have felt like at times; a superficial, shallow goldfish bowl of visual connections with other people. A breeding ground of insecurity and anxiety where we compare ourselves, often unfavourably, with other women, who are also putting only their best foot forward, showing a glamorous and exciting life while only ever looking impossibly beautiful. Marilyn told the photographer Lawrence Schiller, who took photographs of the famous pool scene on her uncompleted film *Something's Got to Give*, 'I never wanted to be Marilyn – it just happened. Marilyn is like a veil I wear over Norma Jeane.'[4]

A condition of photographing Marilyn was that the photographer accepted that she had full control over her image and expected to see negatives and contact sheets before any photographs were released. Many photographers were confronted by Monroe wielding pinking shears. One photographer in particular, Bert Stern, who is famous for what is now called 'The Last Sitting', experienced Marilyn's hatred for his work in 1962 as she took a hairpin to the negatives, angrily scratching at the images she didn't like and crossing them out with a red pen until they were rendered unprintable. However, she hadn't bargained for modern-day technology, as many of the images have since been Photoshopped and are readily available for the public to view in books and online.

Lawrence Schiller revealed that Marilyn used a full-length mirror during photoshoots to help her strike a pose that she was happy with. He asked her, 'Do you pose for the photographer or the mirror?' Her answer was categorical: 'The mirror,' she told him. 'I can always find Marilyn in the mirror.'[5]

Marilyn's relationship with the camera was comforting and empowering. After the disaster and trials of filming *The Prince and the Showgirl*, Olivier talked about Marilyn's confidence in front of the camera. In his 1970 interview with Michael Parkinson, Olivier told the interviewer that Milton Greene had approached him for a publicity photoshoot with Marilyn. Olivier responded, 'Oh no, no thank you very much – anybody else can replace me,' but Greene was insistent.

Olivier told Parkinson:

I did [the photo shoot], and he [Greene] knew how to treat Marilyn, and right early on I remember Irina Baronova, a marvellous dancer, a darling friend of mine, and she said, 'I know what's a matter with that girl, inside somewhere she does not want to act, she wants to show herself, that's another thing. She is a model, by accident or by villainy of nature forced to be an actress – that's the answer to her.' And I thought about that and said, 'Well that's fine, but it's not helping me to get through.' However, I did get through, I simply dreaded it, and she was like an Angel! And he would say, 'Marilyn, just show a little bit more of that right titty. Just look up at Larry, stick your ass a little bit more into him.'

Olivier went on to say:

You never saw a child so happy in your life and I realised then she really and mentally wanted to be a model and there was something in her that resisted being an actress in that she had to go onto the floor and do it. You would never know it, when it was easy for her, when she got it by some glorious circumstance or other, I don't know, I very seldom got it, I didn't make the best of Marilyn, other directors have done much better with her than I did.[6]

Whilst Olivier's language was somewhat patronising, Irina Baronova did possibly have a significant and valid point. Marilyn always appeared more confident and relaxed about her photoshoots. She was in total control; she understood that the technical details, the light, the poses, everything was within her power, and she had uncontested approval of the resulting photographs.

The still camera was a joy to her, but on the movie set she reached a point of paralysis and at times would be rude and surly. There are countless stories of her being called to set and responding with 'fuck off'.

During the making of *Some Like it Hot* (1959), her lateness and her moods became legendary. Wilder said, 'I didn't like being dependent on her moods. I could never understand what made her tick. It wasn't her heart.' He said, 'You could always count on her – to be late. You could set your watch by it.'[7]

Wilder was asked why her behaviour on set didn't make him visibly angry with her. He replied, 'Because Miss Monroe has a brain of cheese, tits of steel, she is very good in her part and I'm getting paid a quarter of a million dollars.'[8]

Marilyn had been incredibly difficult on set and was unhappy with many of Wilder's comments about her. When filming finished, she phoned him intending to offer an olive branch, but instead of speaking to Wilder, she talked to his wife, Audrey. Audrey explained that Billy wasn't home yet, so Monroe asked her to take a message, 'Would you please tell him' – she was putting her words together slowly, thoughtfully – 'would you please tell him to go and fuck himself?' A slight pause again, and in a gentler voice Marilyn concluded, 'And my warmest personal regards to you, Audrey.'[9]

Marilyn's behaviour must be put into context; her monsters were driven by many things, not least her very femaleness that was working against her – her gynaecological and hormonal problems, including her chronic endometriosis and inability to have a child. It has been documented that Monroe suffered from painful, heavy periods immediately that she began menstruating in the autumn of 1938 when she was 12 years old. Periods came as a nasty shock, causing severe cramps, and they were also irregular, catching her out unexpectedly and always inconveniently, a situation that did not improve with age.

Eventually, endometriosis was diagnosed, a condition where the tissue that makes up the uterine lining is present on other organs inside the body. Endometriosis is usually found in the lower abdomen or pelvis. This was to have a significant impact on her life. It caused severe fatigue and depression and made it difficult for her to get pregnant and sustain a pregnancy. It is likely she also suffered from common symptoms such as painful sex, pain on going to the toilet, nausea, constipation and diarrhoea. Marilyn had several gynaecological procedures in the hope of easing the pain and enabling her to conceive successfully.

Marilyn lived and worked in a male-dominated environment. This was an era when 'women's problems' were not discussed, menstruation was seen as unhygienic, and few would consider or admit to having sex during a woman's period. It was a subject very much kept in the taboo category. No exceptions would have been sanctioned by her male colleagues.

During both *The Prince and the Showgirl* and *Some Like It Hot* Marilyn was pregnant, and she miscarried both times; her third and final pregnancy with Arthur Miller also resulted in a miscarriage. This was something that Arthur and Marilyn would have struggled to talk about.

Marilyn had traded her whole life on her femininity. In her last interview, with the journalist Richard Meryman, he asked her if she had ever wished that she was tougher. She answered, 'Yes, but I don't think it would be very feminine to be tough. Guess I'll just settle for the way I am.'[10]

Marilyn found herself caught between the drive to remain available, adored and sexual, and the ultimate feminine mystique – finding her happiness through marriage and motherhood, which in the 1950s was incompatible with being a bombshell. One of her co-stars on *Some Like It Hot*, Jack Lemmon, summed up Marilyn's dichotomy perfectly when he said, 'Marilyn had a fatal flaw ... she didn't believe it would last, and she had to have it – the success, the fame, all the attention. She squeezed life too tightly.'[11]

Attempting to deal with her demons by seeing psychiatrists on practically a daily basis and taking an ever-increasing quantity and assortment of prescribed medication, Marilyn made her problems immensely more challenging to overcome.

In early 1960 Marilyn had her first consultation with Dr Ralph Greenson, and at the same time became deeply embroiled in an unethical doctor–patient relationship with the psychiatrist. Post-war America embraced psychoanalysis, with many Americans having daily sessions as both a therapy and a social status. Being able to afford your own psychiatrist was something to aspire to.

In 1950 Greenson was a founding member of the Freudian Group, a clinical professor of psychiatry at UCLA Medical School and a supervising analyst at the Los Angeles Psychoanalytic Society and Institute. He was also a showman; he enjoyed giving lectures and had a deep interest in celebrity. His patients included Frank Sinatra and Tony Curtis.

For Marilyn, her life had been a succession of transient relationships – she had told Jack Cardiff, 'I was abandoned right at the beginning, and where it really matters, I'm still being abandoned.'[12]

Trust was always an issue, and she had few safe outlets for her demons. Dr Greenson appeared to be the answer; not only did he counsel her, he invited her into his home to become a member of his family. Married with two teenage children, Greenson broke every rule of psychiatry, every doctor–patient code, and eventually many believed he broke Marilyn.

WHEN YOUR VIRTUE IS LESS IMPORTANT THAN YOUR HAIRDO

In 1954, it was suggested to Marilyn that she should have her auto-biography ghostwritten to increase her income and for extra publicity. She agreed, on condition that she had full content approval. Her agent swung into action and contacted Jacques Chambrun, who acted for Ben Hecht, a prolific and speedy writer; Marilyn was delighted when Hecht accepted the commission. Meeting several times, she took her friend Sidney Skolsky along with her for guidance and advice. Marilyn was already familiar with Hecht, whom she had met two years earlier. She felt confident talking to him, and she knew he would do a great job.

Within weeks he had a draft for her approval (which was eventually published under the title of *My Story* in 1974). Unfortunately, his agent, Chambrun, also had a copy of the manuscript, which he sold without the permission of Monroe or Hecht, to an English publication, *The Manchester Empire News*, which serialised the work between May and August 1954. Chambrun pocketed the fee, while Hecht had to return his $5,000 advance to the publishers Doubleday and Marilyn abandoned the project.

The resulting manuscript has been a subject of controversy for years over what Marilyn did or did not say. The published segments were an exposé of what is commonly known as 'the casting couch' in Hollywood. The casting couch was a method by which (mostly) young women (star-lets) were encouraged to trade sexual favours for a chance to advance their career.

In the article published in England, Marilyn talked about her expe-riences as a starlet in Hollywood. She denied ever succumbing to the casting couch, but she did mention the 'wolves': 'the talent agents with-out offices, the press agents without clients, the contact men without contacts'.[1] Marilyn went on to say, 'I met them all ... Some were vicious and crooked. But they were as near to the movies as you could get ...

And you saw Hollywood with their eyes – an overcrowded brothel, a merry-go-round with beds for horses.'[2]

Much of what Marilyn and the other young hopefuls dealt with in the Hollywood of the 1950s still resonates with people today. It is not just a Hollywood problem, and it has become the centre of news in what is now known worldwide as the #MeToo movement. The phrase quickly went viral in 2017. It became a global movement against sexual harassment and appeared to begin in Hollywood in the wake of allegations against movie mogul Harvey Weinstein that quickly accelerated into a debate about workplace sexual harassment, with an ever-increasing list of mostly high-profile men being exposed for sexual harassment and abuse within the film industry in particular.

The 'me too movement' actually began very differently from the call to action on social media in 2017 by the actress Alyssa Milano, who said, 'If all the women who have been sexually harassed or assaulted wrote "Me too" as a status, we might give people a sense of the magnitude of the problem.'[3] The movement actually started in 2006 and the founder of Me Too, Tarana Burke, who was born in 1973, is an African–American civil rights activist.

With her own experience of being raped and sexually assaulted as a child and a teenager, Burke was encouraged by her mother to become involved in her community and help others who had experienced hardship and sexual abuse. In 2006, after listening to yet another horrifying disclosure of sexual abuse, Burke wanted to share the message with survivors that 'You're not alone. This happened to me too.'[4, 5]

Would this have helped Marilyn? If she were alive today, would Marilyn be an exponent of #MeToo? It is, of course, possible, as she felt strongly about any kind of injustice. However, if the casting couch had been obliterated during her time in Hollywood, would Marilyn have made it on her own? While, rightly so, people now demand equality with no trade in sexual favours, this is, without doubt, the right way forward, but for Marilyn, who did not have an innate ability to act, would this have meant no possibility of a career in films?

When asked by the journalist W.J. Weatherby during one of their conversations whether the stories about the casting couch were true, Marilyn responded:

They can be. You can't sleep your way to being a star, though. It takes much, much more. But it helps. A lot of actresses got their first chance that way. Most of the men are such horrors; they deserve all they can get out of them![6]

In the 1950s, female virginity before marriage was highly valued by both men and women, with mothers making it clear to their daughters the advantage and importance of innocence, and waiting until marriage before embarking on a sexual relationship was very much expected. With the wolves of Hollywood, Marilyn, as a divorced woman who had already been sexually active, would have been fair game.

Marilyn said, 'In Hollywood "being virtuous" is a juvenile-sounding phrase, like "having the mumps".'[7] But she was still insisting that she turned down offers, and even suggesting that this 'ran' her 'price up'.[8] Monroe said that she didn't take the wolves' money and that they didn't get past her front door, but she went to their parties, drove in their limousines and ate their food.

There are, of course, different paths to the casting couch scenario. Marilyn may or may not have gone down the usual route of sleeping with a casting director for a part, but she did advance her career via people in her life and the use of favours given to such people as her agent and lover Johnny Hyde. With different accounts and times for their first meeting, it is hard to establish the exact date, but it is probable they most likely met on New Year's Eve 1948.

Hyde was widely respected in Hollywood; he frequented the best establishments and had a track record of successful clients, including Lana Turner. He told Marilyn she was going to be a big star. Thirty-one years her senior, he was a short man of 5ft 3in and married with children. Within months of meeting Marilyn in the spring of 1949, he had left his wife and family.

Hyde rented a house in North Palm Drive, Beverly Hills, and Marilyn moved in with him. He wanted to divorce his wife and marry Marilyn, but she wanted to further her career. She told Hyde that she did not love him, and therefore she rejected his proposal. Hyde was not fazed by this and continued to ask her to marry him. The roles began rolling in. After Marilyn was dropped by Fox in March 1950, Hyde persuaded Darryl Zanuck to take Marilyn back and sign her to a seven-year contract. Hyde wanted Marilyn back at Fox because he had heard about the role of Miss Caswell in *All About Eve* and believed this could be an important part for her.

By the end of 1950, Marilyn had six films in release and was a rising star, but Hyde's efforts had taken their toll on his already fragile health.

The constant round of parties, dancing and social networking was simply too much. When his first heart attack occurred, Hyde went to the Cedars of Lebanon Hospital and was advised to slow down, but he just couldn't bring himself to follow doctor's orders. With his desperation to establish Marilyn, he increased the pace. To induce her to marry him, he expressed how anxious he was to provide for her financially and, feeling that he didn't have much longer to live if she were his wife, Hyde would ensure she was financially provided for.

Of course, Hyde could very well have chosen to leave Marilyn a considerable fortune in his will without the necessity of being married to her, but he didn't. He did, however, while he was alive, take care of her meals, clothing and beauty treatments and some minor cosmetic surgery. Although she denied it in later years, for a short time Marilyn was in fact a kept woman. This was also repeated with Milton Greene, who took care of her living expenses, beauty treatments and clothing, etc., in 1955 when she arrived in New York.

On 16 December 1950, Hyde stayed in Palm Springs to rest, while he encouraged Marilyn to go on to Tijuana with Natasha Lytess to do some Christmas shopping with his money. While they were there, Hyde had a massive heart attack and died on 18 December in Los Angeles. Marilyn did not reach him before he died.

For a while, Marilyn's Hollywood protection ceased and she was again subjected to the wolves. Shortly after Johnny Hyde's death, Marilyn began her relationship with the director Elia Kazan.

Many biographers cite Marilyn's story of her turning down Harry Cohen's attempt to get her alone on his yacht for sex as proof she did not submit to using what was necessary for favours in the industry. It seems possible that they are either naïve or in denial. It does a great disservice to Marilyn not to try to understand the complexity of the time she lived in and not to credit the intelligence with which she dealt with such circumstances. It is as if it would be a shameful notion that Marilyn could do such a thing, rather than see it in the context of how she negotiated the shark-infested pools in which she swam.

Marilyn would choose those she would gift with her favours very wisely. The notion expressed by a producer that, 'Marilyn never slept with a man who could do her any good,'[9] was simply nonsense when it is looked at and questioned, given the evidence regarding her relationship with Johnny Hyde. Marilyn was intelligently selective. Over the years her sex life has been grossly and elaborately over exaggerated; Marilyn was very careful with whom she shared her body.

During a conversation with the journalist, W.J. Weatherby, Marilyn expressed her feelings about her sexual activity as a starlet:

> There was a period when I responded too much to flattery and slept around too much, thinking it would help my career, though I always liked the guy at the time. They were always so full of self-confidence, and I had none at all, and they made me feel better. But you don't get self-confidence that way. You have to get it by earning respect. I've never given up on anyone I thought respected me.[10]

Mamie Van Doren, actress and cult icon of the youth scene in the 1950s, was another blonde bombshell who experienced the 'casting couch' first hand. In her autobiography, *Playing the Field*, Van Doren begins her prologue by covering the casting couch. She identifies the favourite question of interviews as, 'Is there a Hollywood casting couch?' and, 'Did she ever find herself on it?'

Van Doren is delightfully frank and honest as she reveals, 'Many of us who made a career in the movies did – many, many more than want to admit it.' She also said that while she was asked this eternal question, she was never asked about how she felt when she was on the casting couch.

Van Doren's view could in some factions be seen as being unacceptable today, but she is pragmatic and also gives voice to women having sexual desires and not being afraid to accept them when she says:

> The phrase 'casting couch' implies that an actress has to have sex with someone as the *necessary* price for being cast in a film. Fortunately, it was not necessary for me. If you are young, healthy, energetic, and possessed of the normal set of biological urges, the casting couch can also be fun with the right person. Fun, I believe, was where I excelled …
>
> Marilyn Monroe once told me, not entirely in jest, that she believed I was smart enough to sleep with the 'right' person. Without regret, I can tell you honestly that I was not. All too often, I bypassed the casting-couch activity that would have furthered my career and followed the instincts and urges of my heart. By and large such romances did nothing to advance my career … I also turned down the advances of several powerful and important men in the industry because they simply didn't appeal to me.

Hollywood in the 1950s exhibited double standards and repressed sexual mores of the rest of the country – it was okay for men to play around, but nice girls could not. The difference in Hollywood was that if nice girls did sleep with the right guy, they could get ahead in the business. That was the game you had to play.[11]

In 1954, Marilyn reportedly said:

In Hollywood, a girl's virtue is much less important than her hair-do. You're judged by how you look, not by what you are. Hollywood's a place where they'll pay you a thousand dollars for a kiss, and fifty cents for your soul. I know, because I turned down the first offer often enough and held out for the fifty cents.[12]

Almost seventy years later, we are still hearing the same sentiment.

FROM HOLLYWOOD TO WESTWOOD

The year 1961 saw momentous changes in Marilyn's life, which had, in a way, come full circle. Contracted to complete another movie for Fox, Marilyn was reluctant to go back and desperately wanted to get it over with. Returning to Fox was a temporary necessity. New York was now her home, and she had every intention of returning. Expressing her feelings about Los Angeles, she told her friend, the writer Truman Capote, 'Even though I was born there, I still can't think of one good thing to say about it.'[1]

Time was Marilyn's nemesis, working in an industry that was ruthless about age. The role of Lorelei in the 1953 film *Gentleman Prefer Blondes* was planned initially for Betty Grable, but Marilyn was the new blonde on the block and ten years younger than Grable. For the studio it was a natural choice to cast Marilyn; she was younger, less of a financial outlay and becoming increasingly more popular.

When both Grable and Monroe were cast together along with Lauren Bacall in the 1953 production of *How to Marry a Millionaire*, the 36-year-old Grable had seen the writing on the wall after *Gentleman Prefer Blondes*, and she told her young rival without any malice but more in acceptance, 'Honey … I've had mine – now go get yours.'[2]

Even magazines of the time were mocking the female ageing process while glorifying older male actors with euphemisms such as debonair and distinguished. In the 14 July 1956 issue of *Picturegoer*, they ran an article 'Be your AGE, Girls', asking why older female actresses accepted romantic leading roles opposite younger actors. It declared that watching older actresses in these roles was 'embarrassing' and that the cinema-goers 'laughed out loud' watching an older actress play opposite a younger man. It contrast, the writer admired 48-year-old Bette Davis for knowing her place and playing 'a washed-out, drab middle-aged Bronx housewife' in *Wedding Breakfast* (also known as *The Catered Affair,* 1956), stating 'How one admires her for no longer trying to kid either picture-goers or herself that she is still an ingénue.'

The 1957 film *Kiss Them for Me* had the male lead, 53-year-old Cary Grant, sandwiched between his two leading ladies, 24-year-old Jayne Mansfield and 25-year-old Suzy Parker. When the film did not make its box office expectations, it was Mansfield's career that suffered as a result, not the older Grant.

Marilyn, fast approaching 35, was very aware of how the industry viewed the female ageing process. She also had health issues that resulted in a return to New York for the removal of her gallbladder on 29 July 1961. Her half-sister, Berniece, spent time with her as she recuperated at home in New York. By 8 August Marilyn was fit to travel and returned to Los Angeles. Her ex-husband Joe DiMaggio met her at the airport. They had reignited their friendship and after Marilyn's death there were rumours that the couple had been about to remarry; however, there is no evidence to back up the theory, and after her death DiMaggio refused to speak about her in public and rarely in private.

On arrival in LA, Marilyn's figure was the centre of attention, as gossip columnist Louella Parsons wrote, 'I thought I hadn't seen her look as well since the first time I knew her – years ago. She's taken off so much weight that all those bulging curves have gone.'[3] At her heaviest during *Let's Make Love*, Marilyn had weighed exactly 140lb (10st), hardly bulging with curves, and by today's standards she would have been comfortably in a healthy weight range for her height. However, she was now approximately 117lb (8st 4lb), which is at the very lower end of a healthy weight range for Marilyn's height of 5ft 5½in.

Back in LA, Marilyn was seeing quite a bit of Frank Sinatra. She had also been seeing friends Peter Lawford and his wife Pat, the sister of Jack and Bobby Kennedy. Marilyn met both brothers and was alleged to have had an affair with both of them. However, it is a complicated knot of rumours that is impossible to untangle and not helped by unreliable narrators such as Robert Slatzer and Jeanne Carmen, who came forward several years after Marilyn's death. Neither one can prove they even knew Marilyn personally, but by making unsubstantiated claims about affairs that can never be verified, it left a whiff of smoke in the air.

As filming of *Something's Got to Give* commenced, it became central to Marilyn's life and her unhappiness. The actress hated the script but, regardless of her feelings about it, Fox made it clear she had no choice.

Her therapist, Dr Greenson, told her it would be good for her. This was the beginning of an avalanche of upsetting events in her life that included news in December that Arthur Miller was planning to marry Inge Morath, the photographer he met on the set of *The Misfits*. Marilyn was deeply affected by the news, and it was soon compounded by the revelation that Inge was pregnant and expecting Arthur's baby.

That February Marilyn agreed to pose for a spread in *Paris Match* with the photographer Willy Rizzo but, feeling unwell, the first appointment was cancelled by Pat Newcomb on Marilyn's behalf. After several false starts, a four-hour shoot finally took place on 10 February. Marilyn drank throughout and Rizzo remembered that she had done her own make-up and made a bit of a 'hash of it', recalling, 'Marilyn was immensely sad … and that sadness was very visible on the pictures.'[4]

It is unlikely that Marilyn saw many of the photos, which show her the worse for drink. Fortunately for Rizzo, the ones he did put forward Marilyn loved and with her approval *Paris Match* published the article about her on 23 June 1962, leading with a beautiful soft focus Rizzo photograph of Marilyn on the cover.

Her therapy sessions with Dr Greenson were also becoming a nightmare. People who knew Marilyn well suggested the more involved she became with her therapist, the more miserable she was. Despite Marilyn wanting to return to New York, Greenson firmly encouraged her to buy a house close to his, engaging a housekeeper companion on Marilyn's behalf – Eunice Murray.

Murray found a home for Marilyn that was a miniature version of Dr Greenson's house, which incidentally, he had purchased fourteen years earlier from her. DiMaggio helped her with a loan for the deposit. Monroe's finances had been depleted by her living expenses and the people that were working for her, such as Greenson, the Strasbergs, her publicist Pat Newcomb and now Mrs Murray – amongst several others.

Life was growing ever more complicated as a direct result of the people surrounding her. Marilyn's own words echoed this on her last visit to New York, when she told the journalist W.J. Weatherby, 'Sometimes I think the only people who stay with me and really listen are people I hire, people I pay. And that makes me sad. Why can't I have friends around me all the time, friends who want nothing from me?'[5]

Something's Got to Give was becoming a self-fulfilling prophecy with illness and setbacks, but on 23 May Marilyn was on form and the photographer Larry Schiller was there to capture her in all her glory. She agreed to do nude shots on the set, on the condition Schiller ensured her photos knocked her rival, the reigning movie queen Elizabeth Taylor, off the magazine covers. Schiller said, 'Her wet skin glistened. Her eyes sparkled. Her smile was provocative. She was a week away from her thirty-sixth birthday, and she looked as good as she'd ever looked.'[6]

Marilyn was doing what Marilyn did best. She appeared confident; this was her domain, the still camera and striking a pose. No lines to remember, and she understood all the moves.

Celebrating her thirty-sixth birthday on 1 June, after a full day's work, her stand-in Evelyn Moriarty organised a birthday cake and champagne. Directly from the set, Marilyn headed to the Dodgers stadium for a charity baseball event. She never returned to the film again.

The following day, 2 June, Marilyn was overcome with depression and unable to work. Greenson was on holiday with his wife in Europe. Dr Milton Uhley was covering for Greenson and was called out to see Marilyn. While there he removed what he felt was a surprising amount of pills, and Marilyn asked Eunice to contact Greenson.

Returning early from his vacation on 6 June, Greenson went immediately to Marilyn's house. The information isn't clear, but what is known is that on 7 June Greenson took Marilyn to see the plastic surgeon Dr Michael Gurdin, who observed that Monroe was 'dishevelled' and under the influence of drugs.[7] Greenson told the doctor Marilyn had fallen in the shower. Her eyelids were black and blue, and she was fearful that her nose was broken. Gurdin took X-rays and reassured Marilyn there was no fracture.

Over the years it has been questioned as to how the injuries actually occurred and to what extent Greenson may or may not have been involved.

On 8 June, Dr Greenson spoke to Fox executives, with promises of being able to return his client to the studio immediately. However, by this time, the executives and crew were no longer in the mood for disruptive, unmanageable behaviour. Marilyn was promptly fired and issued with the threat of a lawsuit.

Although this was a difficult time for Marilyn, she may have felt some relief as she ploughed on with photo sessions and interviews in an attempt to keep a high profile with the public.

As the *Paris Match* spread hit the newsstands on 23 June, Marilyn met the photographer Bert Stern to work on a photoshoot for *Vogue*.

Of meeting Monroe for the first time Stern said, 'I took a deep breath and said, "You're beautiful".' Looking straight at him, she responded, 'Really? What a nice thing to say.' Another surprise to Stern was her voice: 'it wasn't tiny, the breathy baby voice you hear in her movies. It was more natural, yet distinctive and feminine.'[8]

Stern had the foresight to order plenty of Dom Pérignon, Marilyn's favourite champagne. His aim was nude photos, and he manipulated a drunken Monroe into removing her clothes and using sheer, diaphanous scarves to obscure her body from total nudity. But at the end of the shoot, he captured the photograph he'd intended from the start: a fully naked Monroe.

Throughout the session, Marilyn sought reassurance from those around her, 'How's this for thirty-six,'[9] she asked Stern, and to her hairdresser, she appealed, 'George, how does this look,' and he replied, 'Oh how wonderful, how beautiful.'[10]

After the shoot, photos were sent to *Vogue*, but the magazine was not happy with them. It still wanted Marilyn but not semi-nude. A further shoot was arranged, and an editor, Babs Simpson, was sent along with a selection of fashion garments to oversee the shoot, which was a successful and elegant production.

Several days later, when Marilyn hadn't received the proofs, Pat Newcomb contacted Stern and asked how the pictures were. She told him, 'You know, don't you, that Marilyn has the approval of all her photographs?' Stern was not happy and he writes in his book about the session, 'Approval had not been part of the deal, and even if they had asked for it they almost certainly wouldn't have got it.'[11] Which was rather arrogant of him, as were he to deny Marilyn photographic approval it is more than certain she would not have agreed to shoot with him.

He told Newcomb, 'It's one thing if I agree to give her approval, but I can't speak for *Vogue*.'[12] Pat insisted that Marilyn wanted to see all the photos anyway.

Craftily, Stern did not send the entire shoot, but Marilyn was horrified with what he did send. Many of the photographs were not flattering; her surgery scars were visible, the light was harsh, signs of age showed in noticeable lines around her eyes, her teeth were tinged yellow, and her skin had a deathly pallor. Her dislike of the photos was evident when she returned them to him with the images on the contact sheets crossed out in magic marker and the transparencies scratched out by a hairpin until they were mutilated and destroyed.

These photos would have been a devastating blow to Marilyn. In later years Stern published the photos Marilyn scratched out and now they are often seen on the internet as beautiful, though heavily Photoshopped, works of art.

Before receiving Stern's photographs, Marilyn had spent three days with her photographer and friend George Barris. From 29 June to 1 July he took photos for a *Cosmopolitan* photo essay. Marilyn was relaxed; she drank Dom Pérignon, but unlike the *Vogue* and *Paris Match* shoot, she did not look the worse for wear in the photographs. In fact, she looked beautiful and in control of her life.

Over five days, 4 to 9 July, Marilyn gave her last interview for *Life* magazine, with the journalist Richard Meryman. Taped over eight hours, she was articulate and honest, talking about the effects of fame and her life under the spotlight. She told him:

> Fame has a special burden, which I might as well state here and now. I don't mind being burdened with being glamorous and sexual. But what goes with it can be a burden. I feel that beauty and femininity are ageless and can't be contrived, and glamour, although the manufacturers won't like this, cannot be manufactured. Not real glamour; it's based on femininity. I think that sexuality is only attractive when it's natural and spontaneous … We are all born sexual creatures, thank God, but it's a pity, so many people despise and crush this natural gift. Art, real art, comes from it, everything.
>
> … These girls who try to be me, I guess the studios put them up to it, or they get the ideas themselves. But gee, they haven't got it …
>
> It might be a kind of relief to be finished. You have to start all over again. But I believe you're always as good as your potential … Fame will go by, and, so long, I've had you fame. If it goes by, I've always known it was fickle. So at least it's something I experienced, but that's not where I live.[13]

Marilyn was always concerned with how her public saw her; therefore, it is even more difficult to comprehend that somewhere between 9 p.m. on 4 August and 3 a.m. on the 5th, this beautiful, vital, seemingly fragile and yet doggedly determined woman died in her bed of an apparently suicidal overdose of sleeping pills and barbiturates in a messy room, with dirt under her fingernails from gardening that day, and with tousled hair that needed the roots retouched.

Marilyn's funeral was a low-key affair with around thirty mourners, most of whom were on her payroll. She was interred at Westwood Village Memorial Park, within sight of Aunt Ana and Aunt Grace. The arrangements were made by Joe DiMaggio, with the help of her sister, Berniece Miracle, and her former business manager, Inez Melson.

Her friend and make-up artist, Whitey, kept his promise. With the support of a flask of gin, the grim task of transforming the body in front of him back into the woman the world would recognise took place. A blonde wig, green scarf and a gift of baby pink roses completed the story. During one of her last phone conversations with her close friend, the poet and writer Norman Rosten, Marilyn told him, 'Let's all start to live before we get old.'[14]

PART FOUR

DIANA DORS

19

ONE AND ONLY

Diana Dors was the mistress of mistakes, but she rolled with them, showing true fearlessness. She stood up, dusted herself down, pushed back her sleeves and got on with the job of life, and the public loved her for it. This was no dizzy, empty airhead of a bombshell – this was the woman who put the 'bomb' into the shell. She knew what she wanted, and looks had little to do with it.

Straight talking, humorous, and with an abundance of glamour, Diana was a real person. No untouchable goddess, she dived into life and didn't always come up smelling of Je Reviens, but she did know her worth! With all the prerequisites of being a bombshell – figure, face and hair – she also had something else; she was a talented natural-born actress with confidence that saved her from the perils of the profession on many occasions.

A proficient and able writer, Diana wrote columns for magazines and completed five books before she died. Two were autobiographical and the other three were A–Zs of her experience of celebrity life. Diana could tell a tale in such a way that you would simply never forget it; honest, often shocking but always entertaining. With wit and intelligence she showed you that, although some of her relationship choices with the opposite sex were not the wisest, she enjoyed her mistakes to the full and never let them stop her from making another one!

Diana Mary Fluck came as a surprise to her parents, Albert Edward 'Bert' Sidney (also known as 'Peter') and Winifred Maud 'Mary' Fluck. After thirteen childless years of marriage, they could have been forgiven for thinking that the future was going to be just about them until on 23 October 1931 and at the age of 42, Mary gave birth to a daughter, who they called Diana, at the Haven Nursing Home in Swindon, Wiltshire.

The birth was complicated; Diana wasn't breathing, but more of a concern to the doctor was that Mary was in grave danger of dying. While the doctor and nurse worked to save Mary, baby Diana was taken into another room, and with dedicated care the nurse looking after her managed to get her breathing. Both mother and baby survived the ordeal, to which Diana attributed her lifelong claustrophobia.

The Haven Nursing Home, in a Victorian terrace, was a base for the community midwives; it had an interconnecting door through to the neighbouring property, which housed the GP surgery, so help was at hand when needed. With no National Health Service available until 1948, if the Flucks had been poorer, Diana would have almost certainly been born at home, and it is unlikely that either mother or baby would have survived the ordeal.

Returning home to recuperate, her mother's sister, Kit, moved in to take care of Diana, and Bert became surplus to requirements. Bert may well have resented being pushed out, and the changes brought about by this tiny bundle. Growing up, Diana had a close relationship with her mother, but in contrast, there was an abiding personality clash with her father, possibly fuelled by Aunt Kit, who alluded to the possibility that Diana's father was perhaps not Bert but her godfather, 'Uncle' Gerry Lack. This rumour created a wedge of doubt between Diana and her father. Gerry Lack had been a close friend of both Bert and Mary, but he had left the scene by the time Diana was a toddler.

Intolerant of Bert as she grew up, Diana recognised as an adult with the benefit of experience and hindsight that he wanted what was best for his only child and she realised how difficult it must have been for him. Diana was wilful, confident and not afraid of asserting herself.

Writing about her father in her autobiography *Dors by Diana*, she said, 'Within me was an inborn resentment and opposition to this man … I don't know why, yet it was as if the mould of my attitude towards men set itself then.'[1]

Diana recognised after a great deal of time that they simply did not understand each other and she drew the conclusion that '*he* was the first man with whom I had to cope and, as in each emotional relationship involving men throughout my life, I made a hopeless mess of it.'[2]

Man trouble ran in the family; both of Diana's grandmothers were farmer's daughters, and both had complicated relationships with the men in their life. Her paternal grandmother, Catherine Carter from Gloucestershire, was a seamstress model with an 18in waist. Widowed at an early age with Diana's father to care for, she remarried a farmer who was also a widower, with five children of his own.

Diana's maternal grandmother and eventual namesake, Georgina Dors, was from Somerset. Married at 16 to a farmer, she quickly had four children, including Diana's mother and one little girl who sadly died aged 2 years old. As she reached her early twenties, Georgina fell in love with her husband's handsome brother, James, and was soon running away to Wales with him, which caused her to be ostracised from her family for her despicable behaviour.

Life was harsh and money scarce, but Georgina went on to have three children with James. While in the beginning it was a passionate affair, romance and joy didn't last. Repeating history, James left her and ran off with the young fiancée of Georgina's son from her marriage to James's brother.

Diana's formative years were set against complex relationship issues on both sides of her family tree. It also came to light that her mother, Mary, had been married before; her husband, William Padget, had been killed in the First World War.

Diana remembers her mother complaining bitterly in moments of discontent that Diana's birth had changed her life, but that it hadn't changed her father's life one iota. This was a common resentment for women with children in the 1930s as their husbands continued on with relatively unchanged lives after a child was born. They would continue working and socialising at evenings and weekends, while women found they had less opportunity than ever for leisure time. They were still trapped by the belief that a woman's place was in the home rearing children, while the husband was head of the household and providing financially for his wife and children.

Diana remembered her parents arguing continually, mostly over her. Growing up, she and her mother became a formidable team against her father. Despite her mother's occasional annoyance, they shared a very close bond, and Diana by her own admission was the best-dressed child in her neighbourhood, indulged in dancing classes, lavish birthday parties and regular trips to the cinema from as early as 3 years old. After Diana started school, when Mary collected her for lunch she found it easy to persuade her mother to take her to the cinema instead of returning to school for the afternoon session. Their cinema trysts were kept a secret from her father.

Sent to private school but uninterested in her school work, much to the irritation of her father and her teachers, Diana would daydream about the stars she had seen on the big screen. Maths was a problem for Diana, but English was her best subject. In a school essay entitled 'What you would like to be when grown up' the star-struck 8-year-old wrote that she 'was going to be a film star, with a cream telephone and a swimming pool'.[3]

Diana knew from a very early age what she wanted to do with her life and while her father made her shudder with his conservative, traditional values, telling her she should be a secretary and 'I'd like to see you marry some decent sort of chap,'[4] Diana had other ideas, and set on a path that she didn't deviate from. Drawn in by a regular diet of glamour from an early age, Diana adored the beautiful clothes, luxury and a way of life she knew was within her reach. This little girl really was going to grow up to be a movie star.

As an only child, she was independent, wise beyond her years and highly successful in those things she enjoyed and wanted above all else. Mary persuaded Bert to allow Diana to have elocution lessons. She knew that a thick Wiltshire accent would hold her daughter back. In no time at all, Diana was entered into poetry festivals and competitions and was on a winning streak. Her name appeared regularly in the local newspapers. Diana lapped up the attention and excelled in the spotlight.

On Sunday, 3 September 1939, Diana's life and millions of others was about to change as they heard the announcement at 11.15 a.m. made by Prime Minister Neville Chamberlain telling the nation that a state of war now existed between Britain and Germany. Not understanding the implications, Diana was excited by the change in the atmosphere. She'd always hated boring Sundays, but this was a decidedly thrilling Sunday.

Bert would not be called up for military service as he had been invalided out of the army during the previous war and on leaving the service he had become a railway clerk. As the war progressed it began having an impact on everyday living, including holidays, which were always important to the Fluck family. Previous holidays were spent with Grandma Dors in Wales, but she had died in 1937. After her death, they vacationed in Weston-super-Mare, but now it felt unsafe to be there. So they began staying with her mother's uncle, Joe Dors, on his farm in Somerset.

Joe also had a younger brother, who was seen as a bit of a character, and somewhat eccentric. According to Diana, Uncle Arthur, as he was known, had a thick Somerset accent, swore a great deal and enjoyed guzzling cider at every opportunity.

Unfortunately, Arthur also had a lustful eye on his 8-year-old great-niece, and Diana recalled that he made an attempt to rape her. Diana was in the stables on her own, watching the horses eat, when Arthur stumbled in, grabbed her and held her uncomfortably tight. In her book *Dors by Diana*, she writes, 'I couldn't understand why this elderly relation was suddenly displaying such affection. Until then, he had never seemed to notice me, or so I had thought.'

Diana continues, 'even as a child of eight, I sensed something was not as it should be … he kept pressing his mouth on mine with kisses decidedly dissimilar from those I'd received from my other uncles.'[5]

Managing to push him away from her, Diana fled the stables in a confused and upset state, trying to figure out what had just happened. She said, 'I daren't tell my mother. I felt too embarrassed. As for my father! God knows what he'd have done.'[6]

Diana didn't let this horrible experience destroy her confidence or her self-esteem. As the war continued, she found the perfect channel for her theatrical dreams. With an influx of American soldiers to Wiltshire, concerts were staged to entertain the troops. Diana's father would accompany fellow entertainers on his piano at a variety of venues, and at every possible chance, if there were a gap to fill, Diana would jump on stage with glee and sing such tunes as 'Ma, I miss your apple pie', throwing in a tap dance. The soldiers, of course, encouraged and rewarded this tiny powerhouse of talent and determination with roaring applause.

By the age of 13, Diana's ambitions, encouraged by her mother, were unstoppable. She had transformed from a chubby child who had to wear an eye patch to correct a lazy eye, into a stunning young woman who would pass herself off as being 17. Mother and daughter attended the GI camp dances. Both had the gift of charm; as Diana flirted with the GIs, Mary flattered and cajoled the cook, returning home at the end of the evening laden with rationed supplies from the camp kitchen.

With her mother's support, Diana entered a beauty contest. *Soldier* magazine was in search of a new pin-up to feature in a future issue. Posing in a two-piece bathing suit, endeavouring to look like Betty Grable, Diana was thrilled to come third. Once again her photo was in the local newspaper and was seen by the professor of a local college, who asked Diana to pose (in a swimsuit) for art classes. Diana was happy and was soon attending drama classes, letting it be known to everyone that she wanted to be an actress.

Given parts in college productions, she was receiving excellent reviews in the campus paper. Now aged 14, she enlisted her mother's support in leaving school and convincing her father that it would be beneficial to take private acting classes in London. Bert felt the full force of mother and daughter manipulation and eventually agreed, although not without considerable reluctance, on the condition that Diana would study for a diploma to teach elocution lessons.

Soon Diana was making weekly trips to London with her mother chaperoning her; Mary was living vicariously through her daughter and loving every minute of it. With her mother's approval, Diana moved to London to become a full-time student at the London Academy of Music and Dramatic Art (LAMDA) while living at the Young Women's Christian Association (YWCA) in Kensington.

Around this time she also began to earn a little extra money towards her living expenses with evening work modelling for the Camera Club. Inevitably perhaps, they requested that she posed nude. After discussing it with her mother, who surprisingly wasn't horrified at the suggestion, her father shrugged his shoulders, knowing Diana would do what she wanted to do anyway. Her father was right and Diana agreed to pose in the nude.

One of the photographers told Diana about the Pearl Beresford Modelling Agency and also gave her a letter of introduction. After being interviewed by the agency, Diana began accepting modelling jobs, but she found the waiting around for lights to be adjusted simply dull and it made her even more determined to get into films.

Her determination paid off as she was cast in the film *The Shop at Sly Corner* (1947). She was told to keep quiet about her age as the part was that of the villain's girlfriend. Pretending to be 17 was no problem for Diana, she was used to it – all she could think of was that Hollywood was coming closer. Her agent suggested it was time for a name change; Fluck just wasn't suitable, which upset her father, but her mother suggested 'Dors', and with almost unanimous agreement Diana Dors was created.

This bombshell was about to explode, and she wasn't going to let anything stop her.

Harlean Harlow Carpenter aged 6 in 1917. The little girl had a strong bond with her mother, Jean, and eventually discarded her own name Harlean in favour of taking her mother's name 'Jean Harlow'. (Alamy)

Lighting the torch – Jean on loan to Columbia Pictures in 1931, where she played the lead role in a film titled *Platinum Blonde,* two words that would be forever associated with her and would become synonymous with her icon status. (Alamy)

Jean with the love of her life, William Powell, in 1937. It was becoming clear that her illness was taking a toll on her. She died shortly after this photograph was taken at the age of just 26 and without the wedding ring she had so desired from Powell. (Alamy)

Ruth Ellis (first left) appears as a beauty contestant in *Lady Godiva Rises Again* in 1951. Diana Dors, the star of the film, is tenth left. Ruth's dreams were once again thwarted when she found she was four months pregnant and was unable to pursue the career she longed for. (Alamy)

Believed to be taken at the Little Club in 1954, Ruth loved her job as it gave her the opportunity to be an actress on her own stage and enjoy a lifestyle that she would otherwise have been excluded from as a working-class girl in London. (Getty Images)

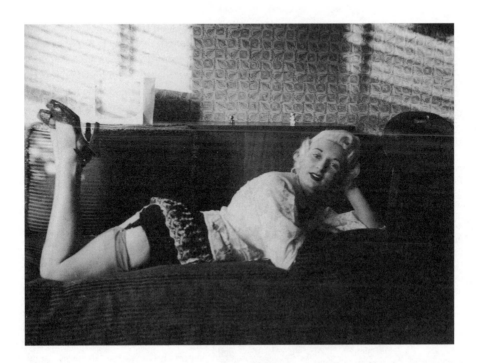

Ruth modelling for a Captain Ritchie in 1954. It is quite likely that she is in her flat above the Little Club where she was the manageress on the Brompton Road in Knightsbridge, London. Modelling brought in much needed extra cash. She gave a considerable portion of her earnings to her parents. (Getty Images)

Striking a glamorous pose c.1955. Ruth loved modelling and being the centre of attention – it's easy to forget how young she was. At 28, when she killed her lover David Blakely, her future died too. Her last performance would be in the execution cell of Holloway Prison. (Getty Images)

Under the make-up and the blonde hair Ruth was a finely featured elegant beauty. When she arrived at Holloway, members of staff were surprised by her youthful appearance and pretty and delicate looks. (Getty Images)

Ruth and David Blakely c.1955. Their attraction was fatal, costing both of them their lives within two years of meeting each other. Ruth's mental state at the time of the shooting was ignored and provocation by Blakely was barely touched upon during a trial that lasted less than two days. (Getty Images)

Ruth with 'alternative lover' Desmond Cussen – did he encourage Ruth to shoot his rival? Cussen was a witness for the prosecution. He emigrated to Australia in 1964, becoming an alcoholic, and, after a fall that ironically resulted in a fracture dislocation of his neck, he died on 8 May 1991. (Alamy)

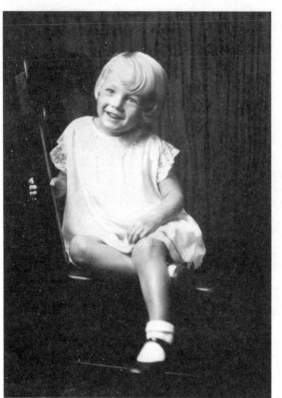

A posed studio shot of a 3-year-old Norma Jeane Baker in 1929 bearing an uncanny resemblance to 6-year-old Harlean Carpenter in 1917. Photos of Norma Jeane as a child show a pretty, well-nourished and cared-for child. (Alamy)

With second husband Joe DiMaggio, at the El Morocco restaurant, New York. Marilyn and Joe were seemingly the perfect couple and when Joe put a ring on her finger in January 1954, he thought he had it made. However, Marilyn's idea of being a wife didn't correspond with Joe's expectations. (Alamy)

Mrs DiMaggio set her sights on playwright Arthur Miller before the ink was dry on her marriage certificate to DiMaggio in January 1954. Her dream became a reality in June 1956 when she married Arthur. Here they are arriving in London on 14 July 1956 to film *The Prince and The Showgirl*. (Getty Images)

On the set of *Gentlemen Prefer Blondes* in 1953, Marilyn's miniature co-star was 7-year-old George Winslow (Wenzlaff). Marilyn always wanted a child of her own, but it wasn't to be. She and Arthur experienced several miscarriages during their marriage, the pressure and distress contributing to the failure of their relationship. (Alamy)

Marilyn would often pose with a book in her hand, appearing to be reading titles such as Arthur Miller's *An Enemy of the People* and James Joyce's *Ulysses*. Miller himself stated that Marilyn was not the great reader photos implied, although she had an extensive home collection of popular intellectual reading. (Alamy)

With acting mentor Lee Strasberg and his wife Paula, Marilyn's acting coach, in February 1962. Both had significant influence on Marilyn. She left her clothing and personal effects to Lee in her will, requesting he distribute them to her friends and colleagues. He didn't and her estate eventually went to auction. (Alamy)

Marilyn's last film became an albatross. Unwell during the making and eventually fired, she fought back and there was talk of her returning to the set, but in Marilyn's last interview for *Life Magazine* in July 1962 she raged against the studio. The article was published two days before she died. (Alamy)

First husband Dennis Hamilton was instrumental in forming Diana Dors' career path, simultaneously moving her forward and holding her back. It was a volatile marriage in a time when domestic violence was more often than not an uncomfortably accepted and ignored abuse. (Alamy)

Diana possessed all the ingredients of the ultimate blonde bombshell: hair, beauty, figure and a driving ambition with a hidden intelligence, fearlessness and tenacity that few women were allowed to reveal in the male-dominated society of the 1950s. We have since come a long way – or have we? (Alamy)

Diana's acting ability was showcased in *Yield to the Night*, in which she threw off the shackles of the bombshell to play Mary Hilton, a women awaiting execution for murder. The film contributed to the anti-capital punishment movement in the wake of the Ruth Ellis trial. It was the film of which Diana was most proud. (Alamy)

Against advice from friends, Diana married comedian Dickie Dawson in New York, setting up home in the USA where Diana worked to earn the family income. The marriage lacked the passion and excitement she craved. Despairing of Dickie's long silences and depression, Diana sought solace in affairs. (Alamy)

Motherhood was difficult for Diana. In an age when women were expected to stay at home and care for husband and children, Diana had not only divorced their father, but she then returned to England, leaving her sons in the USA with Dawson and thus challenging society's view on the meaning of 'Mother'. (Alamy)

Diana married actor Alan Lake in 1968, and their son Jason arrived in 1969. Although a stormy marriage included battles with Alan's alcoholism, the stillbirth of their second son and Diana's illnesses, their love was strong. Diana died in May 1984, and Alan killed himself in October of the same year. (Getty Images)

In February 1978 Diana launched her book *For Adults Only*. Diana had always yearned to be an author; she knew her bombshell days were now behind her but the future looked secure and happy with a new career as a writer and offers of character acting parts. (Alamy)

Diana's weight had increased gradually. Becoming an object for ridicule by the press, Diana would refer to her size with self-depreciating humour. In 1983 she accepted a diet slot on *Good Morning Britain*, successfully losing weight but sadly dying of cancer just fourteen months after this photo was taken. (Alamy)

Jayne Mansfield aged about 16 months in 1934–35. Two years after this photo was taken, she lost her beloved father, Herbert Palmer. Herbert died of a heart attack while driving with Jayne and Vera as passengers; Vera's quick action in controlling the vehicle saved lives of mother and daughter. (Alamy)

The epitome of glamour – Jayne presented as a bombshell. She had a cast iron self-belief and explosive confidence, but the 1960s were to shatter the image she had so painstakingly constructed during the previous decade. (Alamy)

Having it all? With second husband Mickey Hargitay, daughter Jayne Marie, sons Mickey Jnr and baby Zoltan 1960. Jayne proved to a society unable to adjust to the concept of a woman being both sexy and a mother that they were not mutually exclusive but an integral part of womanhood. (Alamy)

ayne leaving hospital with her daughters Jayne Marie and little Mariska, and sons Mickey Jnr, Zoltan and baby Tony, whose father was her third husband Matt Cimber (far right). The marriage was just weeks away from an acrimonious ending, and a fierce and messy custody battle lay ahead. (Alamy)

wo tenacious bombshells working to survive the 1960s, Jayne and Diana Dors pose with Jayne's hihuahuas while staying in the same hotel in Wakefield. Both were playing the northern clubs in ngland during 1967 but, according to Diana, Jayne appeared to be oblivious to the downward spiral f their careers. (Alamy)

Jayne performing at a club in England in 1967. Her personal life had been ruinous for her career and her prospects were looking grim after the fabulous Fifties and the heady days of Hollywood with hits such as *The Girl Can't Help It* and *Will Success Spoil Rock Hunter*? (Alamy)

Jayne with her lawyer and lover Sam Brody in Germany on 5 May 1967. The couple met the previous year when Jayne engaged Sam as her divorce lawyer. It was a less than harmonious relationship; Jayne was often seen covered in bruises. Both were killed in the car crash on 29 June 1967. (Alamy)

20

RESOLUTELY BLONDE

As a child with mousey hair and suffering the indignity of having to wear glasses with a patch over one eye to prevent it turning inwards, Diana had already developed a love of blonde. Her best friend at school, Christine, was a natural platinum blonde, and Diana envied her friend's hair, along with her ability to excel at maths and the fact that she had two brothers. Diana, an only child, had always wanted a brother. 'All this must have had an enormous effect on me,' she wrote in her autobiography, and she was already dreaming of 'becoming a blonde, alluring film star, a woman who enchanted men and lived a life of glamour and fame'.[1]

During the early 1940s, the most popular hairstyle was sported by the diminutive Hollywood film star Veronica Lake. A shoulder-length honey blonde, Lake's hair cascaded down in waves, with a soft drape over one eye in a seductive 'peekaboo' style that was loved by both men and women.

Diana was by now a precocious 12½-year-old who suddenly found she had the hairstyle of the moment and lightened her own locks to a similar honey colour. The results were striking, and Diana was thrilled, recalling, 'I walked about the town, cries of "It's Veronica Lake" rang out from passing GI trucks.'[2] Diana loved the initial attention and was delighted and flattered, but gradually hearing the name 'Veronica' everywhere she went, started to bore her; this girl was never going to be happy walking in anyone else's shadow!

As she developed, she became more eager to take on the image of the blonde bombshell, seeing it as an integral key to the Hollywood life she was ready to live. At 14 years old, Diana thought acting was synonymous with glamour, and during this era it certainly opened doors and it was beneficial to have that added allure.

Initially, Diana did not understand the dangers of being 'typecast'. She was young, beautiful and enthusiastic. Sexual attractiveness was a given, it came naturally to her, it was who she was. While glamour can, to a certain extent, be created, the type of appeal Diana had is not a quality bestowed on every female just because they are in a certain age bracket. She had innate confidence, but she didn't have the experience that comes with age or hindsight, and therefore she didn't realise just how difficult it would be to lose the bombshell tag when her sell-by date expired, as it inevitably would.

Standards of beauty, of course, are socially and culturally based, and with the expansion of Hollywood the influence was primarily glamour. With people's aspirations to live a certain kind of lifestyle after years of austerity during the rationing of the war years and beyond, the 1950s saw an excess of everything – including sex. The headscarves of the female factory workers were released and the tight victory rolls were shaken out.

Women of the 1950s could indulge in being feminine, with less of an emphasis on mend and make do. While many women embraced the freedom to dress for comfort and appreciated the ability to be part of the workforce, for others the workplace was not where their aspirations lay. Many women considered their most significant asset was their image and the effect it had, primarily on the opposite sex.

In her first autobiography, *Swingin' Dors* (1960), Diana talked about her time under contract at the Rank Organisation, which was founded in 1937 and soon began producing and distributing films. Rank also attempted to manufacture its own stars, as Gainsborough Pictures and the Hollywood studios did. Rank conceived a system that began life as 'The Company of Youth' grooming young contract players for stardom. It was better known as the Rank Charm School, with such illustrious alumni as Claire Bloom, Christopher Lee, Joan Collins and Maxwell Reed.

Students of the Charm School were expected to attend weekly cocktail parties full of important people in the industry including producers, casting directors and other people with influence. During these events, a system of networking took place. The objective was to be seen by the right people, with the hope of being cast in the next big upcoming production.

Diana observed, 'Some girls had no talent, but wonderful bodies. A few unscrupulous men had the power to cast the girls in minor roles.' As Diana saw it, 'It was a fair exchange, I suppose.'[3]

The girls were obviously thrilled with the results of their efforts and would boast about the things they had done and with whom. Of course, this was just another version of the casting couch, which was prevalent in various forms as equally in London as in Hollywood.

It was against such circumstances that only the brave and tenacious survived. Diana Dors ably dealt with the notion of sex and image. She admitted during an interview that she owed her screen popularity to 'sex and good publicity'. Diana also understood that she had to set herself apart from other blondes vying for position in the same industry, telling the reporter Joe Hyams. 'To the average Englishman a girl like Grace Kelly is the summit of a mountain – cool and unattainable. I am like the valley. Attainable.'[4]

Creating the 'attainable' bombshell illusion brought substantial financial rewards for Diana and by 1956, at the age of 25, she owned a yacht, Rolls-Royce and a country estate. Honest with the press from the very beginning, they appreciated her directness and the fact that she didn't take herself too seriously. 'She could laugh at herself, and her sense of humour never seemed obstructed by her own ego.'[5]

'There are hundreds of girls in England with more attractive individual characteristics than I have,' she told the reporter Joe Hyams. 'But I don't think anyone tried to make herself into a more attractive package … I know sex is a dangerous tightrope to walk, but I figure if I'm lucky I can last for another five years.'

When Hyams asked her the secret of her glamour, she replied, 'I'm a woman in a man's world. I find men much more interesting than women, and I let them know it. It's as simple as that.'

When she was interviewed in America by the journalist Mike Wallace in 1957, he wanted to talk about her appearance. Diana told him it was essential to keep the public interested and a huge part of that was creating the best possible image.

He asked her about a publicity stunt she took part in, wearing a mink bikini and travelling down the Grand Canal in Venice. She explained she had been due to attend the Venice Film Festival in 1956. Hounded by the press, she was asked to reveal what she would be wearing to the event. Knowing she needed something sensational, the idea of a mink bikini was concocted. Designed by costume designer Julie Harris, it was a hugely successful PR stunt. The fur was actually rabbit, as mink was too difficult to get hold of. After the event, the top half of the bikini was reused as a collar on one of Diana's suits, while the scraps of what was left over lined her cats' bed!

Wallace asked if she enjoyed making an 'exhibition' of herself. She explained that Diana Dors, the film actress, was different from Diana

Dors, the person. Going to events, being seen by the public at premieres and nightclubs was part of her job. The public expected to see her wearing 'low-cut gowns and striking provocative poses', but the other side of her would much rather 'stay at home, invite friends down, talk, swim, play tennis and generally just loaf around not have to get dressed and made up'.

Wallace's interview became an interrogation about the way Diana looked. He asked if she liked her appearance and her blonde hair and if she ever yearned to have it cut off. She told him she tried to make the most of herself, and that she tried 'to appear in the best way possible'.[6] Her hair was long because she felt it suited her that way.

Asked what she thought made her interesting to the public, she replied:

> I don't know, I think maybe it's because I am representing a larger than life kind of character, one that is completely detached from the every day normal kind of life that most people lead ... maybe some people have a secret yearning to do the things that I do, and wear the kind of clothes that I wear.

After asking her if it was 'all that it's cracked up to be?' she responded with her usual honesty and forthrightness:

> No ... when I first began, I had dreams of being a glamorous film star, like the film stars I had seen on the screen and I had read about. And I thought, what a wonderful life it must be; you don't work hard, you lie around in satin and silks all day, and you have everybody sort of fawning over you. But ... you realise nobody gets there in the first place without a lot of hard work, disappointments, and heartbreaks ... everything in life has its price.[7]

The price Diana paid, amongst others, was two failed marriages, but by 1968 she had married her third husband, the actor Alan Lake, who was nine years her junior. The wedding was quickly followed by the birth of their son Jason in 1969.

Diana did not find it easy to lose her post-pregnancy weight; she put it down to 'contentment' and being 'superbly happy'. She also said that she felt 'more womanly' with the extra pounds and that Alan was the 'big culprit' as he couldn't stand 'skinny birds'.[8]

With the weight gain, there was a dramatic upturn in Diana's career; she put this down to no longer having pin-up proportions, which meant attention was now diverted to her acting ability. She hoped that people would go on taking her more seriously and she felt it would be 'worth getting really fat for that'.[9]

Adjectives such as 'deliciously plump' were now used to describe Diana and in 1975, at the age 44, she acknowledged, 'I know my days as a sex symbol are over, and the thought doesn't worry me at all … it's given me the chance to prove I'm a good actress.'

However, the media were bewildered by the switch from sex symbol to character actress and found it hard to accept. At this time, Diana and Alan were expecting a second child. She told the famous columnist Marje Proops, 'I wouldn't want to go through all the misery and terror of being young again … I'm getting as fat as a house, and I don't give a darn. Fat and happy that's me.'[10]

Diana faced much adversity during her life, finding out she had cancer in 1982. After what appeared to be a successful operation for ovarian cancer, it seemed she was ready to deal with the battle of regaining her bombshell curves.

In an article on 12 December 1983 for *People Magazine*, Diana, then aged 52, was once again drawn into discussing her weight. In Diana's heyday of pin-up and films, she weighed 120lb (8st 8lb), but now she had reached an all-time high of 213lb (15st 3lb).

Diana loved food, especially biscuits, and she also admitted:

I'm the best gravy maker in Britain. I love potatoes, and sugar and cream in my coffee and fruit pies with that lovely ReddiWip they sell in the States. I never knew what the word diet was. Everybody else was always watching my figure, particularly men, but the last person to watch it was me.[11]

In July 1983, with the incentive of the TV-am breakfast show *Good Morning Britain*, for which she had been hired to do an agony aunt section, she was given a dieting segment called 'Dors' Dozen'. Diana announced a plan to lose 1lb for each of her 52 years; twelve overweight members of the viewing public were invited to join her on a high-fibre, calorie-counting mission with weekly weigh-ins at the studio. Talking about her motivation for the weight loss, she told journalist Roger Wolmuth, 'I was tired of being described as pleasantly plump, matronly, buxom, and all the other adjectives we use to describe fat.'

With the added bonus of boosting TV-am's ratings, Diana successfully managed to lose 54lb by October 1983. Her final weigh-in saw her reach beyond her target to 159lb (11st 5lb). Building on her dieting success, Diana was hoping to go stateside the following year and sell her dieting plan to the American public.

Sadly, the weight loss was not entirely down to Diana following a sensible eating regime. One of her co-hosts on TV-am, Anne Diamond, said that when Diana first began the diet she wasn't really following it. Diamond said, 'She would lose a pound a week, but it was because she took off jewellery that she wore, huge jewellery and she'd just take off a bracelet and a couple of rings.' However, as the show progressed, Anne remembered, 'What was upsetting was that she was noticeably losing weight, and she must have known it was because she was ill.'[12] The cancer had returned with a vengeance and contributed to Diana's weight loss.

Even undergoing treatment for cancer, Diana had an eye on her image. She didn't care for the natural look and she felt that her platinum hair was a lot more interesting than the real colour. Diana thought it might be dark brown, but wasn't sure and said for all she knew it might even be grey, 'but I feel like a blonde, and that's the way I'll stay'.

We currently live in an age where a great deal of effort has been made to avoid overt sexual objectification of women in adverts, television and film. There is a war on body shaming, but also a shaming of women who want to look a certain way and project a particular image that is becoming more and more unacceptable in our society.

Diana Dors went against 'feminist values' and yet here was no shallow image of a woman being explicitly objectified by men – here was an actress, a bombshell who delighted in being female, whose appearance was once the living epitome of sex.

She found women's lib amusing:

They don't approve of me and I don't think they ever will. While I believe that a woman should have the same opportunities as a man, I also believe that she has a duty to the opposite sex to make the most of what she's got.[13]

Talking about her image to the journalist Suzanne Thomas in an interview just before she died in 1984, Diana still upheld the values and principles of the concept of being a bombshell:

> I think it's important ... not so much to me but to the public. If they saw me slopping around in dowdy old clothes with my hair perhaps grown out another colour, I think that would shatter an illusion and that would be a pity.
>
> Everyone has to have illusions. It's what gets us through a grim world, and if I provide a glamour fantasy, then I'm perfectly happy to continue it.

Diana added, 'If I let it down, I would depress myself. I would feel that I was deteriorating, so it wouldn't help me either. Also, bear in mind I'm an actress first and foremost.'

'You see,' she said. 'I am Diana Dors and I will always be Diana Dors.'

A SCANDALOUS WOMAN

Sex in the 1940s was a minefield of misunderstood and misappropriated information. The general attitude of society to sex concluded that it was an activity only to be undertaken during marriage. While men would often pressurise women, young girls were invariably warned by their mothers that sex was something unpleasant to be endured for the procreation of the species.

Women would often find themselves in a no–win situation – while they were coerced and cajoled into sexual activity, a woman who gave in to the demands was 'easy' and worthless, while the more sexual experience the male could gain gave him a superiority among his peers. 'Female virginity, followed by male-initiated sexual awakening'[1] was the prized goal, with the male taking on the status of a sexual educator to the female.

As a 15-year-old negotiating an independent life in London, Diana felt sex 'was still a frighteningly strange place where I had never dared to tread'.[2] Despite her outward appearance of grown-up sophistication and beauty, and her skilful art in flirtation practised under the supervision of her mother at the American GI dances, Diana had been fully versed by her mother on the dangers of an illegitimate pregnancy.

While sex itself was never explained, Diana understood the warning, with her father making it clear to her men's opinion of 'easy meat' and reminding her that every man expected his bride to be a virgin on their wedding night.

These were days when contraception was haphazard, to say the least, and the pill had not yet made its debut. While Diana may have been left in ignorance about the actual details of sex, she was under no illusion about the dangers of 'finding oneself destitute and disgraced'.[3]

A young Diana was cast in *A Boy a Girl and a Bike* (1949), which was filmed on location in Yorkshire. She fell for a 19-year-old cameraman by the name of Gil. Diana decided the time was right and experienced her first lover. With great disappointment, she wrote:

Once the act of lovemaking was over, I was left wondering what all the fuss was about. Sex and all its glory had been far from ecstatic for either of us! How awful, I thought, that once upon a time girls really waited until their wedding night. What if they had discovered they didn't like the man they had married for better or for worse?[4]

Diana had written 'once upon a time' but that time of waiting for the wedding night was still very much expected for most girls in the late 1940s. Diana, without realising it, was daring and breaking ground that the average unmarried girl of 16 would not dare to break.

Diana's career was starting to make steady progress, with parts in films such as *Diamond City* (1949), *Dance Hall* (1950) and *Worm's Eye View* (1951).

She now entered into a few short-lived relationships, which included the actor Anthony Newley and Michael Caborn-Waterfield, aka Dandy Kim (a nickname given for his good looks and dapper dress sense). Diana met Michael on New Year's Eve 1948 at the Cross Keys pub in Chelsea. Recalling that first moment of seeing him, Diana remembered:

I glanced away from my friends to see a boy with the most disturbing eyes that seemed to pierce right through me ... His dark good looks were almost beautiful ... I half-smiled in his direction, but abruptly he turned away as if he hadn't seen me. I was not used to being given a hard time by the opposite sex.

Diana called him 'courteously arrogant', but they soon become lovers. Diana's parents were not impressed with the new love of Diana's life, and they would have been even less enamoured of the relationship had they known what their only daughter was about to go through.

Diana, at just 18, found herself pregnant with Michael's baby, and she was about to pay what was commonly known as the 'wages of sin', which in this case was £10 and took place on a kitchen table in Battersea.

During Roman times, the embryo was considered part of the maternal body and not a separate entity until birth had taken place. Abortion was standard practice. If a woman aborted her pregnancy against her husband's wishes, he could have her punished, although the punishment was not for the abortion per se, but for the wilful disobedience of her husband. It wasn't until Christianity remodelled the idea of the embryo by bestowing a soul upon it that it was decided abortion was a crime against the foetus.

At the time Diana was seeking her first abortion, in 1949, *The Second Sex* had just been published, a book of feminist philosophy by the French existentialist Simone de Beauvoir, who said of abortion:

> Few distressful situations are more pitiable than that of an isolated young girl, without money, who finds herself driven to a 'criminal' act to undo a 'mistake' that her group considers unpardonable. Illegitimate mother-hood is still so frightful a fault that many prefer suicide or infanticide to the status of unmarried mother.[5]

Pregnancy was not an option for Diana and neither was giving up her baby for adoption; illegitimacy was a disgraceful shame and a social stigma on both the mother and the child. It would have finished her career and her life. The decision Diana took wasn't made lightly. Abortion remained illegal in England until the law was reformed in October 1967. Before then, the procedure was most often performed by what were known as backstreet abortionists. The procedure was usually carried out by unskilled people who had little or no knowledge of physiology. Both the physical and emotional repercussions of such terminations were immense. With little support and no aftercare, the result of such horrifying episodes were far more painful than normal childbirth and often resulted in internal injury, or a fatal haemorrhage.

In the UK it is now accepted that a woman is entitled to be granted an abortion if she requires it, for whatever reason. She can expect support and a safe termination, with aftercare and counselling available post-abortion. However, abortion laws still vary across the world, with some countries and religions banning a woman from seeking an abortion with no exception, while others accept only life-saving abortions, where the mother's risk of dying is high.

The fear of dying was very much on Diana's mind. It took her several hours to miscarry and a great deal longer to recover mentally and emotionally.

Less than two years later, Diana began working on the film *Lady Godiva* (1951). On one particular day she had an afternoon free from filming. Her relationship with Michael had all but fizzled out, it was a warm day in May, and she was about to meet the man she would marry within five weeks.

Dennis Hamilton Gittins (he dropped the 'Gittins') was a 26-year-old, smooth-talking, good-looking charmer, who won Diana more by his personality than his appearance. As they talked, they soon learned they shared many coincidences, such as the same birthday and living in the same street. Hamilton, a water softener salesman, had also tried his hand at part-time acting work, but soon found he was camera shy, while away from the cameras he could deal with any situation head on, with a strong character, drive and audacity that few possessed.

Dennis had a tendency to fly into violent rages, having once beaten up the headmaster at his school. He had also dropped a hod of bricks on a foreman who had been giving him orders that he didn't appreciate while he was working as a labourer on a building site. A natural-born risk taker, Dennis had been caught riding a motorcycle without a licence. He quickly applied for one after the fact; however in July 1949 he was fined £6 for the offence and gained an endorsement for his newly acquired provisional licence at Bedford Magistrates Court.[6]

Diana loved excitement but was soon to learn from experience that life with Dennis was perhaps too exciting, frightening and unpredictable. She later professed that she had never been in love with Dennis during any stage of their relationship, but she said of that time, 'I was the fly caught in the spider's web.'[7] However, she had always been attracted to 'bad boys' and Dennis was probably as bad as she could get.

Dennis was also a misogynist, possibly due to his mother taking him with her when on trysts with her lover when he was a young child. As an adult, Hamilton spent much of his time bedding wealthy married women during his job as a salesman; he was far more successful at that than selling the water softeners that opened the door for him.

As is often the case, Diana thought he was different with her. He seemed to worship her and on 3 July 1951 they married at Caxton Hall in London, after some discrepancy over the legal documents. Diana was 19 years old and needed her parents' signatures, but at the time they were on holiday. The signatures were queried by the registrar, who claimed they appeared to have been forged. Forged or not, Dennis persuaded the registrar, with more than a little menace, that it was in his interests to marry them. Before the wedding, Diana had already realised she was not making a good move and desperately wanted to walk away; however, she was caught in the moment and reluctantly went ahead with the ceremony.

Shortly after the wedding, Diana took her first punch from Hamilton, when he called her a 'faithless whore'.[8] She had enraged him by giving Michael some money, which she did partly through guilt at leaving him for Dennis. While this changed Diana's attitude towards her new husband, she remained sucked in somewhat by fear and partly by charm, soon learning that Dennis's jealousy knew no bounds.

Feeling as if she was 'held in a web of dangerous fascination twenty-four hours a day',[9] Diana could cope with this more than she could handle boredom, and by her own admission Dennis Hamilton was never dull.

An American producer offered Diana a Hollywood contract, her lifetime dream and ultimate goal, but she watched it disintegrate before her eyes when the condition of the deal was made clear. Diana would be required to divorce her husband; single meant marketable. Marilyn Monroe had divorced her first husband for the same reason without hesitation, but in the face of Hamilton's rage, Diana knew it was not an option for her.

The couple had been living beyond their means, debts were mounting, and the company Dennis worked for was on the verge of liquidation. Unable to pay the rent on their London home, they escaped to the country. Their debts continued to mount, and Diana began to feel her career was in the doldrums.

In February 1952, Diana was pregnant again, and this time she was married and prepared to have the baby. Dennis, however, had other ideas; he saw it as an obstacle to their glorious new future and demanded that Diana have an abortion. The procedure was carried out at the house of a doctor whose wife was also present, for the sum of £50.

With this situation, knowing what was ahead of her, Diana was more terrified of having an abortion than she had been in 1949. Later in her life, talking about her experience, she said, 'The depression any woman feels after such an ordeal is indescribable.'[10]

Dennis gave his wife no time to dwell on the decision to abort their child. Instead, he was determined to swing into action. He became her self-appointed business manager and publicity agent, some would say Svengali. Often referred to as 'Mr Dors', which he loved, he had promised Diana that she was 'going to be the female Errol Flynn, always in trouble'.[11] But Diana didn't want to be the female Errol Flynn, and she certainly didn't want to be in trouble – she wanted to be a serious actress.

True to his word, Dennis did indeed present Diana to the world as a scandalous woman. In July 1953, she became embroiled in a prank that went wrong. She, Dennis and a man named Freddie Markell broke into the flat of a mutual friend and emptied his cocktail cabinet of six bottles of booze. Diana found herself arrested along with Hamilton and Markell, and they were eventually released on bail. Dennis and Freddie were fined, but Diana was given an absolute discharge as it was her first offence.

The publicity generated by this prank was phenomenal, with newspaper headlines such as 'Diana Dors is put in a cell'.[12] This was not her first scandalous headline and nor would it be her last; Dennis would make sure of that.

Occasionally exaggerating, often inventing both her exploits and her income, in May 1954 Dennis invited a reporter from the *Daily Mirror* to their sumptuously decorated home in Chelsea and boasted of having earnings of up to £1,000 a week, a property portfolio worth more than £75,000 and owning an American sedan and a Rolls-Royce.

The reporter quoted Diana as saying, 'All this … on three valuable dimensions – thirty five-inches (bust) twenty-three inches (waist) and thirty-five inches (hips). That merchandise – and boy, how it sells!' She added, 'Variety is the thing for me. Now I can choose my own films. I can be independent. I feel so happy – in love with the world.'

Dennis added, 'I'm pining for the days when Diana can retire … we shall soon own enough property to make that possible.'

'I love the girl.' he said. 'So gay, so down to earth … but not very good at figures.'[13]

The interview led to the authorities questioning how Diana could afford to live so affluently, with a visit to the house by the taxman.

The headlines continued to roll out, and Dennis continued to hit out. After one argument, Hamilton punched his wife in the face. Diana later wrote, 'It was one more nail in the coffin of this marriage that I often hated so much.'[14] Some weeks after this event, Diana's mother died at the end of April 1955, suffering a sudden heart attack after an operation.

In an attempt to combat the sadness and the emotional turmoil she found herself in after her mother's death and the difficulties of living with Dennis, Diana threw herself into her work. She began filming *An Alligator Named Daisy* (1955) at Pinewood Studios with the director J. Lee Thompson. Thompson would soon be directing her in a film that showcased her talent to perfection and remained Diana's favourite of her entire career.

BRITAIN'S ANSWER

While promising Diana the world, Dennis also pledged to make her 'Britain's answer to Marilyn Monroe'. Almost immediately, it became a tag that would irritate and irk Diana throughout her career. What made it even more ironic was that, after Marilyn's appearance in the 1950s film *The Asphalt Jungle* a British film magazine had observed 'How much like our own Diana Dors this new Monroe girl is.'[1]

As the 1950s rolled on, Marilyn was clocking up the big glamour films such as *Gentlemen Prefer Blondes* (1953) and *How to Marry a Millionaire* (1953). While Dennis's publicity drive was bringing in work, it wasn't necessarily of the sort that Diana desired. It bothered Diana a great deal that Dennis was pushing the physical comparisons with Marilyn when for her it was the film opportunities she craved. She was also disappointed that she was earning so much less than Monroe.

The British public, after the austerity of the war years, lapped up the blonde bombshell glamour Diana presented them with. But it left her frustrated; she was not earning the sort of money that could be compared favourably with Marilyn, and when she auditioned for epics with American producers, they acknowledged her similarities to Monroe, but she never got further than listening to them talk about the American star, each one claiming they had discovered her.

The year 1955 was looking to be a watershed one for Diana. She was starring in more high-profile films, including *A Kid for Two Farthings* (1955) and *Value for Money* (1955). However, she also found herself pregnant again, and on this occasion Diana made her own decision to terminate the pregnancy without any input from Dennis.

She was about to play a part that would have the biggest impact on her life and one of which she would be forever proud. It would also be a film that would influence the social and political fight against the death penalty in England. In *Yield to the Night*, released in 1956, the central character, played by Dors, was a young woman called Mary Hilton. Mary had been condemned to death for shooting the woman who drove her lover to suicide. The majority of the film takes place in the grim bare cell, while the prisoner is waiting to hear if her appeal has been successful. Her reprieve is refused, and she must face the ultimate punishment for her crime – death by hanging. It was reminiscent of real-life events the previous year when Ruth Ellis was executed for the murder of David Blakely.

Diana loved playing her first dramatic role and hoped that after watching the film the public would see her as an actress and not the dumb blonde that Dennis had sold to the press. Her focus was changing, and Dennis was about to lose his grip on her.

With headlines such as 'Forget the glamour – This is Dors the actress', the newspapers were praising her performance. They told her to stop the publicity stunts and pronounced, 'If she will concentrate on being an actress she will have a great future.' The press loved her and and *Yield to the Night* would remain Diana's favourite film.

The film contributed to a change in public opinion against the death penalty. Sir Keith Joseph, who was a member of the Howard League for Penal Reform that opposed the death penalty, told the *London Observer*, 'Diana Dors may help to abolish the death penalty.' Joseph said, 'I believe this film will earn her an Oscar and that the film will cause a terrific outburst against hanging.'[2]

Unfortunately, Diana did not win an Oscar, but she was presented to the Queen at the Royal Command Performance. *Yield to the Night* was the only British film to be chosen for the Cannes Film Festival and was also nominated for a Bafta. In 1956, Diana received the highest accolade by the Variety Club when she was named 'Show Business Personality of the Year', and she was feeling positive about her future.

A few weeks after the awards, during a dinner party at home, Dennis was fuming. One of the reporters present at the awards ceremony had described him as a 'suede-shod Svengali', which sent him into a fit of rage in front of their guests. The atmosphere deteriorated and Diana excused herself and went to bed.

Around midnight, two newspaper reporters arrived; they had been drinking and their somewhat inebriated condition gave them the bravado to ask to interview Diana. Dennis called his wife, who was not happy and refused to see anyone. In a flash, Dennis angrily rushed upstairs, grabbed Diana and told her, 'You'll do what I say and come down to see the press,' hurling her down the stairs. She landed at the bottom, to the shock of everyone present. Dennis told the silent and horrified reporters, 'Now fucking interview her.'[3]

Even this incident wasn't enough to make Diana come to her senses. Like many people caught in the trap of an abusive, controlling relationship, she was manipulated with 'gifts' and 'generosity'. Dennis allowed Diana to take the driving lessons she had wanted for some time that he'd previously refused. However, he drew the line at allowing her to have the mink coat she had coveted, telling her she'd 'look like a whore' in it.[4]

Dennis continued to convince her that she needed him and could not function without him. Even years later after Hamilton's death, Diana was still telling the world, despite her knowledge of his infidelities throughout the marriage, that she thought his control was a sign of his great love and need for her.

Although Diana was lauded for her strong leading role in *Yield to the Night*, she was not being offered comparable scripts. In eight months she only did one television show, but that was to be the next turning point in her life. Diana was filmed in England for the US *Bob Hope Show* and when it aired it caused much interest in her. On the strength of it, she was offered a part in the film *I Married a Woman*, which was being made by RKO. Coincidentally, as Dors packed to leave for America, her nemesis Monroe was heading to England, to film *The Prince and the Show Girl* with Sir Laurence Olivier.

Diana and Dennis sailed to America on 21 June 1957, from Southampton on board *Queen Elizabeth* because Hamilton had a fear of flying. Arriving five days later in New York, photographers swarmed the ship in anticipation of meeting 'England's answer to Marilyn Monroe'.

In an attempt to shake off the association with Marilyn, Diana informed the press that she had been in the industry for a long time and that she had a high-profile career in England, having appeared in significant films such as *Yield to the Night*. However, the American press were not interested; their focus was on her looks.

Asked if she had met Monroe, Dors replied 'I have never met her, but I would like very much to do so.' A reporter suggested she could be a bridesmaid to Monroe, who was about to marry Arthur Miller, but Diana responded, 'No, not a bridesmaid for anyone, but as to the comparison, I don't mind. There are a lot of worse people to be compared with.'[5]

Initially, she was the darling of the press with headlines such as 'Diana has curves AND brains.' The New York reporter Stan Mays said photographers and reporters 'voted her more brainy, more curvy and much more friendly than Marilyn Monroe'.[6]

Diana had made a great first impression, with press comments such as 'it was Diana's high spirits and frank, cheerful conversation that delighted American radio and television interviews.'[7]

Television newsreel director Danny Heenan said, 'She's a beautiful girl with better features than Marilyn,' while radio announcer Burt McCoy beamed, 'What curves! – and she is a brainchild beside Marilyn.'[8]

Dors was delighted with her reception despite her frustration with the comparisons to Monroe. This at times made her feel like they were suggesting she had copied Marilyn, making her feel 'extremely insecure and as if she were a British blonde without any talent who had jumped on Monroe's bandwagon'.[9]

Once in California, the Hamiltons embraced LA living with understandable excitement, but unfortunately for Diana and her career, Dennis was a problem. Behaviour that had been questionably tolerable in England was seen as obnoxious and insufferable in Hollywood. Dennis also turned down roles on Diana's behalf, such as *The Girl Can't Help It* with Twentieth Century Fox, which became a big hit for Jayne Mansfield.

Dennis was a liability, which came crashing in on Diana during a pool party. The event was held in honour of the arrival in the US of Diana's favourite hairdresser, Raymond Bessone aka 'Teasy-Weasy'. The intention was to launch Raymond's career in Hollywood and use the event as a publicity junket for Diana, which it indeed became but not in the positive way it was intended as it practically annihilated her Hollywood career.

While standing by the pool chatting to guests, Diana, Dennis and two other guests were pushed into the pool by a photographer looking for some sensational photos. Dennis climbed out of the pool in white-hot rage and proceeded to beat the photographer responsible unconscious. Instead of the positive publicity they had courted, it was the breakdown of their relationship with America as headlines such as 'Miss Dors go home – and take Mr Dors with you!' appeared in all the newspapers.

Diana had walked a fine line by trying to please the American press without offending their English counterparts, but it didn't work. Her marriage to Dennis was drawing to a close and there was a separation on the horizon, with Dennis returning to England and Diana shortly to follow.

When Diana confessed to being homesick, the British press – with vitriolic spitefulness – made a great effort to take her down more than a peg or two. 'So poor Diana Dors is so homesick she is coming back to England,' wrote Donald Zec for the *Daily Mirror*. The article carried a list of comparisons between their own home-grown movie star and America's Marilyn Monroe. In Zec's opinion, Marilyn was way ahead of Diana in the popularity stakes and good behaviour abroad:

> Look at the raucous, capricious trail blazed by the dizzy Dors since she sailed to America last July … The peek-a-boo blonde took one sip at her first mint julep (a famous American drink) and drooled 'America is wonderful your Cadillacs are better than Rolls Royces.'[10]

Diana herself told *Picturegoer* magazine, 'I was always misquoted … If I said I liked a Cadillac, next day the headline would read: "Dors says Cadillacs are superior to Rolls-Royces" or something of the sort.'[11]

Zec stated that Dennis and Diana moved into a £100 per night suite at the Beverly Hills Hotel, implying it was the height of decadence. When they eventually moved into a house in Hollywood, as they intended to live between America and Britain, Zec talked about a £50,000 property with five bedrooms, seven bathrooms and two swimming pools as if it was just simply tasteless and vulgar, and quoting Diana as saying, 'Only the best for Dors.'[12]

In contrast, Zec wrote that Marilyn and Arthur Miller stayed in an 'unpretentious house at Englefield Green, Surrey' on their stay in the UK. In truth, it was hardly unpretentious; the eighteenth-century Parkside House, set in its own grounds, was a large mansion owned by Viscount Charles Moore, the 11th Earl of Drogheda. The house backed on to Windsor Great Park, with not five bedrooms like Diana's house in California – no, Parkside House had nine bedrooms and seven bathrooms at £120 per week plus expenses for servants.

Zec then went on to claim that Diana and Dennis, who already had a Cadillac and Rolls-Royce, 'rushed off to buy an all-white American convertible for £4,000' and that, 'In England, Marilyn and Arthur bought a couple of bikes.'[13]

Marilyn was, in fact, presented with a bike at a press conference after she'd announced, 'I intend to cycle a lot in your English country lanes' when she arrived in London. Towards the end of this press conference at the airport, she was overwhelmed. A reporter said, 'Marilyn was crouching in a corner almost in tears looking as if she had been hauled through a hedge backwards.' Arthur Miller was clutching at her arm muttering, 'For heaven's sake, this is worse than New York darling.'

When Marilyn was asked what she thought of Diana Dors, the response was, 'Well … she's not very well known in America you know. But from what I've heard I'm sure she's a very nice girl.'[14]

Zec completed his article with, 'Miss Disillusioned Dors, she could learn a lot from Marilyn.'[15]

In 1979, during an interview in America with the chat show host Merv Griffin, Diana told him:

> I've been Britain's answer to everybody … there was a point in my life I just used to answer to 'come here Britain's answer'.
>
> I've been 'Britain's answer' to Veronica Lake … Betty Grable, Lana Turner and of course Jayne Mansfield – I was so tired of being 'Britain's answer'. I wasn't really 'Britain's answer' to anyone, I was me, you know. But I came over here on that sort of sex symbol glamour thing, and it was the tail end, more or less of Hollywood as it was in those days.

Diana had a rough ride with the press, but she never gave in; she never let them defeat her. Their cynicism that her split from Dennis was a publicity stunt because they got back together very quickly was proven misjudged when the couple had another acrimonious split, only this time it would be permanent.

For a short while Diana was seeing other people until she met the comedian Dickie Dawson, who was to become husband No. 2. Dickie had dreams of America, so 'Britain's answer' went back to New York. While she was there, she received the shocking news that Dennis had died in a London hospital on 31 January 1959.

The initial cause of death was thought to be heart disease; however, the truth was worse than could be imagined. Dennis had died of tertiary syphilis, and he'd left the miserly sum of £800 in his will to his parents; Diana inherited nothing but his debts to the Inland Revenue.

PITFALLS OF HAVING IT ALL

In just two months, Diana went from being a widow to a newly married woman. Dickie, who had been a bus conductor from Gosport, Hampshire, and whose real name was Colin Lionel Emm, met Diana at the Stork Club in London. When she was preparing to tour with the Diana Dors Show in variety, it was suggested she sign Dickie as part of the act. Diana was unsure, but her agent signed him anyway. Fortunately, despite her misgivings, the show was a great success, and Diana loved working with Dickie.

Within a short space of time, they fell in love. Although close friends warned Diana against the relationship, it was already too late; she was smitten. Diana flew to London to attend Dennis's funeral and when she returned to New York, Dickie asked her to marry him. Initially she was reluctant, as it seemed too soon after Dennis's death and she wanted to marry in England, but Dickie's powers of persuasion were considerable and she eventually agreed to marry in New York. The ceremony took place on the evening of 12 April 1959 directly after she had appeared on *The Steve Allen Show*.

Years later she wrote of this time:

> On reflection, as I continually look back while writing about my life, it is difficult to imagine how weak-willed and stupid I was. Everyone makes mistakes, but I made more than my fair share and have no one to blame other than myself.[1]

From the outset, Diana doubted her decision to marry Dickie, who by now had changed his name by deed poll to Richard Dawson. Almost immediately after the wedding, he went from a fun-loving, happy person to withdrawn, moody and silent, until Diana discovered she was pregnant.

Much to her delight, Dickie was as thrilled as she was, and she was at last expecting a baby that she could keep. The prospect of being a mother excited her, although she hadn't thoroughly thought through the practical aspects of motherhood. Dickie's work was casual and at this point in their lives he was not able to bring in the kind of money Diana was able to achieve.

It seemed Diana was destined to be a working mother as Dickie engaged the services of a new agent, with whom he worked closely, to quickly build up a work portfolio on behalf of his wife with one cabaret engagement after another. The nature of the assignments meant that Diana was working late at night, exhausted from both her pregnancy and her work. She also suffered from sickness, which was impossible to combat.

Returning to England, she was offered £35,000 for her life story to be printed in the *News of the World* in the form of a twelve-week serialisation. Very soon Diana understood that the readers were only interested in gossip and smutty scandal, but it was an offer she couldn't resist. Disclosing details of Dennis Hamilton's sexual inclinations and voyeuristic tendencies, once published the article caused a great deal of distress for Diana, both at the time and over the coming years.

When the story began running, one dissenting voice in particular, Baroness Stocks, a campaigner for decency, stated on the radio that the best thing Diana could do for her unborn child was have it adopted. Diana later said, 'I had sold my soul to the Devil ... England was not yet the free-thinking, unconventional country of the permissive society and the Swinging Sixties.'[2]

Worse still for Diana, the Press Council condemned the memoirs, saying, 'In the opinion of the Council, these articles sank below the accepted standards of decency and the Dors Hamilton articles in particular contained material that was grossly lewd and salacious.'[3]

The public wanted a sex romp, and that's what Diana obliged them with, but they also wanted to hold the moral whip hand.

Already feeling vulnerable, about to give birth to her first child, Diana was under a great deal of stress. She was upset as 'friends' jumped on board the gravy train. Sandra Dorne and her husband Patrick Holt gave a story to the *Sunday Pictorial* titled 'The Shocking Mr Dors'[4] that was published just as Diana was due to give birth.

Amidst all this pandemonium, a pregnant Diana went into labour. After twenty-seven hours of intense pain, she gave birth to her son, Mark Richard. Although she had quietly hoped that the baby would be a girl, she was overwhelmed with love for Mark. With no postnatal blues to follow, Diana said that she felt 'just relief that it was all over and, after such a horrendous ordeal' and 'thankful to God'[5] that her son was healthy.

Within a month of Mark being born, Dickie and Diana's agent travelled to America to negotiate a contract with the Dunes Hotel in Las Vegas for Diana to appear in cabaret with a fee of $7,000 per week. At this time she was also offered a part in a British film, *Saturday Night and Sunday Morning*, but her agent turned down the role as the lead actor Albert Finney was an unknown quantity and the fee was £500, a drop in the ocean compared to what Diana could now earn.

This was one of Diana's major career regrets. *Saturday Night and Sunday Morning* became a huge hit and would have seen her repeating her success in *Yield to the Night*. It was just the sort of gritty, dramatic role that suited Diana's acting talent and she also felt it would have helped her overcome the negative publicity from the newspaper serial that had plunged her into a 'social abyss'.[6]

The £35,000 for the serialisation was fast dwindling as, after it was divided between the agent, writers and lawyers, Diana's share shrunk, and she was expected to get back to work as soon as possible to earn money to keep the roof over her new family's head.

She desperately wanted to stay with her new baby, but the bond was about to be severely tested. Diana had employed a nurse/nanny for her son named Amy Baker. Initially, Amy appeared to be the answer to the new mother's prayers. Most importantly, Diana felt complete trust in Amy, she could clearly see that she and Mark were happy and comfortable in each other's company as there was a mutual rapport. It was the biggest relief to Diana, who had to fly out to America and leave her precious baby behind, and she felt sure he would be safe and loved in Amy's care.

With no choice open to her but to fulfil the contractual obligations that her husband and agent had negotiated, Diana left for America.

One can only imagine the pain Diana felt, and the mixture of emotions must have been excruciating for her. She felt the love for her son, the joy of having a healthy newborn; this was the first baby she had carried full-term in her womb and worked so hard to give birth to, and yet the pleasure of those early newborn months was given to another woman.

Diana, like most new mothers, felt inadequate and useless; having no experience of childcare, she was out of her depth in the domestic sphere. On top of her feelings of insecurity, she was heaped with guilt. Perfect mothers were supposed to stay at home and nourish their babies mentally, physically and emotionally. Working mothers were frowned upon as if they put their own selfish needs before those of their child, and from here on in guilt would be Diana's constant companion. Not only had she spent most of her career feeling like a second-rate Monroe, she was now feeling like a second-rate mother.

The memory of leaving Mark so soon after he had been born would stay with Diana forever. When she looked back on it, she wasn't sure if her reluctance was just heartache or a premonition that this was the beginning of losing her son to the woman to whom she had entrusted him

Arriving in New York, she and Dickie spent a week working on her act with a musical arranger and producer before heading to Las Vegas. In the desert heat Diana began the round of shows: seven nights a week, three times a night for a month. 'It was a peculiar existence,' she recalled, 'one that I didn't much like.'[7] This was hardly surprising, as it was a punishing schedule of sleeping all day, getting up at 6 p.m., on stage for the first show at 8 p.m. until 10 p.m., back on stage for midnight with a final appearance at 2 a.m., finishing at 4 a.m. and then back to bed at 6 a.m.

Still not fully recovered from giving birth, this was too much for Diana, and she began to feel ill, with the overriding pain of missing her baby. Dickie, on the other hand, was thoroughly enjoying being in Vegas, gambling and making contacts, but soon he realised that Diana was unhappy when she missed a couple of performances due to illness. Despite this, her act was so successful that the Dunes wanted to renew her contract with an increased fee of $10,000.

By now, Dickie knew Diana wanted to go home, but he had a plan; he secretly arranged for Amy to bring Mark to Las Vegas. When they arrived, he surprised Diana with a fait accompli – whilst Diana was overjoyed to see her baby, he had the lawyer there with the contract for her to sign, which she did.

When the contract came to an end, both Diana and Amy were more than ready to return to England, but Dickie loved America and had accepted a $12,000 per week engagement for Diana to work at Lake Tahoe and a further two weeks' work in Hollywood at Ciro's nightclub. Her appearance at Ciro's established her as a force to be reckoned with and the film offers rolled in.

However, Dickie's own career was just not getting off the ground, contributing to his sulky, brooding moods with endless 'days of silence'.[8] Diana still wanted to return home; her marriage was under strain and she was having to travel alone for work as Dickie preferred to stay in Los Angeles.

The threat of bankruptcy in England, coupled with the fact that she was earning so much more in America, influenced Diana's decision to stay. Although Dickie was ecstatic to remain in the US, their personal relationship continued to deteriorate. Diana had an affair while working away and sought advice on divorcing Dickie. When she returned from a three-week cabaret tour on her own again in South America, Dickie met her at the airport with Mark and he wanted reconciliation.

Putting a brave face on things, in July 1961 Diana told a reporter, 'My first trip to Hollywood just fizzled out like a glass of champagne that's gone flat. This time I didn't do anything spectacular to draw attention to myself. We lived very quietly, and I just worked.'

Still haunted by the serialisation of her life story in the *News of the World*, the reporter suggested that selling her memoir was cheap. Diana succinctly replied:

> Listen, for £36,000 I don't mind being cheap … I've often done things for the money, but you mustn't forget for a long time I didn't have any … I literally didn't know where my next meal was coming from … in this business it's very easy to be famous and broke.[9]

In September 1961 Amy and Mark accompanied Diana to Spain, where she was making a film, a project eventually abandoned due to financial problems. Diana had noticed that Mark was extremely dependent on Amy and if she left the room he would be inconsolable. This no doubt added to Diana's stress and anxiety, with a sinking feeling that she was unable to appease her own child on top of her brutal work schedule.

The trio returned to London, where Diana had rented a house. She had been given the part of Myra in the film *Mrs Gibbon's Boys* (1962) and also had a cabaret assignment at a London nightclub. In early November Diana discovered she was pregnant again.

Dickie flew over from America for Christmas, and Diana surprised him with the news of her pregnancy. Once again he was delighted, but he returned to America after the festivities, leaving Diana to complete her cabaret contract. When her commitments were fulfilled, Diana settled down at home in the California sunshine to await the birth of her baby and on 27 June 1962 at the Cedars of Lebanon Hospital, she and Dickie welcomed their second son, Gary, into the world.

Within ten weeks of Gary's birth, Dickie had arranged work for Diana, who was still the only one bringing significant money into the family home Diana had purchased for $175,000. Diana had put down a deposit but had to take out a jumbo mortgage to cover the shortfall. Therefore, the pattern of Diana working had to continue, regardless of her having so recently had a baby.

While working alone in New York, Diana received the news that her father had died on 28 April 1963, aged 69. Diana didn't attend his funeral; instead, she fulfilled her contract of work commitments.

Returning home to California when her latest assignment had finished, after just a few weeks spending time with the boys at home, Diana was back out to work again, this time in New Jersey. Each time Diana had to leave the children it became more stressful, not just for Diana but for the boys too, especially for Mark, who revealed in an interview in 1990 that he would do anything to prevent his mother leaving for work:

> I'd remember the time that she would leave, it would be painful … I'd try everything to get her to stay … I'd take all her make-up and flush it down the toilet because I didn't want her to go. I figured if I got rid of all her make-up, she wouldn't leave.[10]

There was a last-gasp attempt to make the marriage work, with a family holiday to Hawaii. The holiday was successful, but on returning the couple were told that the family dog had died, which sent Dickie into a spiral of depression.

A two-month cabaret tour of Australia had been booked for Diana, but Dickie refused to go. Instead, he asked his friend to accompany her. The travel was gruelling and Diana repeated past indiscretions, finding comfort in the arms of a man who wasn't her husband. She had reached the point where the thought of staying with Dickie, growing old with him in silence and indifference, sent her into a 'cold panic',[11] with the notion of facing the taxman in England as preferable to the life she was currently leading.

24

QUEEN OF THE CASTLE

New Year, new start. On 17 January 1964, Diana filed for divorce. However, in spite of her complicated love life and her continued unhappiness in the marriage, by 23 January newspapers were reporting that she had dropped her divorce petition and that for the sake of the children she and Dickie were going to try and save their marriage.

Mark and Gary were now 4 and 2 years old, and as far as Diana was concerned, Amy had well and truly undermined her, entirely usurping her in the mothering role. While she felt immensely bitter and resentful of the situation, Diana was torn, knowing that Amy could be trusted to keep them safe and well, as a mother would. Whereas Diana worked; it was all she knew and no one else in the family could earn at the same level.

However, in March 1964, Diana resumed flying back and forth between LA and London, growing more disenchanted with Hollywood as Dickie dug his heels in, refusing to return to England to live. Diana had work in England and eventually she decided to rent a small cottage in Chelsea on a six-month lease.

As a working mother, Diana was leading from the front at a difficult time for women. Gender roles had been set in stone throughout the twentieth century, with only a handful of women pushing the barriers. People were not generally comfortable with any disruption to the status quo and a woman such as Diana, who subverted the traditional role of motherhood, was seen as a threat.

Men prided themselves on working and bringing home a wage packet, stipulating how it would be spent as far as housekeeping needs were concerned, while their wives had the role of managing the household with the money their husbands allotted them and being responsible for the children. This in its way gave the woman an element of power – they were the authority on the home and children.

Women would often feel possessive of their territory, not wanting anyone else to care for their children – and yet women also found being at home with no financial independence, placing the needs of their husband and family before their own, both mind-numbing and depressing.

Diana never got the chance to find out into which category she would have fallen, as her earning capacity far outweighed most men and her career was already well established before maternity. However, there was a certain amount of stigma and shame attached to Diana as a working mother, who would leave her children for long periods while she worked to provide for them.

Few questioned Dickie's role while they were married; judgement was directed at Diana. If Dickie had been out working and travelling the world as Diana was to support his family, he would have been seen as a hero sacrificing time with his children to ensure that they had a roof over their heads and they were fed and clothed. He would have received admiration and sympathetic understanding for his sacrifices of home and family time, whereas Diana was viewed as gallivanting around and placing her career above her love for her children.

Although she felt undermined by Amy, for Diana making the ultimate sacrifice was leaving her children with a woman who was capable, trustworthy and cared deeply for them. Amy was not caring for them alone while Diana travelled the world; Dickie spent the majority of his time at home with Amy and the boys.

Working in England, things began to change for Diana. Her agent felt he had nothing left to offer her. He was now handling clients with more prominent names and more significant potential, and felt that Diana was 'trading on an old sex symbol screen image'.[1] Moreover, she was no longer relevant to the scene. Diana's personal life was also going through a downward spiral. Her choice in men was questionable and she found herself immersed in some negative relationships.

So amid this chaos, with her now ex-agent implying there was no future in an ageing bombshell, London was experiencing a cultural revolution. In 1965, a 16-year-old Twiggy was propelled on to the scene by her manager boyfriend, Nigel Davies, who changed his name to Justin de Villeneuve and boasted, with familiar echoes of Dennis Hamilton ten years before, 'Twiggy couldn't do anything without me.'[2]

With an image that was opposed to Diana's, Lesley Hornby, aka Twiggy, was born in 1949. Eighteen years younger than Diana, with an almost androgynous figure – 5ft 6in, weighing just over 6st and measuring 31-23-32 – and with short-cropped hair of varying shades but not platinum blonde amongst them, it was impossible for Diana to compete, even if she had wanted to. This was the new vibe in London: youth and unique fashions for skinny, lanky figures.

By comparison, some saw Diana's look as overblown, gaudy and old fashioned. Taking whatever work she could get, still living beyond her means, her career was travelling downhill fast. In America, Dickie was making more positive progress with his career. In 1965, he had a lucky break when he was cast in the role of Corporal Peter Newkirk in *Hogan's Heroes*. It was a new TV sitcom about a prisoner-of-war camp that ran until 1971. (Later he became an iconic household name in America as the host of the game show, aptly named under the circumstances, *Family Feud*, which ran from 1976 to 1985, and then 1994 to 1995.)

Still sending money back to California, she began taking her cabaret act to working men's clubs. From the luxury of Vegas to the indignity of working while being heckled with calls of 'Get 'em off' or 'show us your tits',[3] Diana was missing her children terribly and wanted to have them in England with her, but she felt depressed and quite likely ashamed of the turn her career had taken.

As much as she wanted her children with her, she also wanted what was best for them. In her eyes, she felt the safety and comfort of the only home they had ever known in California, with their father and their nanny, was the best. Diana saw nothing positive in making them live in hotel rooms, in the cold climate of England, watching their mother's career failing miserably.

At the same time, Diana had reached a point where she could no longer afford the flights to America, but no help was forthcoming from Dickie, and she had no choice at that time but to remain in England and endeavour to improve her career.

Already struggling financially, in 1967 the Inland Revenue slapped a £48,413 bill on her for unpaid taxes. In the light of such turmoil, she was advised to sell her Beverley Hills home. When she discussed the possibility with Dickie, he panicked and suggested a better alternative to the taxman taking the property would be for her to sign the house and the contents over to him as part of an uncontested divorce settlement, along with her signing over legal custody of the children to him.

With bankruptcy imminent, Diana knew it was essential to secure a home in England that was close to London for work and suitable to accommodate visits from Mark and Gary as often as possible. It took many negotiations, but eventually Dickie agreed to Diana using the trust fund insurance policies principally from her *News of the World* payout, which she set up for the boys to purchase a house free from the threat of the Inland Revenue getting a hold of it.

Diana was desperately reluctant to give Dickie legal custody of the boys, but she also realised that she could not drag them away from a country and a home they loved. Despite the problems between Dickie and herself, she knew that as a father he loved the boys deeply. When she asked for reassurance, of course Dickie obliged, telling her, 'You know I'd never do anything to hurt or jeopardise them,' adding, 'And this house is yours whenever you come to see us.'[4]

Trusting Dickie's promises, Diana agreed under the condition that she would have unrestricted access to the boys and that the house in Beverly Hills would be put in trust for the children's future so that in the event of Dickie remarrying the house would still go to the boys should anything happen to their father.

With the legal paperwork signed, Diana was disappointed to find Dickie offered no warmth towards her, and they went their separate ways.

On 30 October 1967, it was revealed the house she purchased was Orchard Manor (formally known as The Croft) in Sunningdale, Berkshire, for around £20,000. The accommodation included a playroom and a specially designed play area for children, as well as tennis courts in the grounds. Diana couldn't wait for the boys to see it. That Christmas she went to America, hoping they would be excited when she told them all about Orchard Manor, but of course, they were too young to understand. Children live in the moment and the moment when she had to leave them and return to England was harrowing for them. Diana wept all the way home on the plane.

Society has come to recognise over the years that divorce is sometimes unavoidable, and yet it struggles with the idea of a mother who leaves her children. However, in many divorces, one parent must walk away from the family home and shared parenting is rarely a solution. Often when a father leaves the family unit, he is shown sympathy for his painful situation, but he is expected to go. On the other hand, when a mother walks away, people often believe that she has deserted her children, forsaken them and relinquished all responsibility. When she leaves, she is categorised as being in the wrong.

There is incredible guilt and distress for a parent who makes such a decision. The feelings of regret often last a lifetime, even when the parents have worked through the situation and see it as the best outcome for the children, as in Diana's case. Nevertheless, regardless of it being in the best interests of the children, the grief of making that decision cannot be overestimated.

It was a controversial decision and one that women still struggle with today. While attitudes are a little more understanding, there is always an element of society that is shocked by a mother leaving her children. She is still seen as failing them. Even though the father is sometimes capable of fulfilling the child's emotional, mental and physical needs better than the mother can, it continues to be a perception in some sections of society as unnatural for a mother to leave her child.

It is often other women who are fierce critics of absent mothers, particularly women who have lost children. However, the harshest critic of all is the missing mother herself, whose inner voice will tell her what a failure she is in every possible way.

In Diana's situation, while she had held the financial power, she could not use it. Withdrawal of financial support would not only have caused Dickie great hardship, it would have had a dramatically detrimental effect on Mark and Gary. It would have collapsed their comfortable and settled world. Unfortunately, they lived in an era where the physical distance exacerbated poor communication. It is so much easier for absent parents to stay in touch now, with the internet and mobile phones the technology allows us both sound and visual contact at any time of the day or night.

In the 1960s Diana was dependent on Dickie giving the boys letters and gifts that she sent. She was also dependent on him enabling long-distance phone calls, which were incredibly expensive, as were the cost of flights between the countries.

Diana failed to take time out between relationships. Her lovers almost literally ran into each other. It was as if she had a pathological fear of being alone without a man in her life. It was a strange dichotomy for a strong intelligent woman who dealt with feelings of depression by throwing herself into her work. Always one to square her shoulders, getting on with the practical business of living, she was a modern powerhouse of strength in a time when women were expected to be helpless and incapable.

In the summer of 1968, Mark and Gary flew to England with their nanny, Amy, for a visit with their mother. They loved Orchard Manor, and

Diana started to think that maybe she and Dickie could share the parenting, with the boys living part of the time in Sunningdale with her. On discussing it with Amy, it seemed like a useful idea and Diana started to feel excited at the prospect. However, she'd made a colossal mistake. When Amy returned to California with the boys, she told Dickie that Diana had attempted to prevent them from leaving and that she wanted to keep them there permanently. Naturally, Dickie was enraged, and the consequence of this false disclosure was a breakdown in the already strained relationship between the parents.

The friction Amy regularly caused was difficult for Diana to deal with; it was a double-edged sword. Diana had chosen Amy for the very reason that she had a strong connection to Mark when he was born, which also extended to Gary, but she also reluctantly accepted Amy's role in her life for the sake of the children.

With her divorce now final and the bankruptcy near completion, Diana was ready to get her life back on track. She had been offered a guest star role in a new television series *The Inquisitors*. The show was ultimately fated to be axed, and Diana was eventually fated to fall in love again.

25

WHAT IS A LAKE?

'He is above everything the man I worship, and love.'[1]

Diana said she saw her third and final husband for the first time as she watched TV at 9 p.m. on the evening of 24 July 1968. Alan Lake was appearing in an episode of *Half Hour Story*, written by Alun Owen. The play, called *Thief*, was a philosophical interaction between an attractive female at a party who fills her cigarette case with complimentary cigarettes from the tables, and Lake's character, who steals the case from her bag and then visits her hotel room to return the case, whilst accusing her of being a thief and telling her she is no different from him. Lake gave an 'engagingly insolent performance'.[2]

Impressed with the writing, Diana was also attracted to the competent young man delivering the lines. She was coming to the end of her relationship with Troy Dante (whose real name was Noel Frederickson), a 'would be' pop star/actor who she'd met when she returned to England in 1964. Troy was married, and Diana had found herself in a complicated love triangle.

Diana finally met Alan after she was offered a guest part in a new crime drama that was being piloted for television called *The Inquisitors*; she was to play a stripper in an episode titled *The Peeling of Sweet P Lawrence*. Diana was delighted when she found out that she would be starring alongside Alan Lake. However, Alan was less than thrilled and uttered the now famous line, 'Oh! Madam tits and lips.'[3]

Alan had not seen any of Diana's films. He was a young, RADA-trained, serious actor who visualised her as the stereotypical female movie star: an overbearing bombshell with an attitude and a predisposition to lateness and tantrums. Instead, he was late to the set on the morning of 10 October 1968. Arriving, he found a beautiful woman with soft platinum hair, wearing a wool two-piece and a red leather jacket, glasses perched on the end of her nose as she read through the script.

Diana looked up and there was mutual recognition of something more profound than appearance. Diana had thought she had been in love probably too many times to count but, as she held Alan's intense gaze, this was different. She knew Alan's soul, and he knew hers; this was love. He was everything Diana had ever longed for; she felt she had been searching for him all her life.

With dark curly hair and large brooding eyes, full lips that broke out into the most beautiful smile and a gold earring in his left ear, Alan had been cast in the part of a gypsy in *Sky West and Crooked* (1965), reflecting his heritage as his grandmother was a gypsy.

Within three days of meeting each other, Alan had presented Diana with a family ring, telling her he loved her and asking her to marry him. Diana put up little resistance; she was in love with him too, but first she had to go back to Orchard Manor and speak to Troy. The relationship with Troy had already run its course by late summer 1968, and meeting Alan motivated Diana to ask Troy to leave. She was honest with him, and although he was disgruntled he accepted the situation and left. As a testament to Diana's personality, they remained friends to the end of her life.

Enchanted by Alan's background and fascinated by his dark, dangerous looks, which flickered a warning of a temper when roused that was at odds with his love of the arts, literature and the poetry of Dylan Thomas. Alan had a sense of humour that Diana adored. Laughter had always been a goal in life, not taking things too seriously, and Diana herself had a wicked sense of humour that had gotten her through some difficult times. Diana was also intrigued by the shy man under the brash bravado of the actor.

She said of Alan's proposal, 'I decided this might be my last chance of finding happiness, so I had to hold on tight for fear it slip away.'[4]

They announced their engagement to the press on the evening of 28 October 1968. This was to be Alan's first and last marriage. The media took great delight in referring to the couple's age gap of nine years; Alan was almost 28 and Diana had just turned 37, but they both shrugged it off as unimportant. The press then brought up Diana's bankruptcy hearing, to which Alan responded, 'If you are in love, what's a debt?'[5] He also joked, 'At least no one can say I'm marrying her for her money.'[6]

With great speed, they set a date, 23 November 1968, and just over six weeks from the day they met they became man and wife. Both Diana and Alan were early for the ceremony; Diana wore a white lace mini-dress with a matching cape and she held a bouquet of white orchids, the symbol of hope.

When questioned by reporters about children, Diana responded, 'We want to have a family. I don't mind how many but there is nothing we want more than a baby.'[7]

A champagne reception was held at the Astor Club, but two significant guests were missing from all of the celebrations. Diane had sent a request to Dickie asking him to allow the boys to be present at her wedding. However, possibly because he didn't expect it to last, Dickie ignored Diana and neglected to tell the boys about their mother getting remarried.

According to Diana, Gary saw the news of his mother's wedding on television one evening. In confusion, he asked his father what was happening, and Dickie replied, 'Nothing, just a load of publicity!'[8]

There was no time for a honeymoon as Diana and Alan were busy with work commitments, and Diana needed to earn as much money as she could as she had debts pay.

As 1969 dawned, the newly-weds were blissfully happy and Diana discovered she was pregnant. Although she had told reporters that a baby was very definitely a hope on their horizon and Alan was ecstatic, Diana began to experience doubts. She was concerned about her age and worried about the impact of a baby on what she considered her perfect relationship with Alan. She also remembered the nightmare she went through having to leave Mark and Gary and the conflict she was still experiencing with Dickie, so Diana was apprehensive as the reality of having another child set in.

As always, Diana drew on her inner courage and in February she was telling the media with optimism and brightness, 'I feel like a young girl in love for the very first time.'[9]

The emotional stakes of having another baby were high, but Diana now felt sure of her love for Alan, and at this point, there were no concerns about their relationship. However, the impact of a sibling for Mark and Gary would have meant more emotional adjustment, as contact with the boys was always a significant upheaval on both sides of the Atlantic.

Long tiring flights were unpleasant. Arriving at their destination would have involved a whole new set of rules about behaviour and discipline that would lead to confusion and sometimes resentment, and now they had to adjust to another child who would, unlike themselves, be living with their mother.

Talking candidly about pregnancy and motherhood in May 1969 during an interview with the journalist Patricia Boxall, Diana said, 'Look, love, I'm probably going to be a lousy mother … but I'll do my best.'

Boxall observed, 'Diana's baby is due in August, but typically she acts and looks like everything you don't expect a mother-to-be to be.'

Diana acknowledged, 'I'm just not the twice-a-week-to-the-clinic and flat-heel-shoes type … I've never rated the maternity bit as a great emotional wonderland.'

Extolling the virtues of later motherhood, Diana said that she felt it was a good idea for a woman to have a baby when she was older. Stating that she intended to really enjoy this new baby because she was more tolerant and possibly less ambitious than when she was younger, but she was quick to confirm that she had no intention of becoming a 'cabbage'.

She also admitted what everyone already knew, that she wasn't able to follow the rules and that for her it was best not to make plans as she said:

> Something always crops up if I do … when I had my first baby I made all sorts of rules about being a good mother. I planned this and that, the lot – All according to the book. When my second son came along some of the resolutions were slipping a bit. Now with this one, I've got a strictly take-it-as-it-comes approach.

Diana added, 'My life has been unsettled and really the boys are better off in America. Naturally, I long to have them with me, but what I want is not everything.'[10] But she told the reporter she still hoped the time would come when they would live with her for good.

On 11 September 1969, Diana gave birth to her third son, whom she and Alan named Jason. With the approach of Christmas 1969, Diana put her foot down and demanded that Mark and Gary, whom she hadn't seen for almost two years, were sent over to meet their baby brother and to attend his christening. This time she received a reply, telling her that when she sent the tickets they would come, so the arrangements were made and Amy brought the boys to England.

With all her sons together at last, Diana's new family had a joyous Christmas. When it was time for Mark and Gary to return home, the heartache was more painful than ever as the boys slipped in and out of her life. When they were due to arrive, she'd plan what they were going to do as a family when they were together, and she hoped they would want to stay. When they left, she felt grief and loss, which was almost always followed by recriminations from Dickie on their return as Amy debriefed him, and he would threaten to deny future contact. Diana would then feel frustrated and angry again.

Shortly after Jason's birth, there was an opportunity to return to work with Alan; they were both offered parts in the play *Three Months Gone*, which was to open at the Royal Court on 28 January 1969. Diana engaged a nanny to care for Jason, despite her hesitation after her experience with Amy.

Diana was nervous, as she'd not performed on stage for almost fourteen years, but she needn't have worried. She and Alan were a huge success and the critics loved them. Sir Laurence Olivier was in the audience that night and was eager to see them backstage after the performance to congratulate them. It had been Diana's first attempt at a character role and she loved every moment of it. Diana had successfully shed the bombshell image that had both served her and almost destroyed her. She had watched it end the life of her arch nemesis Marilyn Monroe and the sweet, Kewpie doll Jayne Mansfield.

While she might be the perennial blonde, this bombshell could transform into any character required without a sigh of regret for her vacuous sex symbol days, including the grotesque alcoholic Mrs Wickens, resplendent with a wart on her nose, yellowing teeth and not a platinum hair in sight, as she portrayed in the film *The Amazing Mr Blunden* (1972).

There were, however, troubles on the horizon to overcome. During the pregnancy with Jason, she and Alan had an argument and 'in a fit of passion through a drunken haze Alan took an overdose of pills'.[11] This resulted in him having to have his stomach pumped.

Diana was terrified, but she missed the real warning sign. Diana wasn't a drinker herself, but she was used to being surrounded by heavy drinkers in the business, so initially Alan's drinking didn't register as a serious problem. However, eventually she realised he was, in fact, an alcoholic.

One of Alan's drinking sessions culminated in him being arrested as an accessory to a stabbing. He had got into a bar brawl along with his friend and the temporary relief manager of the pub, who Alan said had incited the fight, was injured. It could not have come at a worse time – both Diana and Alan were contracted to appear in a new television series called *Queenie's Castle*. A car was waiting for them after the court hearing to take them straight to the studio in Leeds.

Alan was advised by his solicitor to plead guilty to speed up proceedings so that he and Diana could get on with their work commitments. As it was his first offence, he was expected to get a suspended sentence. On Friday 16 October 1970, Diana was horrified to hear the judge send Alan to prison for eighteen months. Diana wept, saying, 'It's a savage sentence.'[12]

As ever, with resilience and strength of character, Diana dried her eyes and went to work on her own, while Alan served his sentence. Diana arranged her work schedule so that she wouldn't miss her authorised visits to her husband in prison, which involved travelling a six-hour round trip.

After serving twelve months, on 16 October 1971 Alan was released on good behaviour, much to Diana's delight. When he returned to Orchard Manor, she threw a welcome home party, inviting their family and friends – and gifting Alan a horse called Sapphire, along with £6,000 that she had saved during their enforced separation.

Diana and Alan thought the worst was over, but they were soon to be proved wrong. On 20 February 1972, Alan was riding Sapphire in Windsor Royal Park when he had a severe accident. The party he was riding with got him to his feet and walked him to a vehicle, driving him back to the stables where an ambulance was called. This was unfortunately the worst thing they could possibly have done, as Alan had broken his back and shoulder in five places and had cracked six ribs. He arrived at hospital semi-conscious and the extent of his injuries were so bad the doctors did not expect him to survive. If he did, they warned Diana, he would spend the rest of his life in a wheelchair.

Astonishing everyone and turning the doctors' predictions upside down, Alan was not only walking again six weeks after the accident, but was back in the saddle by the end of summer. But, while Alan was able to exert maximum willpower in most things, he was using alcohol to self-medicate for the intense pain. Diana would return from work to find him drunk and argumentative. On one occasion Alan was hallucinating and thought he was a soldier in the trenches in France during the First World War.

Both Diana and Alan went to war with his alcoholism. It was a long battle, but Diana knew they could win it together, although there would be many setbacks along the way.

TO THINE OWN SELF BE TRUE

'This above all –
To thine own self be true,
And it must follow, as the night the day,
Thou canst not then be false to any man.
Farewell, my blessing season this in thee!'[1]

The attractive, intelligent man Diana had married was a bloated, repetitive bore when drunk and she hated to see him like that. During the 1970s, Alan acknowledged he had a problem and made several attempts to control it with Diana's help, but they were both out of their depth. Eventually, Diana booked Alan into a rehab clinic in Northampton. It was successful for short while, but as it often is with an alcoholic's journey of recovery, each relapse would be worse than the last.

By 1973, both Diana and Alan had begun attending the Sacred Heart Catholic Church close to their home. They both found a feeling of peace and tranquillity that had previously been missing in their lives.

They began taking instructions, and Diana underwent a year-long process of counselling. In 1974, Alan and Diana were officially received into the Catholic faith. During the ceremony, they renewed their wedding vows. Diana was unable to contain her emotion. She broke down and cried, saying afterwards, 'Somehow the words stuck in my throat when it came to "death us do part".'

Tragedy struck yet again when, on their sixth wedding anniversary on 23 November 1974, Diana was suddenly taken ill. She had meningitis and the first twenty-four hours were critical. Alan did not leave her side and, much to everyone's relief, she pulled through. Diana believed her recovery was a miracle, and her faith grew even stronger. A few months later, while still recuperating, she was shocked to learn that she was pregnant. The doctors told her that she was still weak from the meningitis and that her age (she would be 44 when the baby was due) was another factor that indicated a termination would be the safest option.

Diana initially agreed, but as a newly converted Catholic, she was aware that abortion was condemned by the Catholic Church and, after some deep soul searching, she decided to go ahead with the pregnancy. Finally, on 2 May 1975, Diana announced to the press that she was expecting a baby, due in October.

In an interview for the *Daily Mirror*, she told Marje Proops:

I've not had an easy life. I've got into bad scenes, fallen for the wrong men. I was bankrupt at thirty-six, and life, I can tell you, was tough. I wouldn't want to go through all that misery again. It's hell being young. I'm settled now, with Alan and Jason and the new baby coming. I am beside myself with happiness, for I've come to terms with myself as I've got older.

Towards the end of the interview, Diana said:

When you start off as a busty pin-up, and no one ever expects you to be anything more than a sex symbol to whistle at, it's pretty good to end up as an actress and a contented wife and mum ... This wonderful unexpected pregnancy is the great gift of my tranquil middle-age.[2]

Sadly, the gift was to be cruelly snatched away from her. Attending a routine check-up at eight months, the doctor could not detect a heartbeat. He told Diana he was uncertain as to whether the baby was alive or dead. Because of how far advanced the pregnancy was, a termination was ruled out. She found it one of the most distressing experiences of her life, carrying a child that could possibly have died in her womb.

On 27 August, Diana was rushed to hospital in premature labour, but there was no time for pain relief and her baby son was stillborn. Diana never saw her baby, but Alan, who did, told her he was the image of Jason.

It was not until the mid 1980s that losing a baby was understood as significant grief and in the 1970s a stillbirth was almost a taboo subject. As Diana experienced, babies were whisked away without their mothers seeing them and fathers were required to make decisions on their own, to 'protect' their partner's emotional well-being.

Grieving was not encouraged and stillborn babies were rarely given a name. In some cases, the parents were not even told the gender of their child. Incredibly, most parents were not given their child's body for any form of a funeral and more often than not they were not informed about what had happened to the body. Furthermore, a child was not able to be registered if it had been born dead before week twenty-eight of pregnancy. This was not changed until 1992 when a stillborn child could then be registered at twenty-four weeks.

Diana and Alan were perhaps fortunate in their circumstances that they were able to have their son baptised by a priest and arrangements were made for the child to be given a burial.

After the task of giving birth, with none of the joys of being able to hold a healthy baby, Diana wrote that she was 'exhausted and yet relieved it was all over'.[3] However, she had no time to deal with her own grief as Alan was causing problems in the hospital. Still inebriated from earlier in the day, he was weeping uncontrollably. The doctor asked Diana to contact someone to collect him and take him home, which she did; she also discharged herself as soon as she was able and went home. She then contacted her agent to tell him she was available for work.

Fortunately, things have changed for bereaved parents; now, healthcare professionals are trained to be more aware of the intensity of the pain and grief felt by parents who lose a child at birth. Parents are encouraged to hold their baby, have photographs taken and keepsakes made such as hand and footprints, and to hold funeral services and memorials. The pain of losing a baby lasts a lifetime, and this is no longer brushed off and expected to be forgotten as it was during the time Diana and Alan lost their baby.

Diana had hoped that their run of tragedy was over, but sadly, she was to be proved wrong. Jason's best friend was killed in a car accident and a close friend of Alan's died of cancer aged just 34. Alan's mother was also diagnosed with cancer in 1976. Despite appearances, life had never been a smooth ride for Diana; she had always worked exceptionally hard and made some serious personal compromises along the way.

By 1978, Diana was feeling optimistic about the future and excited about the new direction her career was taking. She had always wanted to write and some years before, when she was with Dennis, she had an idea for a script about a young girl who travels to London in search of fame and fortune, but she never got further than a basic outline and the title *Mink and Millions*, which sounded very much like Diana's own life.

Although Diana's autobiography, *Swingin' Dors*, had been published in 1960, she lamented that it had been ghost-written. Diana was a natural-born writer who loved reading poetry and would often write poems, although she vowed never to share them with the public. She was, however, more than happy to write columns and articles for magazines such as *Revue* and *Woman's Own* and, although still working as an actress and TV personality, her long-harboured ambition to become an author was about to be realised.

On Valentine's Day 1978, Diana finally launched her professional writing career with *For Adults Only*, which was in Diana's words, 'A sort of A–Z of life ... my memories, anecdotes, opinions and profiles of people I've met.'[4] It took Diana two months to write and she revealed that she had always been a 'frustrated writer'. She felt rejuvenated by this wonderful turn in the road on the journey of her career.

She loved that she could write in the privacy of her own home and that she could strip off the glamour, be comfortable and still earn a living. Comparing the joy of writing with the satisfaction she got from performing in *Yield to the Night*, she declared with enthusiasm, 'Writing is really all I want to do now. I don't particularly want to act any more,'[5] but she added that she would make an exception if the part was exciting and the director one that she admired.

Having been in the business for more than thirty-two years and being dissatisfied with many of the acting roles she had accepted out of necessity in the past, she also felt that cabaret had taken its toll on her, telling the interviewer, 'I'm afraid I'm a bit past it actually.'[6] Disclosing that she already had a contract for a second book, which would be along similar lines to the first one, she also hinted that she would like to write something completely different in due course.

As 1979 dawned, Diana had achieved her ambition of being a successful author with sales exceeding 100,000 copies. *For Adults Only was* a best seller, with the sequel *Behind Closed Dors* hot on its tracks. *Behind Closed Dors* was a steamy exposé on some of the biggest celebrities in the business, revealing insights into their personalities and gossip about their lives.

As she began another promotional book tour, she continued to exude glamour, but she was also aware of the changes time had inflicted. At a book signing in Coventry she told a reporter that, where once she was compared to Marilyn Monroe and Jayne Mansfield, she was now being compared to her younger self instead. It was an impossible image to live up to, and she admitted, 'I don't think people think of me as a sex symbol now.'[7]

The reporter noted that it was the women at the book signing who were rejoicing the most over the changes that time had wrought on this one-time goddess of sex, but if Diana heard their bitchy barbs she never let on, continuing to sign books with witty banter and a smile. With another publishing contract on the horizon for her autobiography, the future was looking to be a very inviting place indeed.

The decadent decade of the 1980s should have been Diana's. Although they sadly lost Alan's mother to cancer, Alan, with Diana's help, had returned to rehab. He at last managed to maintain his sobriety and was no longer afflicted by the havoc alcohol caused in his life. Gary came to England and lived at Orchard Manor and, while he only stayed for a relatively short time before returning to America, it gave mother and son a chance to get to know each other better.

As Diana's fiftieth birthday approached, she was happy and optimistic; she had completed her autobiography *Dors by Diana* and *Diana Dors' A–Z of Men*, the latter being deemed too libellous to publish at the time, although it did eventually hit the bookshelves in 1984. She had dreamed of giving up acting altogether, but she was still working as an actress, taking TV jobs, opening events, doing anything that required a personality as Diana had personality and glamour in abundance.

It was after one of these events, opening a new hotel, that Diana's life was about to change forever. She'd been feeling unwell and on arrival at the hotel she was in agony but, determined to fulfil her commitment to the job, she shook hands and chatted with people as the ever-consummate professional.

On returning home to Orchard Manor, she collapsed on the stairs and an ambulance was called. She was taken to the Princess Margaret Hospital in Windsor. Once stable, on Saturday 26 June 1982, Diana underwent an operation to have a cyst removed from her ovary, as well as a hysterectomy. Alan was given the news that during the surgery the surgeon had found cancerous tissue.

As with every significant catastrophe Diana had faced previously, she squared her shoulders and prepared to go into battle, this time for her life. Visiting Diana with red roses after the operation, Alan told reporters as he left the hospital that she was laughing and joking with nurses just twelve hours after major abdominal surgery, stating that,

'They should have named the *Titanic* Diana Dors, then the ship never would have sunk.' He added, 'Diana is in great form. She is an incredible woman and is already itching to get back to work.'[8]

A year after the first diagnosis, during a routine scan, more cancerous tissue was found and another operation arranged. Alan, who was filming in Greece, flew home immediately and was with Diana before the operation took place, then stayed by her bedside as she recovered. Another malignant tumour the size of a walnut had been removed from her ovary.

Throughout this time, Diana held on tight to her faith. She was scared of cancer, she didn't feel brave, but she felt assured that God would help her get through it.

In March 1984, Diana began working on the film *Steaming*, about seven middle-aged women who spend time relaxing together in a spa environment. They share their problems and help each other, building a protective world around themselves. That world is soon under threat when the women learn the management is closing the steam room. The women work together, devising a plan to save it.

Completing the film, Diana collapsed on 28 April and was rushed into hospital. The cancer had taken over and caused an intestinal blockage that, on 30 April, was unsuccessfully operated on. The doctor had to give Alan the news; Diana had only a short time to live.

By Friday 4 May, Alan was told it was a matter of hours. A bombshell to the last, Diana wanted to look her best for her final scene. The regulation hospital gown was removed and she was changed into her favourite nightdress, her long platinum hair brushed out and a little makeup applied. The golden '*Dors*' necklace she loved, which Alan had given her years before, had been removed prior to her operation, but now was refastened around her neck.

Diana's last words were to Alan. She whispered, 'Oh my darling, I love you, take care of the boys and say farewell to everyone concerned … This is not the way it was rehearsed.'

At around 9 p.m., surrounded by cards and flowers from well-wishers and with the love of her life holding her hand, the last of the bombshells died.

Leaving the hospital, holding Diana's white vanity case and two cuddly toys, Alan said, 'I have lost my wife and soul mate, and my son has lost a friend and a mother,' adding, 'the world has lost a legend.'[9]

Diana had outlived her competition, but she was just 52 with so much still to do. Her relationship with her sons in America just required a little extra time that she wasn't given, Jason needed her desperately and Alan was unable to live without her, there were too many years in front of him. On 10 October 1984, the sixteenth anniversary of him first meeting Diana and just five months after her death, Alan took his own life; a world without Diana was not a world in which he wished to live.

In a peaceful corner of a small Catholic cemetery, close to Orchard Manor, they now lie side by side in death as they were in life, together forever.

PART FIVE

JAYNE MANSFIELD

.

PINK LOLLIPOP WORLD

It would not be unrealistic to assume that, during her last hours, the self-made Sex Goddess of Cheesecake and Glamour, the Mistress of Mayhem, was haunted by the breakdown of her most precious relationships, and in particular the acrimony between herself and her teenage daughter Jayne Marie, which had caused her untold anguish. Jayne Mansfield's previously good rapport with the press had fallen apart, and she was now the recipient of vicious headlines of a malicious nature. This must have been in her thoughts as she left the Gus Stevens Dinner Club in Biloxi, Mississippi, the club where she had just performed.

With a television interview scheduled for the following day in New Orleans, Jayne decided to head straight there, packing three of her children, two chihuahuas and her partner Sam Brody, who had broken his leg in a recent car accident, into a 1966 Buick Electra. Their chauffeur for the journey to New Orleans was a good-looking young man of 20 called Ronnie Harrison, who has long since been forgotten by all other than his friends and loved ones in the misty murk of that fatal night. Ronnie was about to become a father and needed the money this job would pull in. His fiancée, Elaine Stevens, who was the daughter of the club owner Gus Stevens, told Fox News in February 2018:

> Ronnie was a young man I loved …We were planning to be married in 72 hours. My wedding dress was hung in the closet. A little orange crepe dress. And I was pregnant with my daughter. We went to high school together. We graduated together. It was young first love. My sweetheart.[1]

The TV interview in New Orleans was essential to Jayne; she was still working the publicity hard, the only way she knew how to. The 1960s were not being kind to her; she had attempted to embrace the new era with enthusiasm and optimism, but Jayne had been the Queen of the Fifties – the 1960s was a tough gig for a 1950s blonde to survive.

Born Vera Jane Palmer (the 'Y' in Jane appeared as a child when dressing up and wanting to be a movie star. She thought Jane was far too plain, and so, at her mother's suggestion she added a 'Y' to give her that little something different) on 19 April 1933, in Bryn Mawr, Pennsylvania, to parents Vera and Herbert Palmer, Jayne's ancestry was a mix of German and English.

Vera was a schoolteacher and Herbert a successful lawyer who had drive, ambition and dedication. He saw himself as a future president and may have made it too, had he not died of a heart attack aged 32 at the wheel of his car while on a family outing with Vera and Jayne, who was just 3 years old at the time and sitting on her mother's lap. Vera had the great presence of mind to slam on the brakes and take control of the wheel despite the shock of her husband dying so suddenly next to her in the car.

Jayne and her mother sat for some time in the car with the body of her father – most likely Vera was in shock, and it has to be remembered these were the days before mobile phones were available to summon help.

Later, Jayne expressed her sadness when she said:

My father's death made a great impression on me. I was always asking to go to the cemetery to visit his grave … He was the only man I ever knew who really loved me unselfishly – who never used me for personal gain.[2]

It was around this time that Jayne became obsessed with animals. Her mother was not demonstrative and the death of her husband could undoubtedly have been a significant influence on how she dealt with life as a single parent. Jayne fulfilled her own craving for love and affection by picking up stray cats and dogs, dreaming of a time when she would be a grown-up and she could have all the animals she wanted.

This mother–daughter relationship was complicated, but there is little doubt that deep down her mother loved her dearly. Vera was a strict, no-nonsense woman with an element of control – which is understandable when you learn that, before Jayne was born, Vera experienced the tragedy of a stillborn son who almost cost Vera her life. The pregnancy had reached nearly ten months and it was a distressing time for Vera and Herbert.

Vera was grief-stricken and longing for another baby, but the recovery period was arduous. When she was able to go through another pregnancy, Jayne arrived by Caesarean section weighing a healthy 9lb 10oz. Vera was ecstatic. With total devotion, both she and Herbert worshipped their beautiful daughter. It was also clear that Vera would be unable to have another child, and so Jayne became the centre of her parents' world.

When Vera was widowed in such a horrific way at such a young age it was natural that Jayne should become even more precious, but this resulted in her mother becoming overprotective, sometimes giving the appearance of being too harsh and demanding in her daughter's eyes. Jayne was occasionally spanked, but this was an era of discipline, and children were often physically chastised.

Against the advice of her family, Vera remarried in 1939 when Jayne was 6 years old. Both Vera and Jayne desperately felt the gap Herbert had left in their lives. Harry Peers was able to go some way to filling the void; he loved Vera and Jayne immensely. The only problem was he lived in Dallas and so the new family had to move, which could have accounted for Vera's family and friends encouraging her to stay single.

Vera and Harry were old school; they both believed a woman's place was in the home, primarily looking after her man. They were also steadfast on the line of gender roles; Vera's feminine traits played to Harry's masculine ones, as she appeared to him the distressed incapable female looking for a solid, dependable man to save her.

Harry obliged, sweeping this helpless woman into his big strong arms, placing a shield of protection around both her and Jayne, who witnessed the interplay between the two. She saw how successfully it worked for Vera and how Harry idolised his wife. Vera was also showered with beautiful things that she didn't have to work for. Her job was to keep an immaculate home and enchant and attract her husband, which Vera was able to do with confidence.

Harry was very paternal towards both of them. Jayne was a very perceptive and bright child and had begun to follow the dynamics of her mother and stepfather's relationship. She watched her mother act the part of the damsel in distress, weak and utterly dependent on her mate; a helpless childlike need for attention merged with a fluttering of the eyelashes and an adult promise of what would be given in return for what was wanted.

Jayne also witnessed her mother as a divided personality; she saw the side of Vera's character to which Harry was not exposed. Vera could be critical, possessive and all-powerful; it was a delicate balance that was executed adroitly.

The adult Jayne morphed into the acting version of her mother and took it to Hollywood. It had worked for Vera on her small scale, it seemed natural to her daughter to emulate her mother's success. Only Jayne blew it up out of all proportion, burlesquing to a phenomenal extent.

As a child, Jayne reaped the benefits of Vera's education and teaching experience, especially being an only child, and her vocabulary was far in advance of other children her age. Vera lavished love and learning on her daughter, who was quick to pick up what her mother taught her.

At college, Jayne maintained a B average and in some courses such as philosophy achieved an A. It has also been said that she was fluent in several languages including French; however, during an interview on 30 August 1962, when Jayne was 29, she was asked if she was able to converse with the French-speaking interviewer. She told him, 'I started studying about two weeks ago and I'm only on the first or second lesson … the next time I come back, I hope very much to speak fluent French.'[3]

At around 6 years old, Jayne was clearly expressing a desire to be a movie star. She was a regular visitor to the cinema with her mother; they would watch Shirley Temple movies and, inspired by the tiny tot with a mop of ringlets, Jayne lapped up the fantasy world. Together, mother and daughter would sing Miss Temple's iconic song 'On the Good Ship Lollipop'. During a television appearance when Jayne was the subject of *This is Your Life* in 1960 Vera told the host Ralph Edwards, 'I shielded her from every unpleasantness and built a sort of pink lollipop world for her.'[4]

Harry continued, 'She used to sit in the middle of her big bed surrounded with pillows and make believe she was a movie star.'

As a teenager, Jayne's interest in the movies never faded; if anything she grew more precise about what she wanted to do, but another interest was on the horizon in the shape of boys.

Although it seemed perfectly clear to almost everyone in Vera and Jayne's sphere that Vera loved and indulged Jayne, Jayne seemingly saw their relationship differently as an adult when she told her friend and journalist May Mann, 'I was my mother's pride – and her pain in the neck. I could never please her for long … When I grew older, I gave up trying.'[5]

Jayne professed that she was 'a little afraid' of her mother and that she wanted but never achieved her full approval. Vera kept a neat and orderly house, one in which Jayne felt it was difficult to relax. It didn't help with her mother reminding her 'This is my home.' Jayne vowed that when she grew up she would have her own home that would be a welcoming place 'a pink palace, pink because it's such a happy colour … Everyone would enjoy themselves in my home.'[6]

Reinforcing her mother's perceived position in her life, Jayne said, 'Momma was the important woman of our house. She never let me forget she was boss. I was always in her shadow.'[7]

In fairness to Vera, this was typical of the times; a wife and mother was expected to keep control and showcase an ideal happy home and family. This was Vera's domain and her full-time job on which she stood to be judged, mostly by other women doing the same thing. It was difficult for Vera when Jayne brought a menagerie of stray animals into the house. At one point, after a cat Jayne had brought in messed on the front room carpet, Vera was so cross she rubbed the hapless feline's nose in its own faeces. Jayne was horrified, but she wasn't angry with her mother. Instead, she said 'I felt sorry for her – for her narrow outlook and lack of compassion.'[8]

May Mann, in her book *Jayne Mansfield: A Biography*, tells a shocking and distressing story of Jayne being raped at 14 after her drink was spiked with alcohol at a party, and shortly after she found herself pregnant. Not able to tell her mother, she selected a different young man by the name of Paul Mansfield, whom she felt was suitable to be the father of her baby. She pursued him and they secretly married. This story is flawed, but it is certainly possible that Jayne had a bad experience at 14. However, Jayne Marie was not born until Jayne was 17 years old.

The most likely scenario was that Jayne, who was actually 16 years old at the time, met Paul at her friend's party. Paul, who was 20, brought a date with him. Captivated by this handsome young man, who was equally smitten with Jayne, things began to progress. For all of her grown-up ways and education, Jayne was not as experienced in love as she appeared to be and soon found herself in the frightening situation of being pregnant. On 6 May 1950, in Fort Worth, Texas, aged just 17, Jayne became Mrs Paul Mansfield.

Six months later, on 6 November 1950, after a long but straightforward labour, Jayne Marie Mansfield was born. Vera was thrilled with her new granddaughter.

One thing is certain; whatever the dynamics of the relationship between mother and daughter, Vera loved Jayne and as a mother it is hard to fault her. She instilled in her daughter a strength of character that few are lucky enough to possess, along with confidence and self-esteem that far out-stripped the average child or teenager. In an era and social class where teenage pregnancy was a taboo and a disgrace, Vera openly embraced her daughter and granddaughter with love and affection.

However, having such high hopes for Jayne as her only child, it must have been painful to watch her throw away her best years. Vera under-stood the consequences of marriage and children and her own daughter was still a child, now with adult responsibilities.

As Jayne Marie grew into a teenager, Jayne's parenting style and rela-tionship with her own daughter was about to be challenged as it rocked her pink lollipop world.

BUCKLED DOWN BLONDE

Married life was not exciting, and it was not how the 17-year-old Jayne had visualised it in her romantic dreams. It was in fact rather dull and, with the best will in the world, Paul wasn't able to provide Jayne with what she was looking for. Without ambition and drive, Paul was just happy with his wife and daughter. He was looking forward to settling down just as Jayne was looking forward to taking off and living her best life.

Jayne entered the Miss America contest, but if the judges had found out she was married, she would have received an automatic disqualification. So she told Paul of her plan to keep her marital status secret, thinking he would go along with her. However, instead, he became angry and insisted she give up such a ludicrous idea. Upset, on this occasion Jayne obeyed her husband and abandoned the idea.

In early 1952 Paul had been drafted into the army as the Korean War erupted and was stationed at Camp Gordon, Augusta, Georgia. He wanted his wife and daughter to accompany him, so Jayne laid down the rules. She and Jayne Marie would go with him, but on his two-year discharge he had to make a promise to Jayne. He had to agree to relocate to Hollywood for six months to give Jayne the opportunity of breaking into the movie business, on the proviso that if she failed they would return to Dallas and return to a quiet family life.

Deep down, Paul honestly thought Jayne would forget about the deal. At worse, he believed she would fail in her endeavour to be a movie star, so he readily agreed.

This was a real bargain deal for Jayne. She knew she wouldn't fail in Hollywood; she had innate confidence in her ability and being on a military camp allowed her to perfect her skills of attraction and exhibitionism, with the enlisted men as her captive audience. The war lasted longer than they had anticipated and after a year Paul was shipped out to Korea and Jayne returned to Dallas with Jayne Marie. She began taking her interest in acting further while still entering and winning beauty contests and taking modelling jobs.

She also began working, selling photograph albums door to door. Using her first week's commission of $90 she put a down payment on a car, which enabled her to continue with modelling assignments and get about more easily with Jayne Marie.

When Paul was discharged and returned to Dallas, after a temporary reprieve Jayne called in the debt. Paul had hoped his wife would have forgotten all about her ambition and their agreement or changed her mind, but Jayne was fiercer than ever in her desire to go to Hollywood and it was with great reluctance that Paul fulfilled his promise in early 1954.

The time came to leave Texas and, after filling Jayne's red Buick and trailer with belongings and her two cats, the family set off on the long drive to Hollywood. On arriving, Jayne claimed she got out of the Buick and kissed the ground as she wept, declaring that she was now home. She and Paul secured a small apartment and while Paul unpacked the car, Jayne, who by her own admission was utterly ignorant of how the Hollywood system worked, went straight to the phone booth and called Paramount Studios.

She got through to the secretary of the studio's head of casting, Milton Lewis, and told her, 'My name's Jayne Mansfield and I want to be a star. I just arrived from Dallas, where I won a beauty contest.'[1] Her naïve approach won her an interview, and Jayne later said, 'When I made the direct request for an interview they were too astonished to say no, I suppose.'[2]

During her audition with Paramount on 30 April 1954, she did a monologue from *Joan of Arc*, later recalling the reaction of Milton Lewis: 'He just seemed to think that I was, as he said, wasting my obvious talents,'[3] indicating that she would be most suited to glamour roles. She was also told to return for a screen test when she had lost weight, even though she weighed a healthy 9 st 8lb at around 5ft 7in tall, which was slim by most standards but not slim enough for Paramount it would seem.

Either way, Jayne took the advice on board and began dieting, slimming down to what was considered movie star proportions, although her bust remained large in comparison to her waist and hips; Jayne was soon to become known as the 'bustaceous blonde'.[4] America was fascinated by large breasts in the 1950s and it was a prerequisite for a Hollywood starlet to be well endowed in the chest region. While the censors were not inclined to tolerate cleavage being shown, padding to emphasise the breasts was entirely acceptable and the so-called 'bullet bras' became the choice of underwear for any self-respecting bombshell. The structure of the bra lifted and separated the breasts, jutting them forward with a conical, almost torpedo, silhouette, hence the term 'bullet' bra.

Breasts appeared larger and almost cartoon-like under tight-fitting clothing, particularly sweaters. This gave rise to the term 'sweater girls', a label that became popular to describe the look worn by the 1950s pin-ups and the glamorous bombshells.

America was preoccupied with measurements and no more so than the measurements of the female figure. Jayne's statistics, which naturally varied throughout her life, were on average an astonishing 40-21-35 with a 40D cup size.

The bullet bra's popularity began to decline in the 1960s when feminist activists saw bras as an object of sexism and oppression, and by the 1970s burning bras became symbolic of the feminist movement and its demands for equality of the sexes. Indeed, many women decided at this time to forego bra wearing altogether. Fashion caught the zeitgeist, and as a compromise designers and manufacturers also began to move towards a less restrictive, softer, more natural look and shape.

Meanwhile, Jayne was making phone calls and writing letters – anything at all to further her prospects of becoming a movie star with a studio contract. Soon she had an introduction to Bob Schwartz, a Hollywood talent agent.

Schwartz saw her enthusiasm and potential and agreed to take her on as a client. Assessing her wavy brown hair and hazel eyes, Bob told her, 'Honey, take my advice and get your hair fixed up. You ought to be a platinum blonde.' Jayne had never intended to go blonde, but when it was suggested to her, despite understanding the connotations of being blonde and living with the label 'dumb blonde', she thought anything that would get her to her destination of movie star as quickly as possible was worth it.

Unlike some women in the business, Jayne initially had no problem being thought of as dumb. Her level of personal self-belief and confidence was unusually high, and so a determined Jayne, without question or hesitation, stripped the colour out of her hair and became a blonde the very next day; she would do whatever it would take in the pursuit of her dreams to become a famous movie star.

It is not just men that categorise blonde women as dumb. In her book *The Feminine Mystique*, feminist Betty Friedan argues that an advertising campaign for a hair colour that had the tagline 'If I have only one life, let me live it as a blonde' showed the model to be 'a pretty vacuous woman'.[5] Friedan is suggesting the model is an unintelligent blonde airhead, implying that blonde is synonymous with being dumb. Given this stance, you would assume that the advert was formulated by men, using a pretty model to suck in other stupid women to buy the dye to colour their hair, so they too could be seen as pretty and 'vacuous'. The irony is that the successful advert for Clairol was created in 1955 by a female advertising executive, Shirley Polykoff, in a male-dominated industry. She stood firm and she never underestimated the intelligence of the women who were the target audience. Polykoff not only competed with the top male executives in her work environment, but she also rose above them to become the executive vice president and creative director of Foote, Cone & Belding, one of the largest global advertising agencies.

Polykoff, who was blonde as a child, went darker as she got older. Lamenting the loss of her light hair, partly because she had two beautiful sisters with rich dark hair, she felt her blonde had given her a certain attractive distinction. So when the colour began to tone down, she resorted to hair dye herself, simply because she preferred being blonde, and there is no evidence to prove that she was catering to a woman's longing to be a sex object.

Like Jayne, Polykoff loved being a woman. She gloried in her femininity and was not averse to using it to win over the opposite sex when necessary. She held no secret desire to be a man and frowned on women who tried to emulate men in the workplace. Although she loved her career and was exceptionally good at what she did, she did not put it above her family. She prioritised her husband and daughters and was not ashamed to be a wife and mother first and an advertising executive second. She was proud to be a woman.

While in Jayne's case it was suggested to her that she should go blonde by a man, she had her own agenda and, like Polykoff, she revelled in being a woman and used it to her advantage, reaching heights of which most women could only dream. Glamour was high on her list, not just in her appearance but in the way she lived, dreaming of a luxurious pink palace that she would eventually bring into being.

Jayne could not have arrived in Hollywood at a better time. Her physical appearance was exactly what was required for a glamour girl and a movie star, and she was going to make the most of nature's gift to her. Although it was the key to unlock the door to fame, and she'd mentally signed the contract with herself; ultimately her hair and figure would become a significant obstruction to being taken seriously.

An already unhappy Paul was further distressed by this major change in his wife. He loved her natural hair colour and it contributed to the strain on an already pressurised marriage. By October 1954, the six-month agreement was almost up and Paul felt Jayne had not had any significant success on her chosen path. He therefore pleaded with her to relinquish her dreams and aspirations of a film career and to return to Dallas with him. His plea became an ultimatum, but he had underestimated the powerhouse of determination that he had married. The thought of returning to Texas filled Jayne with horror.

Disappointed and struggling with jealousy, uncomfortable with his wife being ogled by other men, Paul felt he had no alternative but to return to Texas alone. The arguments and recriminations had worn both of them down and Jayne was relieved when he finally left. She filed for divorce on the grounds of mental cruelty and applied for custody of Jayne Marie, which she would be awarded. The divorce was granted on 23 October 1956.

Around this time Jayne received her first payment from an inheritance that had been held in trust, left to her from her grandma Palmer's estate. The trust had been set up in 1945 and Jayne was due a total of $36,340 in instalments, the first being when she was 21. With the first payout of $5,000, Jayne used $4,000 to put a deposit on an $18,000 house in Beverly Hills.

She could, of course, have squandered the money on such things as clothes and socialising, but this was an astute young woman – not such a dumb blonde after all.

The month Paul left was the start of Jayne's new life. It wasn't easy working, looking after Jayne Marie and searching for the acting roles she wanted, but Jayne was tenacious and persistent and wasn't about to accept any kind of defeat. Although being blonde didn't immediately win her a movie contract, she did get a ten-line part in a television programme, which paid $300 and led on to a small part in an independent

film called *Female Jungle*, which gave Jayne some much-needed experience and $150.

Always a quick learner, Jayne realised it was time to part company with
Bob Schwartz. She was ready to move forward with a new agent, and
together they would work the publicity machine in Hollywood as it had
never been worked before.

THE HEART OF IT

Jayne saw her own success clearly in her mind's eye. She was blessed with copious amounts of self-belief and love, but she also knew she couldn't achieve her ambitions on her own, so she began looking for people who were as interested in Jayne Mansfield as she was.

December 1954 brought her first fortuitous meeting with the press agent and publicist Jim Byron. Jim promoted female actresses and models; he was always on the lookout for someone who had star quality and the potential to drive his own career forward and the 21-year-old before him indeed presented the possibilities in an indisputably perfect package.

The pair hit it off straight away and Jim agreed to be Jayne's publicity agent, with his advice and influence making her the darling of the press. She and Jim shared a vision for her career and together they began working on it immediately.

Jim dispatched Jayne in a tight red dress and loaded with bottles of Scotch, looking every inch the sexy Miss Santa. Her brief was to go into the newspaper offices armed with the festive booze and the names of the lucky recipients, who were Jim's best press contacts, and deliver them a bottle of Christmas cheer with a cheeky kiss.

It was the perfect assignment for an enthusiastic and willing Jayne, and the beneficiaries of the gift that was delivered in such an original and fun way were filled with such Christmas spirit that they gave Jayne a gift in return: an impromptu photoshoot that saw this shapely Christmas cracker in all the newspapers the following day.

Such antics in the workplace now would be unlikely to be accepted. The flirtatious nature of Jayne's gift, and the instruction to kiss each man receiving a bottle of Scotch on the back of the neck, would undoubtedly be seen as inappropriate, even offensive, behaviour. Few women now would be prepared to do something in the workplace that would be considered both demeaning and sexually objectifying. There is also the element of sexual harassment for both the man receiving the kiss and the woman being asked to give it. Only in the 1950s could such frankly flirtatious shenanigans be condoned and encouraged.

Jayne was not at all fazed by the request; feminism had not yet arrived to teach her that, as a female, she was being used and that the men saw her for her sexual parts alone. However, if she had been informed of such things it is more than possible that her reaction would have been a wide-eyed put-down. Jayne needed the endorsement; she wanted confirmation of the power she had over men. It gave her a thrill, and she was exhilarated by it.

When Jayne spoke of being whistled at, she said she never took offence. In her book *Jayne Mansfield's Wild, Wild World*, she declared, 'I was grateful. At least someone thought I was sexy. I was almost tempted to turn back and smile, but I didn't.[1]

Byron ramped up her publicity, introducing her to the right people, getting her auditions and sending her off to Florida to make a splash, quite literally, at someone else's press junket. In January 1955, at the press call for the Howard Hughes film *Underwater,* Jayne arrived before the stars, Jane Russell and Debbie Reynolds.

A pool event had been organised and Jayne took full advantage, in a red lamé swimsuit that was too small for her. Diving into the pool, the strap gave way and Jayne surfaced with more than the press photographers had bargained for. They went into a frenzy of snapping their shutters and Jayne made a great play of surprise and a feeble attempt to cover her ample bosom.

By the time Russell and Reynolds eventually arrived, the photographers had already used their film on Jayne. According to Edith Lynch who worked in the publicity department at RKO and was present at the time, Jane Russell's reaction to Mansfield's stunt was to ask, 'Who's the blonde tomato?'[2]

On her triumphant return from Florida things were moving fast for Jayne, with offers and new introductions. She soon met Bill Shiffrin. Bill said Hollywood needed a new glamour girl, Jayne said she was it. Bill believed her and became her new agent.

With rumours that Howard Hughes wanted to sign Jayne after her exhibition at the *Underwater* press premiere, in February 1955 Warner Brothers Studio jumped in and made her an offer. She was advised to wait it out, turn the offer down and wait for a better deal, but Jayne couldn't wait. She was worried that if she missed the bus, another one might not come along.

Of course, Jayne's advisors were right, Warners were expecting a ride on the tail of Jayne generating publicity rather than the studio having to spend money on her promotion. They gave her small parts in forgettable movies and made an announcement that Jayne would be appearing with James Dean in *Rebel Without a Cause*, but it never came to fruition.

She began to feel disenchanted with how her career was proceeding and thought she wasn't getting the star treatment she'd envisaged when signing with Warner Bros. She needn't have worried; just over five months into her six-month contract, Warner dropped Jayne, but she was advised to put a spin on the situation by telling people she wanted out of the contract so that she could be independent and make the movies that she really wanted.

Bill had secured her the lead in a film called *The Burglar*; she was thrilled and travelled to Philadelphia in Pennsylvania to start work. After the movie was finished, Shiffrin suggested she audition for a stage play on Broadway – Jayne was reluctant, she'd set her sights on Hollywood and felt that only there could deliver the life she wanted. However, she agreed to audition for the part of Rita Marlowe in the play *Will Success Spoil Rock Hunter?*, a satirical comedy written by the playwright George Axelrod, who also wrote the play *The Seven Year Itch*. The film adaptation of the play starred Marilyn Monroe, transporting her to the peak of fame.

Perfect for the part of Rita Marlowe, Jayne opened on 13 October 1955 at the Belasco Theatre in New York. She made both the play and herself an overnight sensation.

The story focuses on Rita, a movie star and platinum bombshell who has just started her own production company and divorced her husband, who was a sporting hero. The opening scene has Rita on a massage table undergoing treatment from her masseur. Sound familiar? The part was inspired by Marilyn Monroe, with various references to Marilyn's life throughout the play.

Jayne Marie and the menagerie of animals had accompanied her to New York, but time just wasn't available for Jayne to give much of it to her 5-year-old daughter. She tried to spend time with Jayne Marie as often as possible, and even took her along on 'dates'. Jayne would leave her daughter in the ladies room with the assistant, while she had a drink with her admirer. Jayne Marie was also cared for by her mother's wardrobe mistress, while Jayne's chihuahuas would wait in her dressing room for her.

Amid this madness, Jayne's flings had been fleeting. She'd had an occasional affair but nothing that made her stop in her tracks until she took a legendary night out in the Latin Quarter to catch the Mae West Revue.

The act consisted of Mae's usual sexual innuendos while flanked by a posse of young scantily dressed men with exceptionally muscular physiques. Mae had begun her career in Vaudeville at the age of 14 and had gone on to become the sassy, smart-witted star of the silver screen in the 1930s. Now in her sixties, Mae had no intention of slowing down. She was not quite ready for retirement, the act was a big success, and she adored her young men, especially the 26-year-old Hungarian 'Mr Universe' Mickey Hargitay, who was her personal favourite.

While Jayne was in the club sipping on a strawberry soda, Mickey was on stage doing his thing; usually, the audience was a blurry indistinguishable sea of people and he concentrated on his part in the act, but this night it was different. Jayne, in a white mink coat, wearing a sweater and blue jeans underneath, shimmered in front of him and Mickey could not take his eyes off her. It seemed Jayne was also feeling the glow of attraction as she told her companions, singling out Hargitay, 'That fellow I dig. I've got to meet him. I just love those muscles.'[3] In a newspaper interview, Jayne also claimed she told her friends, 'I'd like that one on the left as a steak for my dog.'[4]

They were soon introduced to one another, and the sexual chemistry between Mickey and Jayne was explosive, but the real fireworks started with Mae West, who was extremely angry, especially with the publicity surrounding the newly loved-up couple. Mae demanded Hargitay end the blossoming relationship before it got out of hand, but Jayne and Mickey were having none of it. A fight broke out in the dressing room between Mickey and another of Mae's men, Chuck Krauser. The fiasco didn't end there; it made the following day's headlines and Mickey filed charges against Krauser.

As a result, Jayne gained even more publicity and fame. The public couldn't get enough of her and the play ran for 452 performances. Impressed with Jayne's performance, Twentieth Century Fox purchased the rights to make *Rock Hunter*, a motion picture with Jayne in the starring role as Rita Marlowe, which she had made her own.

On 2 May 1956, Jayne signed her first contract with Fox. However, by the time screenwriter Frank Tashlin had adapted the play for film, it bore little resemblance to the original script. It kept only one speech delivered by Jayne from the original play, much to Axelrod's disgust.

However, the leading lady could do no wrong. Loved by the press and the public, always agreeable to pose for photographers and give interviews, she charmed the media. The public loved her because, no matter how tired, cold or hungry she was, she would never turn down an autograph.

When the stage production closed on 15 September 1956, Axelrod presented to everyone involved with the play a silver heart key ring as a memento of their time together. Jayne was so captivated by the gift that from then on she claimed the heart as a central theme of her image. When she signed her name, instead of dotting the letter 'i' in Mansfield she put a heart in place of the dot. The symbolic heart grew and became one of her signature features, as she later owned a heart-shaped swimming pool, bathtub and fire surround. Anywhere she could have a heart, Jayne had one.

Jayne returned to Hollywood with Jayne Marie, Mickey and her four dogs on 16 September 1956. Mickey rented an apartment close to Jayne's home to keep up a respectable appearance, as 'living in sin', a term that was frequently used in the 1950s to describe a couple living together and indulging in sexual intimacy while unmarried, was not socially acceptable. The couple both wanted to get married, but at this point Jayne was still technically married to Paul. There had been an error in the paperwork when she initially filed for divorce, and so this did not become final until 8 January 1958.

Furthermore, Hargitay was still married to his first wife, Mary, and was the father of their 7-year-old daughter Tina. When the news of her husband's infidelity reached Mary Hargitay, she immediately filed for divorce, wondering out loud, 'How in the hell can you build an exciting, fresh, young, glamorous sex symbol out of a divorced woman with a child, who is announcing she is going to marry a divorced man with a child? Is that young love?'[5]

Although Jayne's personal life was somewhat chaotic, it didn't prevent her from keeping her career on track. She was a workaholic and continually made sacrifices for her career. Fox had given her the starring role of Jerri Jordan in *The Girl Can't Help It*, but her first day at the studio clashed with Jayne Marie's first day at school. Despite this, she wasn't about to miss her daughter starting school, so she made sure that before she headed to work she personally took Jayne Marie to class.

The Girl Can't Help It was the perfect vehicle for Jayne; it used every ounce of her overt sexuality. Jayne was the embodiment of over-exaggerated 1950s femininity. The opening scene has her walking down the street causing mayhem amongst the menfolk, from a milk bottle exploding in the hand of the man holding it to the shattering of glasses worn by another male who is ogling her.

Jayne appears oblivious to the havoc she is creating in her wake as she sashays down the street on stilettos that elongate her legs, wearing an excruciatingly tight figure-hugging suit that emphasises her hourglass proportions and showcases her cleavage with a low open neckline with a flower placed at the centre of her décolletage. But the viewer understands that she is not only aware of the effect she is having on the male popula-tion, but she is also rejoicing in her power.

Tom Ewell, who starred opposite Monroe in *The Seven Year Itch*, plays the part of Tom Miller, an alcoholic talent agent in New York. A gang-ster hires Miller to make his girlfriend (Jayne) into a singing star, but her ambition is to get married and have several children. The film is a feminist paradox; on first sight full of infantile male sexual innuendos that seem to objectify Jayne's character. However, on closer inspection Jayne is in control; she chooses to be a bombshell. In fact, she plays the part so well, the viewer could be mistaken for believing she invented the term and gave it meaning.

Later, in 1959, Marilyn had a strikingly similar first scene in *Some Like it Hot*. As two of her male co-stars watch from behind, Marilyn walks up the train platform. When two sudden pressurised jets of steam from the train are propelled towards Marilyn's character, Sugar, she appears to be unaware of her effect on the opposite sex and therefore, indifferent to it. Jayne's character, on the other hand, positively makes the most of it.

Fox also had an ulterior motive in securing a contract with Jayne. They hoped it would motivate Marilyn, who was being troublesome and unpro-fessional, to make an effort to turn up on time and know her lines.

Jayne could act, she had determination and ability, but she also failed to see when she was damaging her own career. Jules Styne, a writer and friend of Jayne, observed, 'She has a certain wonderful quality of naïve bouncing enthusiasm … If she would just forget her dogs and her publicity for one year, she'd become a big film star!'[6]

AND BABY COMES TOO

An eighteen-hour day on set was not unusual for Jayne, and any spare moments were spent reading literature for relaxation. The people behind the scenes loved her; for the make-up artists, hairdressers and wardrobe assistants she was a delight to work with and Jayne appreciated them. She knew they were part of her key to success. The only complaint they made was that her dressing room was always full of dogs and sometimes children, with the phone constantly ringing, and they had to work in a lively general state of pandemonium.

Evenings for Jayne were spent reading scripts and offers; she was always ready with her lines for the following day and when she wasn't working she enjoyed being at home and spending time with Mickey and Jayne Marie. Going out nightclubbing at this stage in her life wasn't something she was interested in; she found her social outlet in work.

The year 1957 began with the death of Jayne's paternal grandfather, Elmer E. Palmer, who passed away on 2 January in Pen Argyl, Pennsylvania. Jayne inherited $81,340, a considerable sum at any time, but then it was a vast fortune, the equivalent of approximately $740,000[1] in today's money.

Careful with money, thrifty and budget conscious, once again she invested her inheritance in property and on 21 November 1957 she committed to buying her now famous pink palace, but the purchase did not complete until March 1958.

Fox was becoming concerned about Jayne's relationship with Mickey. They were worried that the relationship was not eliciting the best type of publicity and they were also nervous about their 'investment' becoming pregnant. Jayne had already confided in her friend and journalist May Mann, 'I want to have a baby, Mickey's baby, right away when we get married.' She told Mann, 'I'm a woman first and an actress second.'[2] This was the first time Jayne had relegated her career to second place, behind her personal life.

Partly to break up her liaison with Mickey and to exert some control, Fox sent Jayne off on a forty-day tour, starting in New York, and moving on to cities in Europe. The studio supplied her with a small entourage, including a publicity agent and someone to take care of all her beauty needs. The studio even arranged for her to be presented to the Queen at a Royal Command Performance in London. Jayne was thrilled, but she soon learned it was on the condition she went without Mickey.

Although they were both unhappy about it, it was an opportunity Jayne felt she couldn't turn down. And so Mickey stayed home and took care of Jayne Marie, while also attending to building works at Jayne's house.

The studio was right to be nervous; Jayne was consumed with a need to procreate, despite the experience of having Jayne Marie at such a young age. There is no evidence to suggest Jayne Marie was planned; on the contrary, it seems Jayne had no idea of the biology of reproduction and its consequences. However, once her pregnancy was confirmed, terminating it was not an option for Jayne.

Jayne had continued to attend school throughout her pregnancy, regardless of the name calling and the derogatory remarks from the other students. After Jayne Marie's birth, Jayne took odd jobs such as selling door to door to meet the family's financial needs, but as soon as she was able Jayne enrolled at the University of Texas to continue her education. It was not always possible to get a sitter for her new baby, so rather than not attending class Jayne revealed, 'Many times I would have to take Jayne Marie and her diapers and nursing bottles to class with me.'[3]

Her courage should not be underestimated. Just getting ready for school would have been an enormous accomplishment, as she had to make up bottles and pack nappies (no disposable ones then), and it is more than likely Jayne would have endured sleepless nights and the stress of a screaming baby when she was little more than a child herself.

Jayne eventually took up a place at the University of California, Los Angeles (UCLA), but this time she left Jayne Marie in the care of Vera for the short period she studied there. Jayne missed her daughter so much that after returning home she vowed never to leave her behind again.

When the relationship with Paul Mansfield broke down and he returned to Dallas, Jayne did not let the responsibility of single parenthood destroy her dreams and ambitions or take away her future. She remained resolute, perhaps even more so, to become a movie star.

As Jayne's fame grew, Paul tried several times to publicly shame her, saying in 1956 that 'she is not a fit and proper person' to have custody of their 5-year-old daughter. Jayne responded by saying, 'Despite my stage career and a busy schedule, my little girl has always come first.'[4]

While Fox's publicity department tried desperately to shape Jayne's professional and personal image, she was intent on pulling against them. Instead of allowing them to present her to the public in the best possible way, Jayne garnered her own publicity drive. Her agent, Bill Shiffrin, also experienced Jayne's fierce self-belief and unshakable confidence when he attempted to advise her on her career choices.

Jayne was offered the part in a Cary Grant movie, *Kiss Them for Me*, a comedy farce that was light on laughs, with a poor script and a weak supporting role for Jayne. She was dazzled at the idea of working with Grant, whereas Shiffrin could see the writing was abysmal and that the part would do her no favours.

Ignoring her agent's advice, she took the role but, as Shiffrin had predicted, the movie was an unmitigated disaster and didn't cover its production costs. Jayne was to unfairly shoulder much of the blame as Fox stalled her career as a result.

On 6 November, having just returned from her European tour that Fox had hoped would douse the flames of romance, Mickey presented Jayne with a 10-carat diamond engagement ring, which she enthusiastically accepted. Jayne was not argumentative, and she did not like confrontation. She would rather walk away than fight, and so she paid lip service to the studio while doing the opposite of what she was told. She lived her life on her own terms and sometimes that cost her dearly.

The wedding took place in a blaze of publicity, on 13 January 1958, at the Wayfarer's Chapel in Palos Verdes, California, a beautiful stone and glass building, nestled on cliffs overlooking the Pacific Ocean. The bride wore pink lace, a tightly fitting dress with a mermaid hem that was most difficult to walk in. Jayne had invited Marilyn Monroe to the wedding, along with several other high-profile stars of the day whom she did not know, but Monroe did not attend.

By April, Jayne had returned to Europe, this time with Mickey and Jayne Marie, to make *The Sheriff of Fractured Jaw* for Fox but, as the studio had feared, while in London on 10 July, Jayne announced the news the studio had been dreading: she was expecting a baby in December.

Making personal appearances during her pregnancy up until the time the baby was born, Jayne loved being pregnant. She watched her weight, took care of how she looked, never drank during her pregnancies and positively bloomed, radiating good health. Jayne made pregnancy and motherhood look a breeze, as if it were the most natural thing in the world.

On 21 December 1958, Jayne went into labour. A week overdue, she made the short journey to St John's Hospital in Santa Monica. Jayne insisted on Mickey being at the birth, which was practically unheard of in 1958. A father's place was to pace the waiting room until a medical professional arrived to give him the news that his child had been born. The hospital compromised and allowed him to stay in the adjoining room, from where he could talk to Jayne and offer her encouragement while she was being prepped for delivery.

It wasn't an easy birth; the baby was large and the heart rate was dropping. The doctor fully expected that a Caesarean section would be necessary but Jayne summoned all her strength and at 5 a.m. gave birth naturally to a healthy son weighing 9lb 9½oz, who they named Miklos Jnr after his father. Both Jayne and Mickey were overjoyed with their new baby boy.

Jayne had made it known that she intended to have a large family, and stated, 'Women are much more radiant and happy when they are expecting. After this one arrives, we plan to have others.'[5]

This was not good news for her career and not something any studio would encourage or support in their glamour girls such as Jayne. Motherhood was at odds with being a bombshell. Studios would not renew contracts, sometimes paying the new mother off as they were not comfortable with a mother playing highly sexualised roles, considering it inappropriate.

Jayne knew this, but as she began her career already a mother she thought that it would not be a problem, and she kept to her word when on 1 August 1960, her third child, Zoltan Anthony Hargitay, came into the world. This time, instead of being overdue, Zoltan arrived a full month premature but beautiful and healthy. Once again Mickey and Jayne were delighted. During the pregnancy, she ate carefully to maintain her figure, adding vitamin supplements and not drinking.

Jayne had a strong compulsion towards pregnancy and motherhood. Birth rates had peaked in 1957[6] but with the 1960s and the availability of reliable birth control, and the feminist movement, some women began to opt for smaller families. There was a growing dissatisfaction among women who were looking for a more rewarding way of life. They railed against pregnancy and the responsibilities that were traditionally imposed upon the mother, who was expected to provide the bulk of the child's physical and emotional well-being.

Women frequently found giving birth a degrading and demeaning experience. In Eugenia Kaledin's book *American Mothers and More* she explores the life of mothers in the 1950s and identifies this common theme, quoting an extract from the *Ladies' Home Journal* of December 1958: 'Too many doctors, nurses, and hospitals seem to assume that because a woman is about to give birth to a child, she becomes a nitwit, an incompetent reduced to the status of a cow.'[7]

Through the ages, women have received conflicting information and signals regarding motherhood. The childless woman has received pity if her situation was perceived as out of her hands. The woman who chose to remain childless has been blasted as selfish and unwomanly. With feminism came the pressure to have it all. Betty Friedan, in the *Feminine Mystic*, instructs, 'The only way for a woman, as for a man, to find herself, to know herself as a person, is by creative work of her own. There is no other way.'[8]

Friedan tells the reader that she must be seeking fulfillment in a creative response to life. She must work, but 'any job is not the answer'. For the average woman this was simply unrealistic but Jayne, however, was a pioneer long before Betty began to convey her feminist ideals and instructions to generations of women.

Jayne was already turning responsibility into pleasure, being in control of her pregnancy and birth, choosing to uphold her bombshell values, protecting her sexuality and appearance while having the staff to do the mundane jobs. Jayne could take the pleasures from being a mother, the unconditional love of her young children as they basked in her reflected glory, and she was able to parade them as her own personal works of art. She had created these beautiful creatures.

At the same time, she could enjoy a career of attention, earning the money to deliver this ideal of motherhood, along with creative work that was central to her very being that Friedan suggests women must strive for.

However, things were not all sweet happiness and perfection in Jayne's world. Mickey had become Jayne's manager, gofer and daddy daycare, and as a result, their marriage came under pressure, collapsing under the weight of the strain.

Jayne needed excitement. She relished the euphoria of new love; being worshipped by her fans wasn't enough, and Mickey's devotion had become boring. Jayne, a moderate narcissist, knew she could turn Mickey on sexually and it was no longer a challenge, so she embarked on an affair. She wasn't looking for anyone else to physically ignite her flame, the whole quest for new love was so she was able to conquer them sexually. It was an exhilaration that gave her the power of feeling youthful, feminine and alive.

In May 1962, Jayne filed for divorce from Mickey on account of him not wanting to take the children to Italy, where Jayne was committed to making the film *Panic Button*. Mickey was hoping they could spend romantic time alone, but Jayne had other ideas; she wanted the children and her chihuahuas with her. With leverage applied successfully, Mickey agreed to take the children, so Jayne called off the divorce and the family headed out to Italy.

On 4 July, Twentieth Century Fox, who had been lending Jayne out to other studios rather than making their own films with her, decided not to exercise their option on her contract and, in effect, dropped her.

While they had been in Italy, Mickey had taken care of the children and the dogs, which allowed Jayne to begin an affair with Enrico Bomba, the production manager on the film. Mickey was devastated, but after much toing and froing, in October 1962, Mickey reluctantly agreed to a Mexican divorce (a quicker and easier process than a regular American divorce) so Jayne could marry Bomba. However, by December 1962, she had changed her mind and returned to Mickey.

As 1963 arrived, Jayne began filming *Promises! Promises!*, in which she had a nude scene that Mickey and others strongly advised her against, but she didn't listen. The antagonism in their marriage continued, and Jayne began another affair, this time with Nelson Sardelli, an Italian singer.

Jayne sought a Mexican divorce again and by now Mickey was used to Jayne's fickleness and was tired of the emotional upset, so he did not contest it. After it had been finalised, Jayne and Mickey reconciled again. They did not remarry and insisted that the Mexican divorce had been invalid.

On 23 January 1964, at the age of almost 31, Jayne gave birth to her fourth child, a baby girl weighing 8lb 9oz. The couple named their daughter Mariska Magdolna Hargitay, after Mickey's mother. Some people questioned the little girl's paternity due to both her physical appearance, which was similar to Sardelli, and the timeline of her birth. Regardless of Mariska's biological beginnings, Mickey was her father and they had a close, loving relationship.

Unfortunately, just a month after Mariska's birth, Jayne and Mickey were once again having relationship problems and it soon became apparent that their reconciliation, despite the recent birth of their daughter, was not destined to last.

DOING IT FOR THE PUFF

Jayne's career was not hampered by her bombshell image, her 'dumb blonde persona' or her turbulent love life, and despite earlier in her career feeling that 'being a mother was not an asset for a sex symbol'.[1] This hadn't held her back either. She had received the help of friend and Hollywood columnist May Mann, who deftly put to rest Jayne's fears with an article about her being a good mother and the close relationship she shared with her daughter Jayne Marie.

Far from destroying her bombshell image, with the power of positive publicity the article raised Jayne's credibility and endeared her to her fans and the general public.

It was Jayne's most intense, abiding love affair with what she termed 'Puffblicity', a method of promoting and publicity that kept her to the forefront of the industry and the public's awareness. This was a trade-off that was far more effective and long lasting than any sexual favour on a casting couch, an activity that Jayne expertly avoided by reminding the would-be wolves of Hollywood of both her marriage and motherhood status.

The quest for constant publicity provided a problem that Jayne could not figure out how to solve. Publicity had progressed Jayne's career and paradoxically stalled it, damaging her reputation as an actress even more than accepting poor scripts and making bad movies. Jayne kept the clippings for scrapbooks of newspaper and magazine articles she had appeared in.

Puffblicity was a triple reward for Jayne, who would receive a fee for her appearance at an event. She would get an advertising photoshoot, etc., as well as the goods she was advertising, such as washing machines, fridges, supermarket sweeps, etc. The ultimate bonus would be her picture in the papers and other media, all for just a few hours' work in a tight-fitting outfit, with a movie star smile.

Over time, she saturated the market with her brand, but she was unable to stop. The train was rolling at speed and she was afraid that if she got off, she wouldn't be able to catch it up and get back on again. Her biggest fear was fading out into oblivion, Jayne could not ease up, and instead of slowing down and enjoying what she had already built up, she accelerated to a frantic pace.

Jim Byron had told her at the beginning of her career that she would become a big star with the right kind of promotion and publicity, but over time more often than not the publicity Jayne worked opposed the goal she was attempting to achieve.

Towards the end of her life, Jayne had become more of a 'personality' than the respected actress she had aimed for. Few people can recall the movies Jayne appeared in, but everyone remembers her look from the lavish and abundant publicity photographs that have become part of her legacy.

It was as if Jayne knew that her time would be limited. She had told May Mann that 'she felt she couldn't waste a single minute for she was already going on twenty-three', frequently repeating over and over that 'it's now or never'.[2]

Jayne's skill in promoting goods began early. Before her first screen test for Warner Brothers in November 1954 (although Walter Emeson recalls it as being late 1955), Jayne visited Emeson's, which was a gown emporium in Studio City, Hollywood, that was popular with the glamorous and successful Hollywood actresses who were under contract with Fox, such as Alice Faye and Mary Healy.

Hand in hand with little Jayne Marie, she directly approached Walter Emeson in his shop and told him she was in Hollywood to become a big movie star, but that she had no clothes except those she was wearing that day, a man's white shirt and old blue jeans. She asked him if he could help her.

Emeson explained to her how his business functioned and that he was there to make money and unable to supply free clothing. Jayne continued to persuade Emeson that it would be to his advantage to help her. With the cunning use of charm, flattery and helplessness, she won Emeson over, and he agreed to give her clothing on credit when she promised to pay him with her first pay cheque if she got the contract.

The designer and proprietor must have believed in Jayne as much as she believed in herself. He organised the credit forms for her, on which she signed herself as 'Mrs Paul Mansfield', and then he took her measurements. Jayne's dimensions fluctuated, but on this day they were 40-23-37.

Emeson recalled:

> I chose a sexy, fitted black jersey with a high turtle neck collar and long sleeves with the whole back bare. Otherwise, it had a fully covered effect. She was delighted. Then she said, 'But what can I do for shoes and gloves and a bag? I honestly don't have anything except what I wore in here.'[3]

The slightly perplexed Emeson decided to go the whole way, and fitted her out, head to toe for the then substantial cost of $75 (more than $700 in real terms today). Jayne got the contract with Warner Brothers and was as good as her word, paying her debt the same day she collected her cheque.

This time, however, when the money changed hands, she informed him that she now needed an entire wardrobe. After the sweet talk and promises, Emeson couldn't say no and they began a friendship and business relationship that lasted until the end of Jayne's life.

Although Jayne had a press agent and advisors with whom she was able to generate ideas for quirky, exciting puff, the majority of her publicity she created herself. She had her own personal strategy; it wasn't as haphazard as it sometimes appeared. Puffblicity was the core of who she was. Jayne coordinated events and used every possible situation to her advantage.

When Jayne and Mickey returned from their honeymoon, they moved into their palatial new home and she announced they were sleeping on the floor in sleeping bags. Jayne explained that she and Mickey were working on their act for Las Vegas and that she would soon be filming for Fox. Photos were run in the press of the family sleeping on the floor. In no time at all, the police of Laguna Beach had a whip round and raised funds to buy Jayne, who was their favourite pin-up, a new bed, sending the money directly to her to make the purchase. Of course, she was thrilled and issued the statement:

> What marvellous men … they are really noble to buy me a bed so another man can sleep in it with me. Few men would be so generous. That proves they really love me. They care for my comfort.[4]

Together, she and Mickey were a dream team. The press loved it when they often wore matching outfits, such as leopard shorts for Mickey with a leopard bikini for Jayne, which ensured scoring valuable newspaper space and media attention. They also developed a choreographed act intended to capture attention in public places, where Mickey would lift Jayne above the crowds.

At the premiere of the Warner Bros aviation action film *The Spirit of St Louis* on 11 April 1957, Jayne wore the same dress that received so much attention for Marilyn Monroe at the 1953 Photoplay Magazine Awards. The gold lamé sunburst gown, designed by William Travilla, had had its first outing in *Gentlemen Prefer Blondes*, but due to the nature of the design of the dress it was thought to be too revealing for a full frontal shot and was therefore only shown briefly from the back during a dance scene.

Jayne looked stunning as she and Mickey went into their routine, grabbing the headline the following day 'Plane Jayne puts 'em in spin at movie'.

Jayne stole the show as she was hoisted in the air and held aloft by Mickey to sign autographs, and she explained to the journalists that she and Mickey had practised the pose at home because it resembled an aeroplane in flight. 'And isn't this what this picture is all about?' she asked.[5]

The premiere attracted a host of stars, the biggest gathering in recent memory, but all the attention was on Jayne. Every photographer and film camera was aimed directly at her, and she was happy to pose in any way suggested, saying, 'I guess I'm just a girl who can't say no – to photographers.'[6]

The way Jayne saw it, and as she expressed in her book *Jayne Mansfield's Wild, Wild World*, 'I have always felt that publicity is as necessary to most careers as a ball to a tennis game … I have dedicated much time to publicity. It is the golden gimmick.'[7]

Although their paths must have crossed on numerous occasions, there is only one time that Jayne and Marilyn were photographed together at an event. It was during a benefit party for the Actors Studio following the premiere of *The Rose Tattoo* on 2 December 1955 at the Astor Hotel, in New York.

Jayne approached the table at which Marilyn was seated. The photos show an awkward moment and a churlish Marilyn, who failed to acknowledge Jayne. Unperturbed, Jayne took the opportunity to photobomb Marilyn. The pictures show Marilyn giving Jayne the cold shoulder. She did not show grace towards Jayne, but then this was her rival, whose name was connected continuously with Marilyn's in the press.

On top of that, Jayne was the threat Fox used when they wanted Marilyn to do as she was told. The timing was also relevant. Marilyn was at the peak of her career but was also struggling with her personal goals and professional life. Jayne was less complicated and seven years younger than Marilyn.

On 17 August 1955, Jayne had a photoshoot with Milton Greene, who by now was very much Marilyn's photographer. In the photographs, Jayne looks uncomfortable at times, although they are beautiful. It seemed that Jayne did not have the same rapport with Greene that Marilyn did.

Jayne pulled a similar publicity stunt in 1957 when the Italian bombshell Sophia Loren arrived in Hollywood in a blaze of her own publicity. Fox had purchased the rights to distribute Sophia's latest film, *The Boy on a Dolphin*. A party at Romanoff's favourite restaurant in Beverly Hills was organised to celebrate the occasion. According to Jayne, she didn't want to attend but the publicity department insisted she should go.

The photos taken that night have become iconic for two reasons, one of which was the dress that Jayne wore, which features spaghetti straps and a neckline that was cut so low that when she moved she was in constant danger of exposing her nipples. The second reason was Sophia's side eye glance at Jayne's cleavage; Loren was shocked and slightly horrified at the possibility of Jayne's breasts spilling out on to the table.

Although Sophia showed maximum grace and courage under the circumstances, she does not like to be associated with the memory and refuses to autograph the picture when fans approach her with it even today.

Usually, Jayne would enjoy such events and stay a couple of hours, but that night she didn't hang around once the deed was done, and although she fulfilled the publicity remit, the only real winners that night were the men in the Fox publicity department.

Jayne's promoting knew no limits and she would rarely refuse a request. She would be paid to be seen in restaurants, hotels and resorts while enjoying all the facilities at the expense of the venue. She would enjoy regular complimentary visits to the beauty parlour; it was a lucrative exchange.

However, Jayne's relentless pursuit of publicity almost cost her the life of her son, Zoltan, who on Saturday 26 May 1966 was celebrating his sixth birthday at a party being hosted by Jungleland, Thousand Oaks, California.

During the publicity photoshoot for the park and while posing with his mother in the lion compound, Zoltan was attacked and mauled by one of the lions. A freelance photographer watched the scene unfold, telling the *Ohio News Journal* that Jayne had been moved away from the larger lion, who was looking edgy, so the publicists moved her over to the female. As they were about to take the photo, the photographer said, 'It was yelled the male lion had jumped the boy.'[8]

Zoltan sustained severe head injuries and underwent surgery at Conejo Valley Community hospital. The hospital had to sedate Jayne, who was distressed and in shock. Her son had a compound skull fracture and broken ribs. He was initially given a fifty-fifty chance of survival, but he did pull through despite setbacks along the way such as meningitis. He eventually made a good recovery under the circumstances and was home by Christmas 1966, which became another photo opportunity and publicity event.

Jayne had always swept Mickey along with her; he was used to the publicity stunts and in many ways it suited him as he wasn't able to offer much financially. What Mickey did excel at, and was able to do, was anything Jayne required of him, including hands-on construction work at the Pink Palace while Jayne promoted the contents of the interior. Together they were a formidable team, but things were changing and, as the couple moved into the new decade of the 1960s, Jayne was finding life with Mickey dull and uninspiring, stifling her creativity.

By Christmas 1962, Jayne was relying more and more on publicity to bring in an income. Film offers were dwindling and her previous work was failing at the box office.

A news journalist, Jim Bishop, said of Jayne's obsession with publicity, 'Her massive vanity can be fed only by headlines and a name in lights … Her maternal instinct requires that she put more time in as a mother and wife. The two are not compatible.'[9]

When the media, who had always been her friend, began to turn on her, Jayne was confused. She told May Mann:

> I didn't quite know what to do, I hadn't done anything differently than I had in the beginning … I could feel it, and I read it. Everyone began saying I'd overdone my publicity. But if I stopped – I'd be dead![10]

What the media had failed to acknowledge was that Jayne's career was not accidental like Marilyn's, who was 'discovered' while working in a factory. Jayne set out on a path of study. She made the phone calls without support or guidance from anyone in the business, and she knocked on the doors with a child for whom she was singularly responsible.

After her daughter Mariska was born in 1964, Jayne and Mickey accepted an offer to tour with the stage plays *Bus Stop* and *Gentlemen Prefer Blondes*. The director was a 28-year-old Italian named Matt Cimber, an aggressively ambitious young man whom Jayne initially found quite unpleasant. Within forty-eight hours, her opinion had changed, and so had Mickey's world.

'A WOMAN SHOULD BE PINK AND CUDDLY FOR A MAN'

A new baby was not enough to keep Jayne at home. Less than a month after Mariska's birth, the new mother was desperate to get out and be seen at nightclubs and events, possibly to prove she was still attractive and could command male attention – and she was also drinking heavily.

Having had three babies in less than five years, and despite continually professing her desire to be pregnant and reproduce, the biology of the situation was heavy going. Pregnancy and childbirth had taken a physical, emotional toll, and Jayne was not slowing down. With a frantic fear of work drying up, she was eager to be seen and made herself available for work.

Mickey begged her to slow the pace down and to be choosier with scripts and job offers, but Jayne wouldn't listen to him and had accepted a contract to return to the stage.

The director Matt Cimber, whose real name was Thomas Vitale Ottaviano, had been unemployed until the opportunity to work with Jayne had presented itself. He had previous experience with moderately successful productions off Broadway. He also had the gift of the gab. Jayne was a high-profile movie star and personality who brought with her an abundance of publicity, and it would be a valuable opportunity for any young director who wanted to move their career up a gear.

Before leaving for Italy to film the movie *Primitive Love* (another disaster at the box office), Jayne and Mickey had a meeting with their new director. Mickey requested the role of the cowboy Bo, who falls in love with Jayne's character, Cherie. However, the position had already been cast, but Cimber managed to convince him to accept the part of the bus driver in the play.

On returning from Italy with Mickey, the children and her chihuahua dogs, Jayne was not only two days late for rehearsals, she was also completely unprepared, having not finished reading the script. The other actors thought she was unprofessional until she began to read, whereupon they were stunned; she was the perfect Cherie. Jayne had a natural aptitude for acting when the script was right.

Bus Stop opened at the Yonkers Playhouse on 26 May 1964 to positive reviews. During rehearsals, Jayne had begun to take more than a professional interest in her young director. Jayne, who was always in love with love, fell head over heels for Matt.

The differences between Cimber and Hargitay could not have been greater, and the gulf between Jayne and Mickey was becoming too wide to bridge. It appeared as though Matt had anticipated the split and colluded in the breakdown of the Hargitays' marriage. It had not taken him long to evaluate the circumstances and determine Jayne's weaknesses and how they could benefit him.

Jayne had confided in Matt that she wanted to have fun, and that Mickey was holding her back. She told him that after their successful performance in *Bus Stop* Mickey had wanted to go back to their hotel and relax and get an early night as they both had work again the next day. Jayne, however, wanted to go out and celebrate, to drink and party with members of the cast. Instead of helping her to make sense of Mickey's suggestion, which was entirely reasonable under the circumstances, Cimber allegedly sided with Jayne and encouraged her to do as she pleased.

Jayne was looking for an adrenaline rush; Mickey was offering slippers and a night in with the children. Jayne confided in her friend May Mann, 'I can't stay home every night and eat and get fat and blow my career.' She said, 'Mickey today is not the same man I married. He doesn't want to share my life of pleasure. He expects me to work and stay home or sit in a hotel room and watch TV.'[1]

The problem had arisen because Jayne wasn't what she was selling. That year she had given an interview to a French journalist, who asked her about her image and why she put on an act of not being intelligent, She answered, 'Part of being a glamour girl is being in a way rather naïve ... especially in the eyes of men.'[2] She added that when she began her career, the type of woman she portrayed was 'someone who is in very much need of looking after'.[3]

Jayne had used the classic 1950s stereotypical female and exaggerated traits such as innocence and sexual submissiveness. In a male-dominated culture, she was a caricature of the female role. In the era of post-war prosperity, Jayne appeared to be following the social expectations above and beyond what was required, and what's more, loving every minute of her role as the pink fluffy female available to satisfy every whim of the male in her life.

It was a time when women were expected to step back from the workplace after the end of the war and continue where they had left off, working in the home for the good of their husband and family. In contrast, men who returned from war duties were able to step back into their traditional role of breadwinner and patriarch.

In the *Feminine Mystique*, Betty Friedan talks about how women were presented in the fast-growing popular women's magazines, in particular looking at an edition of *McCall's* (early July 1960) and observing:

> The image of woman that emerges from this big, pretty magazine is young and frivolous, almost childlike; fluffy and feminine; passive; gaily content in a world of bedroom and kitchen, sex, babies and home. The magazine surely does not leave out sex; the only passion, the only pursuit, the only goal a woman is permitted is the pursuit of a man. It is crammed full of food, clothing, cosmetics, furniture, and the physical bodies of young women, but where is the world of thought and ideas, the life of the mind and spirit? In the magazine image, women do no work except housework and work to keep their bodies beautiful and to get and keep a man.[4]

With regular appearances in magazines, Jayne was an exponent of this attitude. In an interview with Robert Robinson in 1960 she was asked to define sex appeal. Jayne responded, 'Sex appeal is a wonderful warm womanly healthy feeling ... To me it's cleanliness and youth and an effervescent desire to enjoy life ... it's sort of the vibrancy you find in a young kitten.'[5]

Jayne wanted to be representative of what was then perceived as the perfect woman. She wasn't fighting to escape the stereotype, and there was no backlash against it; rather she appeared to be cleaving to it and cementing it in white middle-class American culture, while in private she lived a considerably different life. Caught up in a constant state of contradictory flux, when she was asked about her tumultuous life she said, 'Some people are born with a cyclone going on – I'm sure I was because life has always been like that.'[6]

Jayne was selling this ultra-feminine woman, who was subservient to the strong authoritative man; it simply wasn't who she was. As much as

Jayne exuded female perfection, Mickey, on the other hand, who was to all intents and purpose the epitome of maleness, had wholly reversed the gender roles with his wife. He would tend to the domestic needs of the family, following Jayne and doing as he was told.

Taking responsibility for both of their lives, she controlled the family, made all the decisions and earned the lion's share of the family income. The vast majority of Mickey's income was brought about by Jayne, in that she gave him roles in her films and her Vegas nightclub act. Mickey followed her with puppy dog unconditional love, always desperate to please her. Possibly because of this, Jayne eventually came to see Mickey as weak and ineffectual.

In diametric opposition to Hargitay, Matt Cimber offered Jayne the strength and capability she craved, believing he would carry her burdens and responsibilities while also turning her career around. It seems as though Cimber played beautifully into her ego; he read her personality, telling her how intelligent she was. With Jayne's often-talked-about IQ of 160, Cimber came in with his own IQ of 165. In a newspaper report, Jayne said on the subject of their IQs, 'The men always like to have the upper hand in this respect.'[7]

Cimber had observed that Jayne was a strong dominant woman who was tired of her own strength. Telling her she was wasted professionally and that he was the man who could make her into the serious actress she had desired to be, he talked her into believing he had all the answers and the ability to take her to the level she longed to reach. Jayne thought Matt was a gifted director, a talented intellectual.

Where dullness had set in with Mickey and contempt had grown, Matt Cimber was offering a new and exciting dynamic that she could be part of. With Matt, she thought he understood her but, most crucially of all, he made her laugh, and yet, much of the jokes and the laughter were on her or on Mickey.

It could be questioned if Matt Cimber was using humour to humiliate and disparage. Jayne was used to her sexuality, appearance and dumb blonde persona being an integral part of the joke for many comedians that she worked with. They loved her for her timing and the way she would feed them the material they needed, and which they delivered with a smug superiority that reinforced the stupidity and inferiority of women while ensuring the intelligence of men.

As their relationship developed swiftly, Jayne once again told Mickey she was in love with someone else and was ending her relationship with him. The awkwardness of the situation cannot be overstated. On top of the apparent hurt that Mickey felt, Cimber ridiculed him and the taunts often flared up into physical pushing and shoving, to the point that Mickey broke Matt's arm during one altercation. Meanwhile, Jayne thrived on the drama of having two men fighting over her.

Matt had promised Jayne the world; he confidently predicted that he would be able to progress her career to the heights of stardom beyond what she had briefly attained in 1956 and 1957. Jayne likened their relationship to that of Sophia Loren and Carlo Ponti or Marilyn Monroe and Arthur Miller, even though neither alliance produced real box-office success.

Matt Cimber did not have the experience or talent of either Miller or Ponti. Instead of relaunching Jayne's career as a serious actress, all he could achieve was to book her a succession of chat shows and dingy nightclub performances, with a smattering of mediocre stage plays and independent films including *Single Room Furnished*, which was directed by Matt but was not released until after Jayne's death in 1968.

The film did not make a major impact, although Jayne gave a sterling performance by acting three different parts, which eerily ended with Jayne's final character putting her make-up on in front of the mirror, which suddenly cracked and the sound of a car crash in the distance could be heard.

When it was eventually shown, the *Daily News* reported, 'It is Jayne's picture from start to finish. Her first dramatic part … She documents that she could toy with a serious role.'[8]

One thing that did grow out of proportion during her time with Matt was her entourage of Matt's friends and family, which included Marty Levine, Matt's assistant, while her own friends were allegedly kept at arm's length.

Ray Strait, Jayne's press secretary, recalled in his book *The Tragic Secret Life of Jayne Mansfield* that Jayne, for all practical purposes was Matt's prisoner. Even Minda Guild, her best friend, could not reach her by phone, 'either Matt or Marty interceded'.[9]

Jayne, who had always had tight control on her own purse, was no longer handling her own money. She was also mixing pills with alcohol. When Strait asked Jayne what was going on, she told him the new people in her life were so much fun.

On stage, she was ever the professional, but one evening after a show, according to Strait, she had been drinking Black Russians and someone at her table asked her, 'Jayne don't you think you should go easy? People are watching.' Jayne retorted, 'Fuck them! They pay $3.50 minimum to Jayne Mansfield in there,' she motioned towards the theatre. 'They pay to see Jayne Mansfield, and they get Jayne Mansfield. In here they pay me nothing, so fuck them!'[10]

Her relationship with Matt was volatile and passionate. Both Strait and her friend and Hollywood columnist May Mann reported seeing bruising on Jayne, which she blamed Matt for, going further by telling May that she 'loved it'.[11] Matt apparently told Strait that Jayne would get drunk and beat herself on the arms and legs.

In a private ceremony on 24 September 1964, Jayne married Matt in Mulegé, which is in the Mexico state of Baja California Sur, but by the next morning the honeymoon was over. Strait saw Jayne sitting by the pool and when he approached she asked him, 'Will you tell me something? Tell me why I married Matt?'

Strait replied, 'If you don't know, Jaynie, you've made a big mistake.'

Her sad response was, 'Then I've made a big mistake.'[12]

On returning to New York, Matt's family had prepared a party, Jayne saw all the food and whispered to Strait, 'I hope I'm not paying the tab for all these peasants. I didn't invite them.'[13]

Jayne was uncharacteristically reticent about her marriage, not announcing it officially until 30 September at the Chateau Henri IV, when she told the waiting press, 'We were married last Thursday at a small town in Baja California, in Mexico. I met him when he directed me in *Bus Stop*. He is one of the most brilliant directors in the world.'

When asked about being a sex goddess, she replied, 'I think being a sex goddess is banal. In comparison to being happy it is nothing.'[14]

Jayne's income was decreasing, but money was still being spent. The fights continued, and so did the drinking and pill taking until Jayne found out she was expecting Matt's child. The announcement was made on 11 March 1965, and she told the press the baby was due in September. As with her other pregnancies, Jayne took control of her drinking, and for a short while settled down until their son, Antonio 'Tony' Raphael Ottaviano, was born shortly after 9 a.m. on 18 October in Los Angeles, weighing in at 9lb.

Amidst the joy of childbirth, the flowers and the congratulations, Jayne was about to experience the worst time of her life.

33

NOT QUITE SO DIVOON

Within less than a month of Tony's birth, Jayne was in rehearsals for the stage production of *The Rabbit Habit*, which opened on 1 December 1964. The play was a disaster and folded after just five nights. Jayne had also realised her marriage was a disaster too, telling Ray, 'I don't know what to do. I am the most miserable person in the world. I want out, but I know Matt will never give up the baby without a fight. And I won't ever give him up.'[1]

With Matt's family surrounding her at home and at work, she felt as though she was a prisoner being spied on and, as 1966 began, her marriage was teetering on the edge. She opened her last major nightclub revue, *French Dressing*, on 24 January, in the Latin Quarter, New York. Jayne was overwhelmed by playing to a full house, with rave reviews after the show.

Jayne worked solidly if not always successfully throughout 1966, and by July she had decided being with Matt was no longer viable and she could see no alternative but to separate and seek a divorce. Although initially, she intended to retain Matt as her business manager, she felt let down and disappointed that his promises for her career had come to nothing.

Tony became a bone of contention between his parents and Matt accused Jayne of being possessive of their son. It became apparent that a custody battle was taking place, Cimber attempting to wrestle control from Jayne by taking Tony from her. He used what he considered her lack of parenting skills and her indecent lifestyle as leverage in the battle.

During an interview with the author Martha Saxton, Matt said of Jayne, 'What she wanted for her kids was OK, but I didn't want my son travelling all over the world.'[2]

He continued, saying he was appalled and disgusted with the standard of education that Jayne's children had received. Cimber also told Saxton that Jayne and Mickey had no books in the house, and criticised the fact that their children never stayed in the same school for more than a few months.

It is not difficult to imagine or understand the level of betrayal and hurt Jayne no doubt felt at Cimber's judgemental attack on her parenting skills, as well as the fear his threat to take custody of Tony must have had on her. Almost immediately after announcing the separation, Jayne had filed for divorce on the grounds of 'extreme cruelty and grievous mental suffering'.[3]

In an interview for a television documentary several years after Jayne's death, Matt concludes, 'The only mistake in our relationship was that we ever got married.' On the question of Jayne being a sex symbol, he adds disparagingly:

> Everybody says, 'Boy she must be really a hot number.' I didn't think so. I know more secretaries who are, you know not to negate what she had as a sex symbol you know when you say sex symbol what does that mean? Jayne was never more to me than a pin-up.[4]

Where Jayne had always had strict control, she had handed over her life to Matt Cimber, including her business affairs, but it simply didn't work out as she had envisaged. For Matt, who was teetotal, Jayne's excessive drinking was too much and she was impossible to help as she was in denial. By his own admission, Cimber felt he did not have enough maturity to deal with the situation.

Jayne had accepted a job performing in Venezuela and when she returned Matt decided to take his son on the grounds of Jayne's excessive drinking and what he considered her general bad behaviour. He conveniently forgot that when he met her he encouraged her to ignore Mickey and go out partying and drinking with him, regardless of the effect it had on the life of Mickey and the children.

This chaotic set of circumstances that Jayne found herself in brought Sam Brody into her life and, without realising it, she sealed her own fate. Brody was a successful attorney with a highly respected legal practice and several high-profile and celebrity clients.

Prepared for a bitter battle, Jayne engaged the services of Brody as her attorney. On 23 September 1966, the press reported that Jayne arrived at court 'resplendent in white coat, white mini skirt and white boots'.[5] Brody, acting for Jayne, told the judge that Matt Cimber was using the couple's son as a 'pawn or wedge to obtain a money settlement'.

Brody claimed Jayne had supported Cimber and his family, bought him clothes and paid his medical bills. He also threatened to disclose further information about Jayne's third husband that he felt was 'quite shocking and disgusting and not proper to relate at this time'.[6]

According to Ray Strait in his biography on Jayne, Sam was preparing trumped up charges against Matt accusing him of being a homosexual and behaving improperly towards Jayne's sons, Miklos and Zoltan. However, on arrival at the second hearing on 29 September, when the judge looked at the paperwork, he gave Sam the option of withdrawing the statement and he agreed.

By October Brody had achieved what he had set out to do and Jayne won a court order for immediate temporary custody of Tony.

By now, Jayne and Brody's relationship had already moved from lawyer–client to something much more personal; Brody had fallen obsessively in love with Jayne. As an attorney he had a proven track record, with a highly reputable practice, with highly tuned skills, academic excellence and the ability to thrive under pressure, but this talent and expertise came at a price. Brody's price was expensive, but instead of charging Jayne they began a physical relationship.

He became involved in all of her affairs, both business and private. To begin with, Jayne encouraged his interest and accepted the gifts he lavished on her, such as soft toys and jewellery, despite the fact he was married with two children, and that his 37-year-old wife Beverly had multiple sclerosis and was in a wheelchair.

Brody, who had been married to his wife for ten years, had been having marital problems long before he met Jayne, and in July 1966 he and Beverly had separated and she was suing him for alimony. She claimed that her husband had committed adultery with forty women throughout their married life, but when Sam and Jayne became a newsworthy item, his wife amended her paperwork to cite only Jayne Mansfield as co-respondent.

Both Jayne's divorce from Matt and Brody's divorce from his wife were messy by any standards, but as 1966 came to a close, Jayne, Sam, Miklos and Mariska attended a New Year's Eve party. The new family are seen in a scarce home movie[7] that shows Jayne beautiful in a powder blue outfit. The powerful lights on the old-fashioned camera flood the room and make the children squint. Kissing Miklos, Jayne offers him bites of food. She then turns to kiss Brody and also pops food into his mouth.

Granting chaste kisses to other men in the room, she sits on laps and poses for pictures.

Despite the turmoil in her life, Jayne continued to work, as by now it had become apparent that Sam had been spending money he could ill afford and had mounting debts. Jayne volunteered to work to pay his debts as well as her everyday living expenses and supporting her family.

Soon the newspapers were buzzing with the news that Jayne Mansfield wanted to marry her lawyer. It was reported by the *Miami News* on 20 January 1967 that Jayne had told the dress designer Lily Pearlman that once their divorces were final, she and Sam Brody were planning to get married.

It was almost inconceivable that Jayne could have been contemplating another marriage when her divorce was intensifying with malicious accusations and threats of litigation on all sides. Jayne had left for a tour of nightclubs in England with Sam and baby Tony on 24 March, when four days later it was reported that she was suing Matt Cimber, claiming that he had struck her and bit her and that Cimber had assaulted her four times in the previous April. Using his 'fists and mouth' she said she was unable to work after Cimber allegedly 'kicked and stomped' and hit her 'about the face and body in a fit of rage'.[8]

The irony of Jayne suing Cimber for violent behaviour towards her is that her relationship with Sam was soon to become increasingly vicious and physically abusive.

When looked at on the surface, it seems Jayne found herself in an intolerable situation of repeated physical abuse; a victim of violence; a cycle she appeared to be trapped in. However, different people that were close to her at this time have indicated it was more consensual and reciprocal than it first seems to be.

Ray Strait claims that Jayne and Matt indulged in constant battles. When they were touring on *Bus Stop*, upon returning to their motel room in the evening, a fight would almost always ensue. It would begin with Jayne breaking bottlenecks and thrusting them towards Matt until the fight reached a peak that was followed by noisy and passionate lovemaking – so loud it could be heard by Strait in the adjoining room. The outcome of witnessing their explosive fights caused Strait to wonder if one would kill the other before any marriage could take place.

May Mann is more explicit when she tells of first meeting Matt. Taking a car ride with the couple, accompanied by Mann's own boyfriend, she noticed severe bruising on Jayne's neck, cheek, arms and legs. She questioned Jayne on how she got the bruises. In front of Matt, Jayne glibly replied, 'Oh, Matt beats me. But I love it.'[9] Matt did not say a word and did not appear to make an effort to deny or confirm Jayne's comment.

The violence appeared to escalate in her relationship with Sam Brody. Again, Mann reports that Jayne's maid, Linda, told her that Brody and Jayne had constant fights. Sam was insanely jealous, and Jayne goaded him to the point that he would hit her, split her lip, and cause all kinds of physical injury.

In shock after inflicting such a beating, he would be deeply apologetic and beg for forgiveness, repeating over again, 'What have I done?' and, 'Not again! Why, Jayne? Why do you make me do this to you? I love you!'[10]

Even when Zoltan sustained his injuries after being mauled by a lion, Jayne and Sam fought in the hospital room that had been provided for Jayne to enable her to stay close to her son while he was in a critical condition. Jayne allegedly left the door open and walked around naked in the room while talking to other men on the telephone. In an exasperated fit of jealous rage, Sam snatched the phone from her hand, pulled the cord out of the socket and smashed the phone against the wall.

In retaliation, Jayne threw a pitcher of water at Sam, who responded by 'slapping and bouncing Jayne off the walls and doors'. In the mayhem, Jayne ran down the hospital corridors screaming, 'Please help me. Somebody lock me up away from him. He's trying to kill me.'[11] The fights had also been fuelled by drink and pills and the hospital took action, banning both of them from the premises.

Jayne was engaging in some seriously self-destructive behaviour, and there is photographic evidence of the bruising she sustained, as well as many independent witnesses. On 7 May 1967, reports of her bruises hit the newspapers, which were asking questions such as, 'What caused the blemishes on Miss Mansfield's lily-white epidermis?' and revealing that 'She had a public slugging match with her constant companion, 39-year-old Los Angeles attorney Sam Brody.'[12]

By 1967, Jayne was involved in a cycle of adrenaline rushes that were no longer fed by success in her career, but now provided by booze, pills, fights and sex. It is tricky to try and determine if Jayne was engaging in consensual harmful sexual behaviour, but there are indications that this may be the case.

In 2016, Dr Holly Richmond, a certified sex therapist, was interviewed for an article in *Rebook* magazine on the subject of rough sex, and she said:

> Often, women who like to be dominated by men, and who prefer something that is considered culturally taboo, are in positions of power and/or have a lot of responsibility in their lives.[13]

As uncomfortable as it may be to contemplate, with Jayne's comment to May Mann about being beaten and loving it, and Ray Strait's observation of her regular physical fights with Matt Cimber followed by wild sex, it is possible that the level of excitement she needed to exist was getting more difficult to achieve.

While Brody was physically dominant over Jayne, she reciprocated, and although he had superior communication skills cultivated throughout his career, Jayne would verbally humiliate him at every opportunity. Brody was an attractive man, with grey-blue eyes, and a square masculine jaw. He was in good physical shape, but his Achilles heel was that he was short. Jayne knew just how to make the most of this; she went from wearing high heels to flat shoes and in stage whispers to friends she told them the reason for the change was because 'the little man doesn't want me to tower over him'.[14]

The devil was in the detail, and things were about to get much worse.

THIRTY-FOUR

Where 1966 had been a messy mix of relationship troubles and transitions, 1967 was destined to be the year of destruction. Within less than seven months, Jayne would be dead, and her last publicity drive was the one that took her life and ended in carnage and devastation for many people.

The changes brought about during the 1960s were not easy for a bombshell to acclimatise to, as their skill set was becoming redundant. Where they were proficient in the subtle art of manipulation, women no longer had to rely on the techniques of this cunning form of deception. They were beginning to find their voice and the courage to ask outright for what they wanted, ready to admit dissatisfaction with the lack of equality in their lives.

The tease of the bombshell was no longer necessary. With the advent of the birth control pill, women did not have to live with the fear of an unwanted pregnancy any more. This transformed their sexual outlook, giving them a more equal footing with men as sexual expectations were challenged.

Feminism was gradually sweeping America, and the beauty contests that had been so crucial in progressing Jayne's career were now being criticised by a growing number of women. Just over a year after Jayne's death, on 7 September 1968, a group of women's rights activists protested in front of the Atlantic City Convention Centre where the Miss America Pageant was taking place. The women's banners declared 'If you want meat go to the butcher' and 'Welcome to the Miss America Cattle Contest'.[1] Demanding an end to the objectification of women, this small but significant protest was indicative of the cultural shift that was gradually happening during the decade and one that would take on speed throughout the 1970s to the present day, shaping not only America but many other countries, too.

Jayne was a symbol of curvaceous overabundance, the post-Second World War woman whom the men had been fighting for, with the promise of coming home to the ultimate female: soft, comfortable and submissive. It was a woman who was accommodating while offering up no intellectual challenge, allowing the theory of male superiority to remain intact and incontrovertible.

At the beginning of 1967, despite these changes in the air, an American war was still raging in Vietnam and on 14 February, with a small entourage including Sam Brody, Jayne arrived for a three-day tour of the military bases. She looked every inch the bombshell in a silver miniskirt, brown sweater and black boots and she was as relevant and necessary in this war zone as she had been during her heyday of the 1950s.

The trip was a great success for both Jayne and the morale of the soldiers she entertained. The men adored her, and at one camp she was presented with a unique gift, a pair of steel combat helmets, painted pink and fastened with belts and straps. They were decorated with the emblem of the unit. Jayne couldn't stop laughing; the men had made her a 'combat bra', and she was delighted. When the roar of the crowds died down she told them, 'I certainly want to thank you, boys, for thinking of me. You can be sure I'll never forget you.'[2]

Visiting a paratrooper hospital had a profound effect on Jayne and she relayed her experience in a filmed interview with a journalist on her return to San Francisco. Speaking in a natural voice, with minimal make-up and dressed conservatively in a blouse and trousers, Jayne gave an impassioned plea for the people to understand what was going on in Vietnam.

She spoke eloquently about the senselessness of war and the reality of the situation, becoming emotional when she told the interviewer about a 25-year-old man who had lost his leg. Struggling for the right words Jayne showed compassion, empathy and love. It was a rare glimpse of the woman behind the bombshell myths that had given her a platform but had also hindered her progress as a person.

During the tour, photos and film captured at the time show Sam Brody getting closer to Jayne, not just in respect of their relationship but also in his physical proximity to her. Never further than inches away, his presence was becoming ever more dominating and claustrophobic.

On returning from Vietnam, Jayne continued to hit the headlines, but one story in particular brought a swift reaction from the normally publicity-ravenous Jayne. Back in October 1966, while attending the San Francisco Film Festival, Jayne had a long itinerary of publicity engagements, one of which included a trip to the home of Anton LaVey, the self-styled High Priest of San Francisco's First Church of Satan, which he had established on 30 April that year.

Jayne later told her friend May Mann that she had gone along with the visit because 'it was for laughs', and of course she hoped it would be great publicity. However, there was a certain amount of chemistry between Jayne and LaVey, which triggered Sam's pathological jealousy. During the visit, Sam defied LaVey's instructions by lighting some sacred candles that he was told not to touch, while also mocking the beliefs of his host. This caused LaVey to go into a spasm of anger, telling Sam, 'You are cursed by the devil. You will be killed within a year!' Sam laughed and, according to Jayne, he found it most amusing.[3]

LaVey was precise as to the cause of death Sam would suffer; he predicted several car accidents, with the last crash wiping out Sam Brody and anyone who might be with him. LaVey warned Jayne that the only way she could escape the curse was to rid herself of Sam Brody as quickly as possible.

When LaVey gave an interview to a newspaper, telling a reporter that Jayne had become a member of his First Satanic Church and held the title of High Priestess, she was contacted for a comment. Swift to deny the story, she responded by telling the journalist who had telephoned her, 'Anton is a good friend of mine and we have had some fascinating discussions concerning his religion ... But I am not on the verge of converting and can't understand why Anton said I was. I am a staunch Catholic, and I will always be.'[4]

Desperate to escape her worries, she and Sam were enthusiastic to begin a two-month tour of England. Jayne sought permission from the court to take baby Tony with her, which was granted, but the other children were to remain at home due to schooling commitments. She arrived in Britain on 24 March with baby Tony cuddled in her arms, to a warm welcome from the public and the press.

It was a grand start, but within less than two weeks, she was fired from her seven-week contract. The promoter who had engaged her, Don Arden of Contemporary Records, was arguing with Sam, and when Jayne had previously visited England she had an excellent reputation for being reliable, but now she was arriving late, forgetting to bring her stage costumes to events and was covered in unsightly bruises courtesy of fighting with Sam.

When the news was released that Jayne was available for work, she was able to secure new contracts for the length of her stay, but the controversy continued. She was booked to perform in Ireland, at the Mount Brandon Hotel in Tralee on 23 April, which was a Sunday. Jayne was in a predominantly Catholic country, and the Catholic Church was outraged that she would not only be working on a Sunday, which was a holy day of rest, but that her act was considered obscene.

Furthermore, she was openly travelling with a man to whom she wasn't married, which was a scandal and unacceptable to the Catholic Church. The Church called for the public to boycott Jayne's performances, which resulted in the hotel cancelling her act and Jayne returning to England to continue her tour.

Back in England, Jayne crossed paths once again with Diana Dors, whom she had previously met in Hollywood during the 1950s when they were both considered rival bombshells to Marilyn Monroe. Now, ten years later, their careers had followed similar trajectories, and they found themselves playing the notoriously tricky northern clubs, a far cry from the glamour and the luxury they had both previously known.

Diana observed the pattern of Jayne's relationship with Brody, writing in her memoir *For Adults Only* that 'they would lie in bed all day making love, then she would stagger on to the nightclub floor, go back to bed and resume, have a fight and he would fly off to Los Angeles leaving Jayne in tears.'[5]

The rest of the tour was not without its problems, mostly instigated by Jayne's flirtations and Sam's jealousies, but also including two minor car accidents. Nevertheless, Jayne was not keen to return home and frequently spoke of making a life in England, declaring, 'I've become so interested in the law that my great ambition is to become a solicitor in England. I'm planning to go to Oxford to study.'

An Oxford official responded, 'We have plenty of mature students here. I should say we would jump for joy and so would the students.'[6]

The photo that accompanied the article showed Jayne wearing a plunging décolletage and the tagline 'bursting with ambition'; other newspapers responded with similarly salacious headlines such as 'Jayne may bust Oxford'.[7]

Before she left England, Jayne was filmed at a venue while she changed into her stage costume behind a makeshift curtain (the facilities were minimal, but Jayne was game), and as she peeked between the drapes, the interviewer asked her, 'How much longer, in fact, do you think you can go on being a sex symbol?' Jayne fluttered her long false eyelashes, smiled coyly and replied, 'Forever darling.'[8]

Jayne completed the tour amidst fights and arguments with Sam, who was also throwing drunken punches recklessly at other men. Sam was a liability, and yet Jayne seemed unwilling or unable to extricate herself from him and their volatile relationship.

When she returned home at the end of May, a few days later she received an unexpected guest in the form of Anton LaVey. Jayne was by now terrified of him, but she told Linda, her housekeeper, 'I dare not refuse to see LaVey, I've got to be nice to him.'⁹

LaVey wanted publicity photos, and Jayne had it in mind that if she gave him what he wanted, wined and dined him, she could persuade him to lift the curse. So much had gone wrong since October 1966, and further car accidents had occurred. She knew perfectly well that it could all be a coincidence, but as a precaution she didn't want to take any chances. She wanted to have LaVey on her side and for him to revoke his previous threats.

That evening she and Sam had dinner with LaVey at La Scala and Jayne broached the subject. However, LaVey told her it was too late, much to her distress and Sam's entertainment as he continued with his mocking attitude.

After saying their goodbyes, Sam drove Jayne home, but on the way back he lost control of the car. Unlike the previous accidents, this was a significant collision. The couple were not hurt, but the car was substantially damaged.

The tension was growing at home, and the Pink Palace was no longer the house of love that she and Mickey built. The children were scared of Sam, and Jayne's relationship with Jayne Marie had been deteriorating for some time. On the evening of 16 June it came to a violent crescendo and made headlines across the world when 16-year-old Jayne Marie was taken into protective custody after walking into the West Los Angeles police station and claiming she had been beaten by Sam Brody while her mother encouraged him.

Jayne and Sam denied the charges that were levied against them, but Jayne knew this had the potential to ruin her career and dreaded the pending court case.

The mother–daughter relationship is a tricky one at the best of times, but for Jayne and Jayne Marie the boundaries were blurred and neither one was quite sure of their role in this complicated kinship. Jayne was only 34 and was too involved with her own life to give Jayne Marie the guidance she needed. At times Jayne Marie took over the mothering role, but there was friction when Jayne felt her daughter was trying to emulate her; it became a kind of uncomfortable competition.

The narcissistic side of Jayne struggled as Jayne Marie began to develop. Photographs of the teenage Jayne Marie show a beautiful young girl suppressed in dowdy clothes, such as unflattering pleated skirts and shapeless dresses. It is without a doubt that Jayne loved her daughter, but she was not emotionally available for her. The adult Jayne Marie reminisced about her mother in 1992 and said during an interview, 'When you were in her presence, she ruled the present, and you didn't infringe on that. It was her life, and we were all along for the ride I think.'[10]

On 21 June, Sam was driving to collect Jayne from the Pink Palace when he again lost control of his vehicle, but this time he did not come off so lightly. The car was damaged beyond repair and Sam sustained a broken leg, hip and internal injuries. Just twenty-four hours after the accident, Sam discharged himself, determined to accompany Jayne to Biloxi, Mississippi, where she had a booking at the Gus Steven's Supper Club from 23 June to 4 July.

Jayne had performed there before and the money was good. There seemed to be a glimmer of better things to come when she received the news on the 23rd that the charges against her and Sam had been dropped due to insufficient evidence. Jayne Marie was still refusing to return home, but personal problems were not permitted to interfere with work; Jayne was a professional. Club manager Shirley Scarchilli said, 'Jayne was so happy and carefree in her performance.'[11]

On the night of 28 June, Jayne finished her act just before midnight. She had taken 9-year-old Mickey Jnr, 7-year-old Zoltan and 3-year-old Mariska to Biloxi with her. Jayne Marie, of course, stayed in California, and 20-month old Tony remained at the Pink Palace in the care of his nurse.

Gathering up her four chihuahuas and the children, she loaded the car borrowed from Gus Steven's wife Irene, a 1966 Buick. 20-year-old Ronnie Harrison, Gus's son-in-law-to-be, had agreed to drive the party to New Orleans as Jayne had a television commitment on the afternoon of the 29th.

They made a quick stop at a petrol station along the way, where Jayne called Mickey Hargitay from a pay phone. Mickey said in an interview many years later, 'We had a sweet, very loving kind conversation. She said to me … the last thing I heard, "Honey the kids are going to be asleep don't worry about them I'll put them in the back seat, don't worry about it. I've got to go.'"[12]

Jayne was as good as her word; she moved the children from the front seat into the back of the car and insisted they lie down and go to sleep. In the front of the car, Sam's inexhaustible jealousy would not let up and he wedged himself between Jayne and their handsome young driver Ronnie for the rest of the ride.

It was 2.25 a.m., and they were within just 15 miles of their destination when Ronnie took a curve in the road. He couldn't see the tractor–trailer truck in front of him, which had slowed down behind a truck spraying the area for mosquitoes. A dense white smog drenched the area, engulfing the car and leaving zero visibility. The vehicle hit the tractor–trailer with such force that the impact sheared off the top of Buick, killing all three adults in the front of the car, along with two of Jayne's chihuahuas.

Jayne had saved her children's lives by placing them in the back of the car; miraculously they escaped with minor injuries.

In her last interview, Jayne said, 'Trouble follows me everywhere; it's always around the corner trying to jinx me. But I think I've managed to shake it off.'[13] Jayne was wrong, she couldn't shake it off, but she was right about one thing; she would remain eternally 34 and a sex symbol 'Forever darling'.

CONCLUSION

In our modern age of technology, the forward-thinking world in which we live seems to look back to bygone eras continually. There are a plethora of social media groups that have come together to explore the past, with a huge surge in the popularity of the bombshells and the 1950s and '60s. All genders are equally fascinated by the image, the lives and the deaths of these women.

The groups share photographs and dissect long-departed glamorous existences, yet myths are often reinforced despite the abundance of information and access to facts on the worldwide web. People still claim Marilyn Monroe was murdered by the Kennedys or the Mafia, or that Jayne Mansfield was decapitated in a car accident. One of the most common collective statements regarding all five of these bombshells is that they were tragic victims.

The victim label is possibly even more prevalent in regards to the women in this book than the automatic assumption that their blonde hair was synonymous with stupidity. By interpreting them as victims, we are robbing strong articulate and capable women of their power, placing them on a pedestal for appearances' sake whilst at the same time enabling us to use them as an example. We simultaneously admire them and pity them.

The entrenched and insidious belief is that they were a product of male desires, fashioned for the male gaze. They were helpless victims of their sexuality while simultaneously they were perfect and played no part in the image of the sex symbol that they became, as if being a bombshell was foisted upon them. They were weak and vulnerable women who were moulded for sexual pleasure, entertainment and the amusement of men.

Is this the truth? Well, indeed the feminist movement had not yet found a voice, and all five women in this book used every opportunity their appearance afforded them to advance their careers, but it was not a bottle of bleach or a man that made them cultural icons. They were not always judged favourably on their appearance, as seen in the case of Ruth Ellis, who may have received some leniency in her sentence were it not for her determination to enter the court room looking every inch a blonde bombshell.

It is possible that, had Ruth not been blonde and attractive, she would have faded from history like so many other women who had committed crimes of passion. Newspaper headlines from the time almost without fail mentioned her platinum hair. Studying several newspaper articles relating to infamous male murderers of the 1950s and '60s, such as John Christie or James Hanratty, it is noticeable that reference to their hair colour was generally absent, whereas almost every article involving Ruth Ellis alluded to both her hair colour and her attractiveness.

With the exception of Jean Harlow, who died in 1937, our bombshells maximised their success during the 1950s, seen as a time when female accomplishments were expected to revolve around husband, home and family and the harshest judge of a woman's domestic prowess was another woman.

The bombshell's obvious glamour was both a threat and an aspiration. Women at home caring for families were often tired and sex was a chore to be endured for many, with the constant worry of another pregnancy. At the same time, housewives dreamed of living a glamorous lifestyle shown in magazines such as *Picturegoer* and *Photoplay*, in which Marilyn, Jayne and Diana were featured in almost every edition wearing beautiful clothes and receiving constant adulation, with not a basket of washing or a broom in sight.

The bombshells were leading from the front against a background of oppression, subtly subverting social culture and expectations. They wore the latest styles and talked about sex being fun and not a duty, fully partaking in the pleasure. They shed husbands when it suited them and moved on with hardly so much as a sideways glance from behind platinum hair and through impossibly long and luscious lashes.

The bombshells appeared to be happy to forego any semblance of intelligence and encouraged the jokes made about them. However, they attempted to assert their intellect symbolically; Marilyn carried the right books that were considered to be intellectually stimulating to reveal her smarts, and Jayne would flex the numbers of her IQ as often as possible. Diana Dors was more pragmatic; as long as she received her brown envelopes with a fee, she wasn't overly interested in proving her brainpower, although it was perhaps more instantly visible.

In seeking to analyse these women, the first thing you notice is that there is a constant contradictory thread that pulls their lives together. They share more similarities than differences, yet their differences are in stark contrast. They all sought a presence in the limelight. They were all attracted to glamour and careers that were creative and initially reliant on their physical attributes.

The four actresses all reached a point where they wanted to let go of the sexual side of their image but it became increasingly difficult to forge ahead without bringing the bombshell into play. Each one of them lamented playing the part of the sex bomb, proclaiming that their only desire was to be taken seriously as an actress and play parts with more depth and challenge. They said they wanted to concentrate on roles that were not focused on appearance.

To a certain extent Diana Dors led the way with *Yield to the Night* (1956), when at the height of her bombshell fame she relinquished the constraints of beauty, appearing on screen with her hair tied back with seemingly no make-up and wearing drab prison-standard dress for most of the film. Diana was uniquely prepared to forgo the trappings of a sex symbol to take on unattractive and at times even repulsive characters of substance, such as Mrs Wickens in the *Amazing Mr Blunden* (1972) and Bessy Morne in *Nurse Will Make it Better* (1975).

Marilyn, however, found being in front of a movie camera excruciatingly difficult and hair and make-up was the armour that enabled her to delay going on the set. It also gave her a physical persona to hide behind as she spoke about 'Marilyn Monroe' in the third person.

Their childhoods followed similar paths in that they all had problems with their fathers and complex mother–daughter relationships. Jean was brought up in a wealthy family, Diana and Jayne enjoyed a middle-class upbringing, but poverty was an issue for Marilyn and Ruth at times.

Four of the five women in this book were reputed to have experienced a degree of sexual abuse during either childhood or adolescence. All five women had three significant lovers and they all married young with weddings that ended in divorce. Domestic violence became a reality for Ruth, Marilyn, Jayne and Diana.

There was unplanned teenage motherhood (Ruth and Jayne) along with aborted pregnancies, while the advent of feminism set out a new order of pressure and constrictions. Instead of being urged to look ultra-feminine, women were now expected to assert their right to wear trousers.

As clothing took on a more androgynous shape, the difference between the external appearance of the sexes slowly began to blend and diminish.

Jean, Ruth and Marilyn died before the term 'sexual objectification' became the watchword of a generation and the very embodiment of the bombshell. Jayne lived to see the writing on the wall; Diana experienced it and despised it. Women such as Betty Friedan, author of *The Feminist Mystique* (1963), were principally looking to establish a central theme of equality for women, but somehow it became lost in translation and women who looked like bombshells were no longer admired but were now disparaged for their image.

The irony was that each of these women were pioneers, and while they may have had some elements of what are considered to be primarily female traits such as empathy, sensitivity, compassion and the ability to nurture, their dominant traits inclined towards ones more often associated with men.

They focused on their own needs, often putting their career and selves first. They were significantly competitive and assertive. They worked towards goals with decisiveness and independence, and each woman could be considered a breadwinner, financially supporting themselves and other people within their circle.

Each one was instilled with a resilient personality. They carried on through childhood traumas, adult challenges, mistakes, rejection and, in Ruth's case, she faced execution with dignity and without attempting to make excuses for her actions. Ruth ultimately accepted responsibility for her crime, and she squared her shoulders and took her punishment. While her crime may be deplored, her integrity and courage as she stepped forward to face the consequences of her actions cannot be anything but admired.

We can only wonder at how their lives may have developed had they not been cut so shockingly short.

Would Jean have grown as an actress, developing her skills and possibly making the move from bombshell to serious actress?

It seems more than plausible that Ruth would have eventually owned her own club, possibly a string of clubs. She was enigmatic and business-minded, a charming hostess and a woman with great potential.

It is challenging to imagine Marilyn continuing long-term in the movies. While she had great talent and comic timing, as well as an abundance of beauty, she had deep-rooted psychological issues and a sensitivity that was not shared by her bombshell colleagues. This set her apart but also did not bode well for her survival in the movie industry, which often valued youth over experience. It seems most likely that she would have made an early exit from Hollywood, possibly living semi-reclusively.

Diana had an eye on the prize and it is not difficult to imagine her as a larger-than-life, glamorous Barbara Cartland figure; an author of racy novels with inspiration drawn from her own bombshell life, maybe even writing scripts for stage, television and film.

Jayne said she wanted more children and she was certainly young enough to fulfil that dream. Maybe she would have developed her acting skills, and it would not be out of the question to imagine her as an animal rights activist as she grew older; her love of animals would no doubt have continued to grow with her.

Sadly, we can only guess at the possibilities that the future could have held for each one of them. With the event of their untimely deaths they have each left us with a vision of glamour that cannot be altered, and often blinds us to their achievements, their courage and determination that has contributed to setting them firmly in history for ever more as cultural icons of unashamed womanhood.

BIBLIOGRAPHY

Ash, Niema, *Connecting Dors: The Legacy of Diana Dors* (Seaford: Purple Press, 2011)

Badman, Keith, *The Final Years of Marilyn Monroe: The Shocking True Story* (London: JR Books, 2010)

Baker Miracle, Berniece and Miracle, Mona Rae, *My Sister Marilyn: A Memoir of Marilyn Monroe* (London: Weidenfeld & Nicolson, 1994)

Banner, Lois, *Marilyn: The Passion and the Paradox* (New York: Bloomsbury, 2012)

Barris, George, *Marilyn: Her Life in Her Own Words* (New York: Citadel Press, 2001)

Brett, David, *Hurricane in Mink* (London: JR Books, 2010)

Byars, Jackie, *All That Hollywood Allows: Re-reading Gender in 1950s Melodrama* (NC: University of North Carolina Press, 1991)

Callan, Michael Feeney, *Pink Goddess: The Jayne Mansfield Story* (London: W.H. Allen, 1986)

Cardiff, Jack, *Magic Hour: The Life of a Cameraman* (London: Faber & Faber, 1996)

Casillo, Charles, *Marilyn Monroe: The Private Life of a Public Icon* (New York: St Martins Press, 2018)

Chandler, Charlotte, *Nobody's Perfect: Billy Wilder, a Personal Biography* (New York: Simon & Schuster 2002)

Churchwell, Sarah, *The Many Lives of Marilyn Monroe* (London: Granta Books, 2005)

Clark, Colin, *The Price: The Showgirl and Me* (London: Harper Collins, 1995)

Cramer, Richard Ben, *Joe DiMaggio: The Hero's Life* (New York: Simon & Schuster, 2000)

De Beauvoir, Simone, *The Second Sex* (London: Vintage Classics, 1997)

Dors, Diana, *Behind Closed Dors* (London: W.H. Allen, 1979)

Dors, Diana, *Diana Dors' A–Z of Men* (London: Futura, 1984)

Dors, Diana, *Dors by Diana: An Intimate Self-Portrait* (London: Macdonald Futura, 1981)

Dors, Diana, *For Adults Only* (London: W.H. Allen, 1978)

Dors, Diana, *Swingin' Dors* (London: WDL Books, 1960)

Dougherty, James E., *The Secret Happiness of Marilyn Monroe* (Chicago: Playboy Press, 1976)

Ellis, Georgie and Taylor, Rod, *Ruth Ellis, My Mother: A Daughter's Memoir of the Last Woman to be Hanged* (London: Smith Gryphon, 1995)

Fisher, Kate and Szreter, Simon, *Sex Before the Sexual Revolution: Intimate Life in England 1918–1963* (Cambridge: Cambridge University Press, 2010)

Flory, Joan and Walne, Damien, *Diana Dors: Only a Whisper Away* (London: Javelin Books, 1987)

Faris, Jocelyn, *Jayne Mansfield: A Bio-Bibliography* (London: Greenwood Press, 1994)

Franse, A. and Morgan, M., *Before Marilyn: The Blue Book Modelling Years* (Stroud: The History Press, 2015)

Friedan, Betty, *The Feminine Mystique* (New York: W.W. Norton, 1997)

Golden, Eve, *Platinum Girl: The Life and Legends of Jean Harlow* (New York: Abberville Press, 1991)

Goodman, J. and Pringle, P., *The Trial of Ruth Ellis* (London: Chivers Press, 1990)

Guiles, Fred Lawrence, *Norma Jeane: The Life and Death of Marilyn Monroe* (London: Grafton Books, 1986)

Halliwell, Martin, *American Culture in the 1950s* (Edinburgh: Edinburgh University Press, 2007)

Hancock, Robert, *Ruth Ellis: The Last Woman to be Hanged* (London: Orion Books, 1963)

Hargitay, Mickey, *My Marriage to Jayne* (Chicago: Novel Books Inc., 1965)

Hart, Sara, *A Mother Apart* (Lanham: Taylor Trade, 2007)

Jakubait, Muriel and Weller, Monica, *Ruth Ellis: My Sister's Secret Life* (London: Constable & Robinson, 2005)

Kahn, Roger, *Joe and Marilyn: A Memory of Love* (London: Sidgwick & Jackson, 1987)

Kaledin, Eugenia, *Mothers and More: American Women in the 1950s* (Woodbridge: Twayne Publishers, 1984)

Khein, Leonara, *A Very English Hangman: The Life and Times of Albert Pierrepoint* (London: Corvo Books, 2006)

Koper, Richard, *Affectionately Jayne Mansfield* (New York: Bear Manor Media, 2012)

Kotsilibas-Davis, James, *Milton's Marilyn* (London: Schirmer Art Books, 2001)

Lee, Carol Ann, *A Fine Day for a Hanging: The Real Ruth Ellis Story* (Edinburgh: Mainstream Publishing, 2012)

Mann, May, *Jayne Mansfield: A Biography* (New York: Drake Publishers, 1973)

Mansfield, Jayne and Hargitay, Mickey, *Jayne Mansfield's Wild, Wild World* (Los Angeles: Holloway House Publishing, 1963)

Marks, L., and Van Den Bergh, T., *Ruth Ellis: A Case of Diminished Responsibility?* (London: Macdonald and Jane's, 1977)

Marshall, Cherry, *The Cat Walk* (London: Hutchinson, 1978)

Martin, Pete, *Marilyn Monroe* (London: Frederick Muller Ltd, 1956)

Meyers, Jeffrey, *The Genius and the Goddess* (London: Arrow Books, 2009)

Miller, Arthur, *Timebends: A Life* (London: Methuen, 1987)

Morgan, Michelle, *Marilyn Monroe Private and Undisclosed* (New York: Carroll & Graf, 2007)

Morgan, Michelle, *The Girl Marilyn Monroe, The Seven Year Itch: The Birth of an Unlikely Feminist* (Philadelphia: Running Press, 2018)

Murray, Eunice and Shade, Rose, *Marilyn The Last Months* (New York: Pyramid Books, 1975)

Nicholson, Virginia, *Perfect Wives in Ideal Homes* (London: Penguin Random House, 2015)

Pierrepoint, Albert, *Executioner Pierrepoint: An Autobiography* (London: Eric Doby Publishing, 2005)

Pitman, Joanna, *On Blondes* (London: Bloomsbury, 2003)

Pizzey, E. and Shapiro, J., *Prone to Violence* (London: Hamlyn, 1982)

Rosten, Norman, *Marilyn: A Very Personal Story* (London: Millington Books, 1980)

Russell, Jane, *Jane Russell: An Autobiography* (London: Sidgwick & Jackson, 1986)

Saxton, Martha, *Jayne Mansfield and the American Fifties* (Boston: Houghton Mifflin Harcourt, 1975)

Schiller, Lawrence, *Marilyn and Me* (New York: DoubleDay, 2012)

Scholz, Sally J., *Feminism* (London: One World Publications, 2010)

Spoto, Donald, *Marilyn Monroe: The Biography* (London: Arrow Books, 1994)

Stenn, David, *Bombshell: The Life and Death of Jean Harlow* (New York: DoubleDay, 1993)

Stern, Bert, *The Last Sitting* (London: Orbis, 1982)

Strait, Raymond, *The Tragic Secret Life of Jayne Mansfield* (Illinois: Henry Regnery, 1974)

Strasberg, Susan, *Marilyn and Me: Sisters, Rivals, Friends* (New York: DoubleDay, 1992)

Summers, Anthony, *Goddess: The Secret Lives of Marilyn Monroe* (London: Victor Gollancz, 1985)

Taraborrelli, J.R., *The Secret Life of Marilyn Monroe* (London: Sidgwick & Jackson, 2009)

Van Doren, Mamie and Aveilhe, Art, *Playing the Field: My Story* (New York: G.P. Putnam's & Sons, 1987)

Vevea, April, *Puffblicity: An Appreciation of Jayne Mansfield* (San Francisco: Blurb Inc., 2018)

Victor, Adam, *The Complete Marilyn Monroe* (London: Thames & Hudson, 1999)

Victor Robles, Gary *Icon Marilyn Monroe Vol. 1 & 2* (New York: Bear Manor Media 2014)

Weatherby, W.J., *Conversations with Marilyn* (London: Sphere Books, 1977)

Wise, Damon, *Come by Sunday: The Fabulous Ruined Life of Diana Dors* (London: Sidgwick & Jackson, 1998)

Zolotow, M., *Marilyn Monroe* (London: W.H. Allen, 1960)

SOURCES

Newspapers

The British Newspaper Archives UK (www.britishnewspaperarchive.co.uk)
USA Newspapers (www.newspapers.com)

Archives

Ancestry.com
The National Archives (nationalarchives.gov.uk)
Youtube (www.youtube.com)
www.marilynmonroe.ca
www.lovingmarilyn.com

NOTES

Chapter 1

1 E! Mysteries & Scandals, 11 May 1998.
2 Stenn, David, *Bombshell: The Life and Death of Jean Harlow*, p.69.
3 Ibid., p.67.
4 E! Mysteries & Scandals, 11 May 1998.
5 Stenn, p.36.
6 Ibid., p.81.
7 Ibid., p.45.
8 Ibid., p.80.
9 Ibid., p.69.
10 Golden, Eve, *Platinum Girl: The Life and Legends of Jean Harlow*, p.70.

Chapter 2

1 www.rarenewspapers.com/view/582923?imagelist=1
2 Stenn, p.131.

Chapter 3

1 Golden, p.182.
2 Stenn, p.219.
3 Ibid., p.221.
4 Ibid., p.235.
5 Ibid., p.237.
6 www.youtube.com/watch?v=GBAd7FpE7RY
7 Golden, p.215.

Chapter 4

1 Lee, Carol Ann, *A Fine Day for a Hanging: The Real Ruth Ellis Story*, p.211.
2 Ibid., p.20.
3 Ibid., p.245.

4   Ibid., p.255.
5   *The Sunday Dispatch*, 'The Woman Who Wants to Die!', Godfrey Winn, 26 June 1955.
6   www.britishpathe.com/video/a-short-life-and-a-gay-one

Chapter 5

1   *Woman's Sunday Mirror*, 'My Love and Hate', Ruth Ellis, 26 June 1955.

Chapter 6

1   Marks, L., and Van Den Bergh, T., *Ruth Ellis: A Case of Diminished Responsibility*, p.39.
2   Lee, p.109.
3   'My Love and Hate', Ruth Ellis, *Sunday Mirror*, 26 June 1955.
4   Ellis, Georgie and Taylor, Rod, *Ruth Ellis, My Mother*, p.83.
5   Ibid., p.83.
6   *The Times* Announcements, 13 November 1953.
7   Ellis and Taylor, p.84.

Chapter 7

1   Marshall, Cherry, *The Cat Walk*, p.65.
2   Marks and Van Den Bergh, p.69.
3   Lee, p.168.
4   Marks and Van Den Bergh, p.74.

Chapter 8

1   Marks and Van Den Bergh, p.77.
2   Ibid., p.80.
3   Ibid., p.86.

Chapter 9

1   Goodman, J. and Pringle, P., *The Trial of Ruth Ellis*, p.33.
2   Ibid., p.40.
3   Lee, p.295.
4   *Ruth Ellis: A Life for a Life*, TV Documentary 1999.
5   'It's obvious I meant to kill him: Says Model', *Daily Herald*, London, 21 June 1955, p.6.
6   Goodman and Pringle, p.51.
7   Ibid., pp.116–17.

Chapter 10

1   Marks and Van Den Bergh, p.133.
2   Marks and Van Den Bergh, p.142.
3   Goodman and Pringle, p.65.
4   MEPO 2/9888.
5   Marks and Van Den Bergh, p.144.
6   Lee, p.327.
7   Marks and Van Den Bergh, pp.148–9.
8   'I Will Always be Haunted by Look Ruth Ellis Gave Me', *Daily Mirror*, Ruki Sayid, 1999.
9   Pierrepoint, Albert, *Executioner Pierrepoint: An Autobiography*, p.34.
10 Dors, Diana, *For Adults Only*, p.96.
11 Ibid.
12 Ibid., p.97.
13 Dors, Diana, *A-Z of Men*, p.80.
14 Dors, *For Adults Only*, p.97.
15 Marks and Van Den Bergh, p.31.

Chapter 11

1   Baker Miracle, Berniece and Miracle, Mona Rae, *My Sister Marilyn*, p.52.
2   Spoto, Donald, *Marilyn Monroe: The Biography,* p.62.
3   Summers, Anthony, *Goddess: The Secret Lives of Marilyn Monroe*, p.18.
4   Hecht, Ben, *My Story: Marilyn Monroe*, p.18.
5   Guiles, Fred Lawrence, *Norma Jeane: The Life and Death of Marilyn Monroe*, p.67.
6   Baker Miracle and Miracle, p.102.
7   Banner, Lois, *The Passion and the Paradox: Marilyn Monroe*, p.51.
8   *The Guardian*, 28 June 2018, www.theguardian.com/uk-news/2018/jun/28/it-never-stops-shaping-you-the-legacy-of-child-sexual-abuse-and-how-to-survive-it.
9   Zolotow, M., *Marilyn Monroe*, p.39.
10 Hecht, p.26.

Chapter 12

1   Spoto, p.81.
2   Dougherty, James E., *The Secret Happiness of Marilyn Monroe*, p.27.
3   Hecht, p.30.
4   Spoto, p.232.
5   Zolotow, p.187.
6   Spoto, p.306.
7   Ibid., p.313.
8   'They're sniping at Monroe's marriage', Lloyd Shearer, *Picturegoer*, 30 March 1957, p.7.
9   Spoto, p.321.

Chapter 13

1   Meryman, Richard, 'Great Interviews of the 20th Century', No. 7, *The Guardian*, printed by Quebecor World, 2007.
2   Spoto, p.294.
3   Ibid., p.202.
4   Summers, p.56.
5   Love note, author's collection.
6   www.youtube.com/watch?v=3aNqcMcjuVo, Marilyn Monroe Video Archives.
7   www.youtube.com/watch?v=p8TMBVrZPHE, Marilyn Monroe Video Archives, Marilyn at Press conference with Arthur Miller on his Roxbury farm, June 1956.
8   Chandler, Charlotte, *Nobody's Perfect: Billy Wilder, a Personal Biography*, p.215.
9   Meryman, No. 7.

Chapter 14

1   Spoto, p.39.
2   Ibid., p.41.
3   Hecht, p.10.
4   Victor, Adam, *The Complete Marilyn Monroe*, p.135.
5   Martin, Pete, *Marilyn Monroe*, p.17.
6   Spoto, p.356.
7   www.billboard.com/articles/news/magazine-feature/7385825/shirley-manson-revisits-childhood-sexual-trauma-talks-feminism-new-garbage-album.
8   Spoto, p.50.
9   intothegloss.com/2014/06/marilyn-monroe-quotes/.
10 'Marilyn Monroe: The Talk of Hollywood', *Life* magazine, 7 April 1952.
11 'I dress for men says Marilyn Monroe', *Movieland* magazine, July 1952.
12 Spoto, p.260.
13 Martin, p.33.

Chapter 15

1   www.youtube.com/watch?v=w74jxMEwlhg 1960s interview Marilyn Monroe Archives
2   Strasberg, Susan, *Marilyn and Me: Sisters, Rivals, Friends*, p.15.
3   Zolotow, p.230.
4   Strasberg, p.8.
5   Zolotow, pp.230–1.
6   Guiles, p.284.
7   Ibid., p.244.
8   Chandler, p.215.
9   Strasberg, p.25.
10 Guiles, p.287.
11 Ibid., p.300.

12   www.youtube.com/watch?v=DmFL0hfLBC0, Sir Laurence Olivier, Michael Parkinson interview, 1970.
13   www.livingtrustnetwork.com/estate-planning-center/last-will-and-testament/ wills-of-the-rich-and-famous/last-will-and-testament-of-marilyn-monroe.html.

Chapter 16

1   Spoto, p.104.
2   Hecht, p.8.
3   Cardiff, Jack, *Magic Hour: The Life of a Cameraman*, p.212.
4   Schiller, Lawrence, *Marilyn and Me*, p.68.
5   Ibid., p.22.
6   www.youtube.com/watch?v=DmFL0hfLBC0, Laurence Olivier, Parkinson interview, 1970.
7   Chandler, p.214.
8   Ibid., p.215.
9   Spoto, p.449.
10 'A last long talk with a lonely girl', Meryman, Richard, *Life Magazine*, 17 August 1962.
11 Chandler, p.214.
12 Cardiff, p.213.

Chapter 17

1   Hecht, p.46.
2   Ibid., p.48.
3   www.theguardian.com/world/2017/oct/20/women-worldwide-use-hashtag-metoo-against-sexual-harassment
4   www.biography.com/people/tarana-burke
5   www.youtube.com/watch?v=zP3LaAYzA3Q
6   Weatherby, W.J., *Conversations with Marilyn*, p.186.
7   Hecht, p.53.
8   Ibid., p.55.
9   Zolotow, p.66.
10 Weatherby, p.144.
11 Van Doren, Mamie and Aveilhe, Art, *Playing the Field: My Story*, pp.8–9.
12 Hecht, p.53.

Chapter 18

1   Badman, Keith, *The Final Years of Marilyn Monroe: The Shocking True Story*, p.25.
2   Spoto, p.264.
3   Badman, p.28–9.
4   Ibid., pp.65.
5   Weatherby, p.174.
6   Schiller, p.52.
7   Spoto, p.588.

8   Stern, Bert, *The Last Sitting*, p.39.
9   Ibid., p.118.
10   Ibid., p.47.
11   Ibid., p.173.
12   Ibid., p.174.
13   'A last long talk with a lonely girl', Meryman.
14   Rosten, Norman, *Marilyn: A Very Personal Story*, p.111.

Chapter 19

1   Dors, Diana, *Dors by Diana: An Intimate Self-Portrait*, p.9.
2   Ibid., p.17.
3   Ibid., p.21.
4   Ibid., p.25.
5   Ibid., p.27.
6   Ibid., p.28.

Chapter 20

1   Dors, *Dors by Diana*, p.10.
2   Ibid., p.32.
3   Dors, Diana, *Swingin' Dors*, p.21.
4   Joe Hyams, *Liverpool Echo*, 14 July 1956.
5   Ibid., 14 July 1956.
6   Mike Wallace interview, Diana Dors, 11 September 1957.
7   Ibid.
8   'Plump and happy', Patricia Boxall, *The People*, 19 April 1970, p.7.
9   Ibid.
10   'Why I'm the happiest mum-to-be', Marje Proops, *Daily Mirror*, 3 May 1975.
11   'Her days as a sexpot done, Diana Dors now hopes to become the next big fitness guru', Roger Wolmuth, *People Magazine*, 12 December 1983.
12   *The Unforgettable Diana Dors*, 24 March 2000, Watchmaker Productions.
13   'Diana Dors – Waving the glamour days goodbye with a smile', Ted Hart, *Coventry Evening Telegraph*, 18 July 1975, p.19.

Chapter 21

1   Fisher, Kate and Szreter, Simon, *Sex Before the Sexual Revolution: Intimate Life in England 1918-1963*, p.82.
2   Dors, *Dors by Diana*, p.50.
3   Ibid., p.51.
4   Ibid., p.79.
5   De Beauvoir, Simone, *The Second Sex*, p.505.
6   *Bedfordshire Times and Independent*, 15 July 1949.
7   Dors, *Dors by Diana*, p.109.
8   Ibid., p.114.

9   Ibid., p.114.

10   Ibid., p.123.

11   Ibid., p.118.

12   *Birmingham Daily Gazette*, 22 July 1953.

13   'At home with Miss Dors', Donald Zec, *Daily Mirror*, 31 May 1954.

14   Dors, *Dors by Diana*, p.139.

Chapter 22

1   Dors, *Dors by Diana*, p.132.

2   *West London Observer*, 16 December 1955.

3   Dors, *Dors by Diana*, p.143.

4   Ibid., p.145.

5   *Birmingham Gazette*, 27 June 1956.

6   'Diana – has Curves AND Brains', Stan Mays, New York, *Daily Mirror*, 27 June 1956, p.17,

7   Ibid.

8   Ibid.

9   Dors, *Dors by Diana*, p.152.

10   Donald Zec, *Daily Mirror*, 29 September 1956, p.11.

11   'Dennis, Hollywood and me', Charles Kirschner, *Picturegoer*, 5 January 1957, pp.6–7.

12   Zec, *Daily Mirror,* 29 September 1956.

13   Ibid.

14   *The People*, 15 July 1956.

15   Zec, *Daily Mirror,* 29 September 1956.

Chapter 23

1   Dors, *Dors by Diana*, p.210.

2   Ibid., p.214.

3   'Sex exploitation – Statement by the Press Council', *Birmingham Post*, 31 March 1960, p.7.

4   'The shocking truth about the fabulous Mr Dors', *Belfast Telegraph*, 30 January 1960, p.3.

5   Dors, *Dors by Diana*, p.215.

6   Ibid., p.216.

7   Ibid., p.217.

8   Ibid., p.219.

9   *Evening Express*, 5 July 1961, p.2.

10   'Dors: The other Diana', Gambit Productions, 27 May 1990 (UK). www.dailymotion.com/video/xdrkqg

11   Dors, *Dors by Diana*, p.233.

Chapter 24

1   Dors, *Dors by Diana*, p.250.
2   *Liverpool Echo & Evening Express*, 15 March 1966, p.5.
3   Dors, *Dors by Diana*, p.249.
4   Ibid., p.255.

Chapter 25

1   'What is a Lake?', poem by Diana Dors.
2   *The Stage*, 1 August 1968, p.12.
3   Dors, *For Adults Only*, p.11.
4   Dors, *Dors by Diana*, p.262.
5   *Birmingham Daily Post*, 29 October 1968.
6   *Daily Mirror*, 29 October 1968.
7   *The People*, 24 November 1968, p.13.
8   Dors, *Dors by Diana*, p.262.
9   *The People*, 23 February 1969, p.19.
10 *The People*, 4 May 1969, p.19.
11 Dors, *Dors by Diana*, p.269.
12 *Daily Mirror*, 17 October 1970.

Chapter 26

1   *Hamlet*, Act 1, Scene III.
2   *Daily Mirror*, 3 May 1975.
3   Dors, *Dors by Diana*, p.284.
4   'Now at last Diana finds what she enjoys most', *Liverpool Echo*, 14 February 1978.
5   Ibid.
6   Ibid.
7   *Coventry Evening Telegraph*, 20 March 1979, p.38.
8   'Diana Dors jokes after operation', *Belfast Telegraph*, 28 June 1982.
9   'Diana loses fight for life', *Newcastle Journal*, 5 May 1984, p.1.

Chapter 27

1   www.foxnews.com/entertainment/2018/02/02/jayne-mansfields-fatal-car-crash-changed-elaine-stevens-life-forever.html
2   Mann, May, *Jayne Mansfield: A Biography*, p.6.
3   www.youtube.com/watch?v=h1e1iXF2BtU
4   www.youtube.com/watch?v=aY0WdbjBRn8
5   Mann, p.5.
6   Ibid., p.6.
7   Ibid., p.8.
8   Ibid., p.7.

Chapter 28

1   Saxton, Martha, *Jayne Mansfield and the American Fifties*, p.38.
2   'Jayne Mansfield tells all Part II "I went for publicity"', *Picturegoer*, 1 December 1956, pp.10–11.
3   www.youtube.com/watch?v=roCzDtVKifA
4   *Picturegoer,* 1 December 1956.
5   Friedan, Betty, *The Feminine Mystique*, p.59.

Chapter 29

1   Mansfield, Jayne and Hargitay, Mickey, *Jayne Mansfield's Wild, Wild World*, p.27.
2   Russell, Jane, *Jane Russell: An Autobiography,* p.157.
3   Hargitay, Mickey, *My Marriage to Jayne*, p.11.
4   'Jayne Mansfield picks husky dog lover for next mate', *San Mateo Times*, 30 October 1956, p.20.
5   Mann, p.50.
6   Ibid., p.51.

Chapter 30

1   www.dollartimes.com/inflation/inflation.php?
2   Mann, p.55.
3   Ibid., p.10.
4   *Daily News* (New York), 22 March 1956, p.31.
5   Saxton, p.97.
6   www.infoplease.com/us/births/live-births-and-birth-rates-year
7   Kaledin, Eugenia, *Mothers and More: American Women in the 1950s*, p.179.
8   Friedan, p.472.

Chapter 31

1   Mann, p.37.
2   Ibid., p.35.
3   Ibid., p.26.
4   Ibid., p.77.
5   *The Province*, 12 April 1957, p.3.
6   Ibid.
7   Mansfield and Hargitay, p.95.
8   *The Montgomery Advertiser*, Alabama, 27 November 1966, p.1.
9   'Jayne Mansfield – a hidden hurt', Jim Bishop, *The News Messenger*, 30 November 1964.
10 Mann, p.38.

Chapter 32

1   Mann, p.28.
2   www.youtube.com/watch?v=TMOJn8e8kVM.
3   Ibid.
4   Friedan, p.82.
5   www.youtube.com/watch?v=O7RmQbzhfcI.
6   www.youtube.com/watch?v=TMOJn8e8kVM.
7   *Tampa Bay Times*, 9 May 1966.
8   *The Daily News*, Pennsylvania, 1 July 1968.
9   Strait, Raymond, *The Tragic Secret Life of Jayne Mansfield*, p.142.
10 Ibid., p.143.
11 Mann, p.131.
12 Strait, p.153.
13 Ibid., p.154.
14 Ibid., p.154.

Chapter 33

1   Strait, p.167.
2   Saxton, p.164.
3   Ibid., p.169.
4   *Arena Blondes: Jayne Mansfield*, 24 December 1999, Illumination Films for BBC2.
5   'Jayne seeks to regain son', *Indianapolis Star*, 24 September 1966.
6   Ibid.
7   https://www.youtube.com/watch?v=VK9lItCfJxA, Vintage Powderpuff's Jayne Mansfield, published 9 June 2014.
8   'Jayne accuses hubby of biting, asks $345,000', *Philadelphia Daily News,* 28 May 1967, p.5.
9   Mann, p.131.
10 Ibid., p.181.
11 Strait, p.191.
12 *The Daily News*, New York, 7 May 1967, p.7.
13 www.redbookmag.com/love-sex/sex/a47424/why-women-like-rough-sex/
14 Mann, p.175.

Chapter 34

1   www.wgbh.org/news/local-news/2018/09/07/protesting-miss-america-but-not-in-two-part-harmony
2   *Racine Journal Times*, Wisconsin, 17 February 1967.
3   Mann, p.177.
4   'Devil cultist loses, Jayne won't convert', Marilyn Beck*, Hartford Courant*, Connecticut, 28 February 1967, p.24.
5   Dors, *For Adults Only*, p.153.
6   'Would Jayne fit in Oxford', *Victoria Daily Times*, Canada, 28 June 1967, p.12.

7   *The Leader-Post*, 28 June 1968.

8   *Living Famously*, UK Documentary, narrated by Caroline Quentin, 2003.

9   Mann, p.224.

10 *Inside Edition*, television, 1992.

11 *San Francisco Examiner*, 29 July 1967, p.4.

12 www.youtube.com/watch?v=58NWaLqV6qM, Hollywood Scandals – Jayne
    Mansfield, 1999.

13 *Detroit Free Press*, Michigan, Ivor Davies, 30 June 1967.

INDEX